DATE DUE

S0-AAG-025

17 JUL 1972 D Z

8 AUG 1972 D Z

THE
STRUGGLE
OF THE
UNBELIEVER

ALSO BY JAMES J. KAVANAUGH

There's Two of You
Journal for Renewal
Man in Search of God
A Modern Priest Looks at His Outdated Church

Nihil Obstat:

Berard L. Marthaler, O.F.M., Conv.
Censor Deputatus

Imprimatur:

✠ Patrick A. O'Boyle
Archbishop of Washington

May 3, 1966

THE
STRUGGLE
OF THE
UNBELIEVER

James J. Kavanaugh

TRIDENT PRESS

NEW YORK

This dissertation was approved by Berard Marthaler O.F.M., Conv. as director and by Gerard S. Sloyan and Eugene Burke C.S.P. as readers.

Copyright, ©, 1967, by Reverend James J. Kavanaugh

All rights reserved. No part of this book may be reproduced in any form without permission in writing from the publisher, except by a reviewer who may quote brief passages in a review to be printed in a magazine or newspaper.

Library of Congress Catalog Card Number: 68–22569

Published simultaneously in the United States and Canada by Trident Press, a division of Simon & Schuster, Inc., 630 Fifth Avenue, N.Y. 10020.

Printed in the United States of America

BT
1102
K3

This book is dedicated to Maurice Blondel, who discovered, as have I, that "the cassock is a scarecrow. It forces a man to compromise and is itself made to compromise through him. It hinders and restricts a man's personal act of service."

It is further dedicated to Herbert Alexander who understands the power of an idea.

INTRODUCTION

This book is my doctoral dissertation and is reproduced as it was written almost two years ago. My beliefs are now substantially the same as they were then, although I was obliged, at that time, to revise the last chapter in order to meet the approval of my dissertation director and to receive the *imprimatur* of the church. Otherwise, my conclusions would have been more revolutionary than the ones that appear here. I decided, however, that the reader would be able to draw his own conclusions after he examined the important evidence presented herein.

It is evident now, even to the most conservative, how poorly understood were the documents of Vatican II by the very men responsible for their adoption. Herein lies the tragedy of the modern church. Vatican II spoke glowingly of the rights of modern man. It approved his new understanding of himself, upheld his freedom of conscience, and encouraged him to enter into real dialogue with his world. Yet, the changes effected in the conduct of the Church since Vatican II have been superficial. Consequently, large numbers of men are leaving the institutional Church to find God in their personal search for meaning and genuine involvement in the world.

The Council even asked the question that is on the mind of contemporary man: "What does the Church think of man?" (Par. 11, *Modern World*) The answer, unfortunately, still offers little hope. The Church thinks that the divorced person who remarries is unfit to receive the sacraments. The Church thinks it is right and the rest of the world is wrong. The Church thinks that faith is more a series of truths and moral principles than a personal commitment to God. The Church thinks that man cannot be trusted, that modern society is dangerously anti-God and blindly in pursuit of pleasure. The Church still thinks that sex before marriage is always sinful and that hell stands ominously pointing its anger at man's weakness.

Theologians say in the Church's defense that all of this is changing. And yet, it is not changing in the parishes. It is not changing in the confessional, in the sermons, in the daily lives of the people. It changes only in the minds of the elite and the sophisticated laymen, or in the lecture halls of the liberal theologian, or especially in the lives of the millions who leave the Church in disgust. It does not change in the codified law.

Thus, the most significant religious experiences are taking place outside or in spite of the institutional Church. This is good, for Christianity can become what it was in its origins, a revolution against the legalism of the establishment. It is too hard to reform an entrenched system which has had its own way for centuries. It is too hard to convince an irrelevant institution that the world finds it intransigent and obsolete. It is too hard to "go through channels" when the "channels" are more a vested interest than a reflection of an honest search for faith. A man can only abandon the institution and search for God on his own or with a few friends. In such surroundings he will not fear the categories of the churchmen which reduce complexities to legalistic naïveté.

It is my hope that the publication of this dissertation will give courage to the man who searches in the anxiety of isolation. Perhaps it will give him a sense of history, a sense of himself, so that he will not fear to move with his times, or even to anticipate them. Scheler, Blondel, and Newman have given me courage, freedom, and perspective. I hope they give you the same, for this is the way of restless and creative peace.

CONTENTS

PREFACE

From the time of Paul's visit to the Areopagus until the twentieth-century efforts of a de Chardin, Bonhoeffer, or Bishop Robinson, the Christian world has been concerned, in varying degrees, with the defense of the faith and the struggle of the unbeliever. Serious efforts must always be made to understand the culture of the day and to make Christianity intelligible to each generation. This is the *apologetic problem.*[1] In some sense, it never rests. It will always be a *modern apologetic problem,* since man's view of himself is ever being transformed.[2]

It is our contention that the apologetic offerings of the recent past have been largely an effort to enlighten the faith of the believer, rather than to win the attention of the unbeliever.[3] Yet this distinction has not been clearly made. For the most part the same proofs and programs were proposed for the believer and the unbeliever alike. The usual approach was an historical one, which attempted to show that man must take Christ seriously when he considers the historical facts logically. Thus apologetics began with proofs for the existence of God, worked its way through imperfect forms of revelation, and finally secured the place of Christ by the use of miracles and prophecies as evidence supporting the claims of the Messiah. Our attitude was one of complacency, insisting that any reasonable and unprejudiced man could see the value of these proofs. If the unbeliever found them ineffective, we sometimes changed our psychology of approach, but we merely reiterated the soundness of the proofs. Consequently, the proofs became more and more irrelevant to an unbelieving world.

There were voices that spoke out from time to time, insisting that something must be done for the unbeliever, asserting that the historical proofs did not convince him. Lammenais saw it in the early nineteenth century,[4] but his efforts were largely nullified by his personal condemnation and subsequent defection, and by the pontificate of Pius IX and the *Syllabus*. At the same period, the efforts of Möhler, Drey, and the Tübingen school, hoping to do for Catholicism what Schleiermacher had done for Protestantism, were obscured by the same antiliberal attacks.[5]

At the end of the nineteenth century and at the beginning of the twentieth, other voices were heard, important voices such as those of Cardinal Newman, Maurice Blondel, and Max Scheler. But even their words have only lately become known, because the efforts of Pius X against modernism rendered them questionable and suspicious.[6] We propose to examine the message of these three men, and to show clearly that there must be an apologetic for the unbeliever, that the traditional apologetics will not move him. It is our intention to establish this point historically and to propose a program for addressing oneself to the unbeliever.

In attempting to offer some reflections on the beginnings of a solution to our problem, it is necessary to examine the immediate historical background as the source of the apologetic which we have come to regard as traditional.[7] If we can see, at least in an overview, the disregard of man's changing image of himself and his powers in our inherited Christian defense, we will not be too unwilling, perhaps, to take a bold step forward toward relevance and meaning in apologetics. We shall examine briefly the formulation of the Christian apologetic which still remains in modern textbooks of theology, and, we hope, explain its value and broaden its method and scope. In providing this brief history of the problem, we would like to acknowledge our special indebtedness to the classic work of Roger Aubert on *Le Problème de l'act de la foi*.[8] The clarity of his treatment, the careful bibliography, the omission of tedious details, and the remarkable interweaving of the cultural climate to which the theologians reacted or failed to react—all of these and more command our respect and gratitude.

After offering the general dimensions of the historical background[9] we shall select certain men who, long before our time, questioned the apologetic which we had largely canonized. We were guided in our selection of these men by a careful study of Aubert, and came to the conclusion that these were the unique prophets who saw the obsolescence of past methods of Christian preparation and defense, and proposed programs which we are only now beginning to appreciate. They represented three different countries and three different philosophical backgrounds. Yet, the conclusions of all three will, we believe, reveal a significantly similar approach. We have chosen Max Scheler of Germany (1874–1928), Maurice Blondel of France (1861–1949) and, finally, Cardinal Newman of England (1801–1890). If it seems illogical that we leave Cardinal Newman until last, when most of his work was completed before Scheler and Blondel began to work, we do this because the force of his ideas was so lately appreciated. In treating Scheler, we will note that he was well aware of the power of Newman and shows a similar approach in some of his apologetic insights. But Newman's influence in any direct way was doomed to deaf ears and distortions.[10]

After our treatment of these prophets of apologetic vision,[11] we shall attempt to offer a personal speculation of what a modern apologetic should be in the light of Vatican II. We will stress some of the key ideas of the main figures of our historical research, ideas which, although still relevant, were not received in a Church which trembled before the forces of modernism.[12] We will add insights from Vatican II which continue and develop what these men saw years before we were ready or able to listen. In general it will mark a departure from the apologetic of pure "reason" and cold logic and a kind of continuation of what Congar refers to as the "Augustinian line" of thought.[13]

Also, in the final section of our dissertation, we will offer some personal observations, the fruit of our own dialogue with an unbelieving world. We can only second the assertion of a modern theologian from Ireland:

On the whole, the experience of converts confirms rather strikingly many of the characteristic insights of the "personalist" and "immanentist" schools of thought, a factor which has considerably strengthened the case for a rather thoroughgoing revision of the apologetics hitherto in vogue.[14]

THE
STRUGGLE
OF THE
UNBELIEVER

II

HISTORICAL BACKGROUND

It was only with a good bit of reluctance that Catholic theologians began to abandon the problematic of the Middle Ages and to recognize the atmosphere of unbelief that developed in the nineteenth century.[1] The Middle Ages had taken faith for granted. It was everywhere, in its Gothic towers, in its social and economic framework, in its days of rest and pageants of refreshment. There was little need to examine the nature of the pagan's unbelief. The "heretic" was handled with dispatch, as was the "unbeliever."[2] Even with the explosions of the sixteenth century, the Protestant Revolt, the Renaissance firmly established, and the expanding world of trade and exploration, the force of tradition continued to examine and reinterpret the definition of faith. There was no attempt to justify faith but merely to explain its mechanics to the believer.[3] It was important for man to know that something in the faith experience was verified by "reason," but there was no need to defend the very possibility of faith. There was always great emphasis on the need for moral preparedness for faith, and there was added gradually a rising apologetic against the Protestants. There was always the assumption of the Middle Ages that we were speaking relevantly to the whole world within the framework of a believer's apologetic. One gets the impression that the only real apologetic problem was the failure of the unbeliever or the partial believer to use the gift of "pure reason."[4] This is what we mean by the "problematic," the mentality of the Middle Ages. The Middle Ages, however, had no spoken-of "proofs" from reason in a totally demonstrative sense as did the post-Reformation age of apologetics.[5] This would be a distortion of true Thomism.

The Eighteenth Century: The Age of Reason

In the eighteenth century, the age of reason and enlightenment, our traditional apologetic was actually formed. As Deism grew, aided by the work of Voltaire and Pierre Bayle, the impact of Newtonian physics, the rationalism of Locke and the skepticism of Hume, and the powerful writings of Lessing in Germany, reason was the unique source of truth; on the other hand, revelation was mocked and discredited.[6] The place of miracles was challenged, the worth of prophecies was reassessed. The balance shifted from "what God has revealed to what man has discovered."[7] In the encyclopedia of Diderot (1750–1770), God was seen as the architect of the universe, the great geometrician, and the only valid source of truth was reason and the natural law.[8] It was an age characterized by a violent rejection of authority in Church and State alike, an age upholding the goodness of man and insisting on finding life now, not merely waiting for it in a future world.[9]

At first the Church could only appeal for secular help, or rely on forms of condemnation and censorship, or resort to ridicule.[10] But all of this had little effect. Gradually, early in the nineteenth century, the Church began to meet the rationalists on their own ground. Apologetics, relying on the Cartesianisms of the theological schools—with its clear dichotomy between nature and the supernature—met the rationalists with rationalistic methods. Reason *could* establish the foundations of the Christian faith, and the theological school at St. Sulpice in Paris became the center of such an apologetic.[11] Maistre, Bonald, and Lammenais had seen the futility of such an approach, but the policy of Pius IX would allow their ideas little chance of growth.[12] Lammenais, in his *Essai sur l'indifférence en matière de religion* (1817–1824), had even attempted a daring new approach. In the end he succeeded in showing that man needs revelation and the social structure of the Church. He moved the motif of apologetics from the level of private reason to that of the common reason of mankind. He developed the famous argument of the marks of the true Church. He saw the need for a dialogue with the unbelieving world. He realized that Hume had practically demolished the traditional certainties, and instead of insisting that reason could prove Hume wrong he insisted that no man could live as a skeptic.[13]

Despite such attempts as that of Lammenais, despite the reaction to the rationalism of Rousseau in France and Schleiermacher in Germany, and despite the efforts of the Tübingen school, the dominant apologetics of the Church continued to be rationalist in approach. By the mid-nineteenth century, the Church was a "closed corporation" to an unbelieving world. The apologetic which had little or no effect on the unbeliever was still the only apologetic offered in any formal and universal way, and the dominant presupposition of such an approach was that nothing had changed from medieval to modern times.[14]

The Nineteenth Century and the Neo-Kantians

As the rights of reason were the more severely questioned in the nineteenth century,[15] the apologetic of the Church grew more defensive and upheld more vigorously the capacity of "right reason" to lead a man to faith. The implication became ever more dominant that only pride and obstinacy could keep a man from the faith.[16] Nature and reason could so thoroughly clarify the motives that it became difficult to see the need for grace.[17]

Despite the increasing vogue of the neo-Kantians at the turn of the century, with their emphasis on morality and "value" as the unique concern of religion,[18] faith continued to be treated as something quite apart from the believer.[19] The growing importance of the "scientific method" and the "inductive way" of scientific positivism was recognized only by exceptional men,[20] who understood that the world would not listen to a message of faith or its preparation in the thought-patterns of a past age. The traditional stream, following the lead of Vatican I, was still preoccupied with the apologetic task of the Middle Ages[21] and a dying eighteenth century,[22] asserting that there was no contradiction between faith and reason, and supplying rational proofs to support this assertion. Credibility was still seen largely as an argument supporting the object of faith, and little attention was paid to the way in which individuals would recognize that argument.[23] Perhaps Johann Steffes brought this out as well as anyone, and this a¹most forty years ago:

The middle ages had devoted a deep, valuable, and comprehensive meditation to the Christian religion, both for purposes of defense and for elevating its positive content. But religion itself stood more or less beyond all doubt and question. This had to change completely. . . . Formerly, two pillars upheld the temple of religion, from the viewpoint of cognitive theory, namely nature and history. The former had provided the proof for God's existence, and the latter . . . had given certainty to God's revelation and the absolute nature of the Christian religion.[24]

Steffes goes on to show that "evolution" and the "immanent power" of man himself had replaced "nature" and "history." The "new pillars" led to a "rational empiricism" as the test of truth, and the progress of the world was viewed as a kind of "changing incarnation of the godhead."[25] It was Kant who synthesized these ideas in critical philosophy. While "Copernicus had removed the center of the world from our planet to space, Kant situated the spiritual center of all life within man."[26] The Church continued to talk about "proof" into the twentieth century, and since the word had been adopted by the practitioners of mathematics and natural science (*Mathematische-Naturewissenschaftlicher*), this only led to misunderstanding or indifference.[27] The world of the Middle Ages had disappeared, and at the turn of the century most apologetes were still generally unaware of what had taken place.[28]

The Beginning of the Twentieth Century

In consequence of the foregoing considerations, at the beginning of the twentieth century Catholic theologians were largely concerned with justifying the reasonableness of the act of faith against the attacks of Kant and Schleiermacher, who from the viewpoint of different philosophic systems saw in the religious experience of men mere sentiment and a projection of human need.[29] The work of the apologists was to uphold the validity of faith as truly intellectual knowledge, and to demonstrate to the rationalists of any kind that faith was not supported by intrinsic reasons, but by the revelation of God.[30] Human *reason* was invoked to establish that God is the supreme truth and can speak only the truth to men. Miracles were pronounced to be the unassailable guarantees of the divine message. Only the insincere would not be moved by this *rational* approach, developed in a sophisticated way.[31]

Some were extreme in their assertion that the motives of credibility had a universal probative value, and did not seem to be perturbed by the fact that this belied experience. J. St. Harent spoke of a "chain of reasons without which there would be no demonstration and no apologetical analysis of faith."[32] J. Didiot asserted in his *Logique sûrnaturelle subjective* that the reasoned credibility of the Christian faith is fortified by "more luminous evidence and more solid certitude than philosophy, morality, or history."[33] Even the simple believer could reach the absolute certitude provided by the motives of credibility.[34] Maisonneuve calls apologetics a "demonstration of Christianity."[35] He goes on to stress the disillusionment of science and the "need to believe" (*besoin de croire*) which the scientist experienced. Maisonneuve explains the new ways which had been offered in the face of the futility of the old apologetics. He cites first of all, the "way of authority" (proposed by Balfour in 1899, *The Way of Belief*), which stressed the unstable conclusions produced by the inductive reasoning of men such as Comte and Spencer, and proposed authority as the only answer. Others (for example, Ollé-Laprune, *La Certitude Morale*) took a psychological-moral approach and stressed the marvelous adaptation of Christianity to the needs of human nature.[36] Finally, Maisonneuve mentions the method of the immanentists and calls the Blondelian approach "the most discussed and most important of the new methods." His conclusion to this section is of particular interest to this study:

[New methods] have determined better than heretofore the role of society, authority, heart, and will in our religious beliefs and the support they give the intellect in adhering to revealed truth, but they seem to forget that faith is an asset of the spirit and that rational motives are indispensable and preponderant.[37]

His final conclusion is that the "ancient methods remain efficacious and necessary."[38]

Ambrose Gardeil, O.P.

Along with Rousselot, Ambrose Gardeil made an important and realistic effort to find a middle ground between a rigorous intellectualism and a kind of fideism which saw little or no place for man's initiative.[39] Gardeil had been actively involved in controversies surrounding Blondel and Newman, and he recognized their efforts to make the faith and the approach to faith intelligible to modern man. He began to teach apologetics in 1884 in the Dominican House of Studies in Paris and continued to do so until 1911. (He died in 1931.) It was in 1904 that he was asked to write the article for the *Dictionnaire de Théologie Catholique* on "Crédibilité." As a result of this effort, he wrote a series of articles on the apologetic problem in *Revue Thomiste* from 1905 to 1907, and ultimately, upon request, published the book *La Crédibilité et l'apologétique* in 1907.[40]

Gardeil begins by stressing that "credibility is the likelihood of an assertion to be believed," and goes on to show that it has an objective and rational character and is extrinsic to the truth to be believed.[41] After developing the possibility of intellectual certitude through the motives of credibility and insisting that it is a true demonstration, he moves from tradition and shows the need of a "moral life" before the motives will mean anything.[42] Man must be in search of the truth and must recognize this search as "good" before he can have the necessary *"intention de la foi."*[43]

Gardeil asserted that the truths of faith must do more than satisfy our needs. Ultimately, they must be accepted on the authority of God revealing; consequently, the motives of credibility must be rationally established to lead to this kind of faith. When the Blondelians asserted that Gardeil left little room for grace, he insisted that the ultimate judgment of credibility would be only conditional, and grace would make it effective.[44] His really important contribution was his discussion of the *"morales suppléances,"* the natural helps which made the motives of credibility more than mere rational conclusions. They involve the total man in the search for truth and act as a kind of human reinforcement of credibility.[45] He lists the motives of credibility as varied, for example, miracles, the virtues of Christianity, martyrs, the life of the Church, conversions, and many others.[46] Credibility, he asserts, is naturally knowable either by rigorous demonstration, or by a prudential estimate based on solidly probable reasons, or by certain subjective reinforcements supplying for the weakness of the motives.[47]

The attempt of Gardeil was a courageous and intelligent one. Although, as Aubert points out, he is afraid to let experience lead him to valid insights; he was well aware that the apologetics of the past was a logical conceptualization that ignored man as he truly was.[48] In the end, his traditional roots led him to speak of the "horizons of universal conquest"[49] of the rationalist apologetic. We can appreciate the criticism of Hugeny, that it is dangerous to allow anyone to think that the arguments of credibility are rigorous in their demonstrative force. This is contrary to the pure scholastic tradition and could unsettle the believer, to whom the motives of credibility may mean very little.[50] In a later revision of his thought, Gardeil came closer to the thinking of Rousselot and allowed more room for the activity of grace in the movement whereby man accepts the motives of credibility.[51] Ultimately, however, our evaluation of Gardeil is in accord with that of Blondel, that for Gardeil only the faith of the intellectual seems to be a truly reasonable one.[52] Although we do not believe that Gardeil succeeded in accomplishing what he had hoped—to act as the middle ground between the fideists and intellectualists—still, we think the evaluation of Gustave Weigel is just when he places Gardeil in the line of Rousselot and Marin-Sola as the ancestors of the growing dynamism in theological thought.[53] But when he criticizes Blondel for preparing people to believe by displaying the "goodness" of faith rather than its "truthfulness," he reveals that his heart still belongs with the traditional apologetic, which will serve as "an objective foundation for the true faith."[54] This is why we have selected Scheler, Blondel, and Newman in preference to the more conservative Gardeil.

In fairness to Gardeil, finally, we must remember his involvement in the *crux theologorum* which played such a part in the discussions of his era: How is faith both free and reasonable?[55] Theological development has been such since World War II that the narrow line between faith and reason is no longer of principal concern. Gardeil was not so fortunate as to have been freed of this burden.

Conclusion

Even when the "rationalist" approach in apologetics was moderated, the tendency to view the unbeliever from the standpoint of faith continued. In an admirable article written in 1937, J. Coppens insists that the person of Jesus is "so transcendant and unique in His religious beauty"[56] that anyone, upon contact with the reality of Christ, "will make an act of faith in Him as the best guide that history offers them in the way of religious truth and salvation."[57] Coppens makes use of the traditional apologetic of miracles and prophecies, but believes that the real motive of credibility rests in the person of Christ.[58] He presumes that man will grasp by himself the existence of a personal and transcendant God, and the reality of a human soul called to a life of eternal union with God.[59] Then it is but a short step to establish the transcendant place of Jesus and His foundation of a permanent Church, which would demonstrate in its teaching and members the same unique, religious appeal that is apparent in Christ Himself. His entire approach is a kind of traditional proof, softened against the harsh rationality of previous decades by emphasis on the person of Christ as fulfilling all the religious aspirations of man. This enables us to see Jesus and the Church as the final and fulfilled revelation:

Can we prove it? . . . It seems to us, "Yes." . . . Some will perhaps object to us that we move in a vicious circle in reclaiming those who are on the route of the search for truth and from the time of their departure have the qualities of religious and moral life which make their souls accessible and penetrable to the divine light. Are we not demanding in them a soul already Christian . . . ? We do not think so, for the intellectual integrity which seems indispensable to us from the very first steps on the way of salvation can be born and develop independently of all positive faith. . . .[60]

The effort of Coppens is a far cry from the cold demonstration of the extreme traditionalists, but he still presumes dispositions on the part of the unbeliever that only a beginning Christian would have. He begins his apologetics where Scheler and Blondel would end theirs. He was really not aware of the present possibility (and actuality) that numerous men would question the historicity of the narratives of Christ and would be scandalized by the divisions of the Christian churches which honored the same "transcendant Christ." Nevertheless, the suggestions of Coppens became an important part of the more sophisticated approach to Christianity,[61] an approach which is under severe question.[62] It was again the case of the believer not opening his eyes to the world of the unbeliever.[63]

For the most part, many are still floundering in the world of apologetics. The attempts to justify the traditional apologetics are still heard, but they are accepted with less and less optimism. Almost a century ago, Max Scheler could say:

For, however they regard the logical validity of their proofs of God, there is one question which all supporters of orthodox natural theology must surely ask themselves: How is it that these proofs, really not complex or hard to follow . . . are totally devoid of power to *convince* modern man or any man who has not derived a belief in God from tradition, faith, or some other religious way of knowing?[64]

Blondel, equally aware of the problem of apologetics, would say:

There are two sorts of arguments: those which satisfy ill-prepared and superficial minds; and those which really satisfy. We must resist those who require from us the wrong set of arguments; we must resist our own inclinations . . . the important thing is not to address believers but to say something which counts in the eyes of the unbelievers.[65]

And Newman said almost a hundred years ago:

The fact of revelation is in itself demonstrably true, but it is not therefore true irresistibly; else, how comes it to be resisted? There is a vast distance between what it is in itself, and what it is to us. . . . I cannot convert men when I ask for assumptions which they refuse to grant me; and without assumptions no one can prove anything about anything. I am suspicious then of scientific demonstrations in a question of concrete fact, in a discussion between fallible men.[66]

Now that we have shown in a general way the historical circumstances under which our traditional apologetic was formed and the questionable validity that it has for the unbeliever, we would like to examine the specific proposals of Max Scheler, Maurice Blondel, and John Henry Newman. We hope from this historical discussion to gain insights for a *beginning in the solution of the modern apologetic problem*. We are grateful for the progress in theology and the openness of the modern Church which make such an investigation possible. We proceed in the spirit of every apologete—to strengthen the faith of the believer, to make possible the faith of the unbeliever.

III

MAX SCHELER (1874-1928)

German Catholic theology before the First World War, unlike that of France, was not overly concerned with the modern aspects of the problem of faith.[1] There had been, almost a century before, important stirrings out of Tübingen, but in general these had passed unnoticed. Rousselot's writings were overlooked until 1930, the Blondelians were classed with Schleiermacher and Ritschl as dangerous, and Newman was not really defended (or understood) until the efforts of Father Erich Przywara in the 1920's. It was the rise of Husserl that initiated a new direction in German philosophy, which eventually would reawaken the problem of faith and transform theology.

Specifically, it was a philosopher under the influence of Husserl who was largely responsible for the change of direction in theology.[2] This man was Max Scheler, who applied the phenomenological cry of *"Zu den Sachen selbst"* (to the things themselves) to the area of religious values, and saw as the question of the day, not the mechanics of supernatural faith, but the very possibility of revelation.[3]

It is outside the scope of this book to attempt an explanation or a justification of the phenomenological method. We simply explain it in terms of Scheler's use of it. It will become clear in our treatment that there are critics of Scheler who attack his failure to establish the fundamental relationship between "being" and "value," and his simplistic solution of problems that he did not have the temperament to penetrate or pursue. We are concerned with the thought-patterns of the past, against which he reacted, and the relevant apologetic insights he offered. We do not avoid the issue of metaphysics, and we describe some contemporary efforts to resolve the problem. For our present purposes, we endorse the conclusion of I. M. Bochenski:

There is a certain sense in which phenomenology remains no more than a link between the nineteenth century and our own day. What it lacks is the capacity to grasp concrete being; it is a philosophy of essence and not of being. Even Scheler did not arrive at a genuine metaphysic despite the great progress he made in this direction. . . . Yet . . . the majority of contemporary philosophers are aware of their dependence upon phenomenology. It is one of the main inspirations of philosophical thought today.[4]

Scheler is the key figure in early twentieth century Germany who pushed theologians into the phenomenological dimension, and this has great importance in the beginning of a solution to the apologetic problem.[5]

Max Scheler was born in Munich in 1874. His mother was the daughter of orthodox Jewish parents. His father was from a Protestant family which had produced a number of clergymen.[6] He became a Catholic while attending the Gymnasium, apparently impressed by the example of an outstanding priest. He completed his dissertation at the University of Jena in 1901, moved to the University of Munich in 1907, where he was strongly influenced by Husserl. In 1910, he went to Berlin as a free-lance writer. He was very much involved in the German cause during the war, and had diplomatic posts in The Hague and Geneva from 1917 to 1918. He had left the Church on the occasion of his marriage to a much older woman in 1898, whom he divorced a short time later. He married again in 1910, and was reinstated in the Church in 1916. A short time thereafter, his wife followed him into the Catholic faith. Upon completion of his diplomatic missions, he took a chair in philosophy and sociology at the University of Cologne, where he was "one of the outstanding Catholic laymen of the time, and exercized a great influence, especially upon the academic youth."[7] He broke with the Church again in 1924 when he could not receive permission for divorce and remarriage. The last few years of his life were troubled ones, when his great devotion to the Church was replaced with a kind of "vitalistic pantheism,"[8] and the rejection of a personal God.[9] His exodus from the Church is reflected vigorously in a late work, *The Nature of Man* (*Die Stellung des Menschen im Kosmos*, 1928), in which he says:

We deny the basic presupposition of theism: a spiritual, personal God, omnipotent in His spirituality. For us the basic relationship between man and the ground of being consists in the fact that this ground comprehends and realizes itself directly in man, who both as spirit and as life is but a partial mode of the eternal spirit and drive. . . . In and through this fulfillment, man culminates in the creation of God.[10]

Scheler went to the University of Frankfurt in 1928 and died that year at the age of fifty-four, still unreconciled with the Church.[11]

It is possible that his "apostasy" is in some measure responsible for the hesitancy of Catholic scholars to consider his work seriously. At any rate, the efforts of Scheler have received scant attention in theological circles.[12] The appraisal of I. M. Bochenski is the one that is likely to grow and endure in his regard:

Towards the end of his life Scheler sketched out a philosophy which is largely a repudiation of his earlier notions. In his main thesis he insists that the higher level of beings are [sic] weaker than the lower ones, because the most primitive and powerful sources of energy are those of the inorganic world; blind to ideas and forms and shapes, they are a matrix of unconscious urges. But this phase of his thought remains incomplete and history will continue to regard him as a personalistic and theistic thinker.[13]

Most authors refer to the three periods of Scheler's life as the pre-Catholic period (before 1912 to 1916), the Catholic period (until about 1924), and the pantheistic period (until his death).[14] Recently, Manfred Frings calls the three periods: the one in which he was interested in Eucken and Kant, the period of applied phenomenology, and the period which emphasized "urge and drive."[15] This characterization follows the works that were published during these various times, but hardly indicates the violent distinction between the second and third periods. At any rate, we will be largely concerned with Scheler's thought in the middle period.[16]

The Use of the Phenomenological Method

Max Scheler saw in Husserl and in the phenomenological method "a tool suitable for his own interests."[17] He was not concerned, as was Husserl, with the application of this method to the world of mathematics and logic. He was preoccupied with the sorry state of a world crippled by war and overrun with false values. Scheler reacted to life situations, as is evident from his variety of practical interests in politics, sociology, anthropology, philosphy, and religion. Most of his biographers or commentators see him as a man bristling with personal problems as well, problems that demanded solution.[18] His writings do not reveal his personal problems, but pulse with a restless and insatiable desire to resolve the confusions of a world torn apart and humiliated by war. If values could not be known in themselves, as the neo-Kantians insisted,[19] then there was no way to defend permanent and objective values in men's lives. Scheler once described his contemporary situation in the following way:

Self-deception over guilt . . . through boundless activity, elevating the simple process of work to an absolute value, or self-deception through the headlong plunge into the primitive pleasure-world of sensuality; eternally provisional life, postponing automatically all assessment of life, to the future, to the deathbed, to the "next time," and then seeking a logical and moral justification in the doctrine of the will to "progress"— that is the *kind* of system prevailing today.[20]

Scheler was not a speculative philosopher who made practical applications of his principles from the contemporary concerns of society to exemplify or clarify his theories. He was a man who saw a world that had denied God and worshipped humanity suddenly deprived of its comfortable theory of "progress." It was in this spirit that he began to theorize, to attack the neo-Kantists, Nietzsche, Schopenhauer, Schleiermacher, Comte, Freud, the Scholastics, the pantheists—and anyone else who destroyed values, or who established them artificially or on shifting sand.[21] He did not accept the false optimism of those who insisted that the "Great War" and its consequent horror had reduced man to "repentance" (*Reue*) and readied him for a spiritual transformation.[22] He had very little time for a religion that was born of the moment's need, a kind of passing sentiment that forced man to his knees. This could occasion a search on man's part, but it did not mean that he would find. Scheler insisted:

For however strong may be a pressure, a need, a deeply felt want, an emptiness in the heart that might be filled, the pressure itself, the need itself, have *not* the power nor the means to achieve their own satisfaction. . . . How much easier it is to imagine that so great a need for religious renewal should remain without positive consequence. It is possible for the world's cry of need to hold great meaning only when it generates motion and activity in man's positive springs of religion, only when it brings our reason to act in renewed concentration on the idea of God and opens our mental eye to the positive benefits of revelation and grace which are already *present* in the world, though great multitudes are blind to them. Need, the empty heart, the heartfelt want, can and should have this effect: to that extent they are beacons drawing souls on to explore new ground. But *more* they cannot do.[23]

He was concerned with a special class of "mental acts" which would lead to values.[24] Concern about values was not a unique contribution of Scheler to the thought of his time. Value-emphasis was a preoccupation with the neo-Kantian school which flourished in his student days.[25] His intellectual background was also in great measure influenced by the thought of Rudolph Eucken,[26] who has been called more "a preacher or prophet than a philosopher."[27] The phenomenological method, so effective in Husserl's battles with the conclusions of Kant, was the perfect companion of the value-concern which occupied Scheler. The application of Husserl's methods to the areas of value was an important part of his genius.[28] Before we discuss directly the phenomenological method of Scheler, it would be well to describe the classical approach as developed by Edmund Husserl. I. M. Bochenski writes:

The fundamental phenomenological intuition is that ideal essences are given. It has already been shown how this intuition helped Husserl and his pupils to overcome empiricism, idealism, and even conceptualism— that fundamental doctrine of Kant's which denies the real existence of material essences. Furthermore, phenomenological inquiry cleared the way to a recognition of . . . the objectivity of knowledge (distinguishing between the act of knowing and its object), and of the human spirit's true nature. All neo-Kantians treat the latter as a purely discursive function, as the technical reason (*ratio*) of the sciences; the phenomenologists restored its character as a genuine *intellectus*, an *intus-lectio* which is not limited to connecting perceived phenomena, but brings a capacity for grasping essences.[29]

Well schooled in Husserl,[30] Scheler turned to the problem of values, insisting that all modern theories of value start with the presumption that the very notion of value in general and moral value in greater degree "are only *subjective* phenomena in man's mind which have no independent meaning and existence."[31] This means that any value possessed would be a mere projection of a man's own desires and his fear of adhering to the structure of an objective system of values.[32]

In opposition, Scheler maintained that there was an a priori value-essence that was "given" in things themselves—if man could only be trained to see it.[33] This was primarily a cognitive process whereby man made contact with reality, but it would be wrong to think of it as a cold kind of rationalism, and wrong, of course, to think of it as a subjective feeling. It was, rather, an "experiential knowledge" which involved the whole man, and in which—and this is an important key to his thought—*love actually became an instrument of knowledge.*[34] Rather than a sentimental kind of discovery of values (*Gefühl*), it was an experience-charged contemplation of reality (*Fühlen*), from which values leaped out.[35] The values that were thus given in reality have an epistemological validity as real as that provided by sensory data, and more real than the rational constructions which flowed from this intuition.[36]

The values thus attained were of various kinds, and Scheler arranged them into an ordered hierarchy. At the summit of all values was the religious value or the grasp of the "holy."[37] *Der Formalismus*[38] gives the complete system and *Vom Ewigen der Menschen*[39] applies the original theory to the area of religious values, the highest of values attained and the real key to the attainment of personality.[40] Scheler was well aware of the difficulties that man had in reaching these values. He insisted that there was "a social deposit," a kind of environmental opposition to the grasping of true values (the *Weltanschauung* vs. the *Werianschauung*).[41] This was a problem that he struggled with all his life, and after 1921, as his personal problems mounted, he became increasingly more conscious of the *"Realfaktoren"* that interfered with a man's grasp of the true value.[42] He had always recognized the force of man's weakness and the inner struggle which obscured the intuition of values,[43] but insisted in his Catholic period that through humility and self-discipline man could reach the supreme value.

At times it is confusing in reading Scheler to determine what his thought was, at a given moment, on the struggle between value-contemplation and the social-personal opposition to values, since the problem was a continuing reflection of his own life.[44] For this reason, authors seem to be divided on whether or not his final and "pantheistic" views were merely a *"Ressentiment"* rationalism of his marital problems or the result, as well, of unresolved problems ever present in his thought.[45] At any rate, it is clear that in his Catholic period he insisted that man could attain these a priori value-essences which had a permanent and universal validity,[46] but it meant a consistent effort at seeking perfection.[47]

When he applied his theory of values to the religious problems of the day, he began, as usual, in the practical realm. He asked his contemporaries to take an honest look at the world. Formerly, the value-philosophies of the day—which he summed up as positivistic or as pantheistic—could point to some distant glory of humanity, the *grand être*, toward which man's efforts were directed. Progress was a sacred word, and science the savior to produce it.[48] Now that the illusion of progress had grown dead and its grave site was marked by the smoking ruins and piled corpses of the Great War,[49] the enthusiasm of the progressive scientist, who had mocked religion and explained it away in species of psychological or philosophical symbols, had noticeably waned.[50]

True, there had always been evil in the world, and there had ever been war and suffering, but never before had it existed on a scale that involved all of mankind.[51] The numerous, finespun theories of value had only produced chaos and they removed the very foundation of future reconstruction. Kant on the one hand and Schleiermacher on the other—seemingly far apart in their fundamental approach—had accomplished the same thing: they had reduced moral and religious values to empty symbols.[52]

And Christianity itself had little of which to be proud. It either had to admit its own bankruptcy and emptiness before Europe's self-annihilation, or it had to recognize that Europe was no longer Christian.[53] A short time before, Christian spokesmen had maintained that the commitment to Christ was sound and sincere,[54] as they stood idly and comfortably by in their complacency. And some were still so naïve as to maintain that the Great War could only lead to a Christian renewal, since man would now recognize his need of God.[55] Scheler coldly reminds them that the hunger of primitive people did not invent the fishhook, and that despair was no guarantee that man would return to the true source of hope.[56]

This time Christianity had to speak solidly and realistically to the world. Germany was not a Christian nation, nor was Europe in general a Christian commonwealth. If it were, the fact of the Great War would vindicate those who said that a new religion was the need of mankind, a kind of post-Christian conceptualization.[57] Hence, Scheler offered an approach to Christianity that would found it on solid ground, that would repair the harm done in the vain and shortsighted speculations of the philosophers and lead men to the "holy."[58]

Scheler and Apologetics

This brings us directly to our apologetic concern. Scheler examined the approach of the Christian apologete to the contemporary European mind, and found such efforts ineffective and shortsighted. Efforts had been made to "prove" the existence of God, and Scheler asserts, along with Newman (whom he quotes), that such proofs only convince the man who needs no convincing.[59] In fact, the whole apologetic approach attempted to fortify man's religious experience by extrinsic evidence, when the only answer was to force man to examine and validate the conclusions of his own religious intuition. The Scholastic method had been a metaphysical one, and such efforts center around establishing the "*ens a se*," the impersonal cause. They do not reach the *Summum Bonum*, the idea of the Holy, the personal God.[60]

Scheler's attack on the metaphysicians is long and arduous. He does not deny the place of metaphysics, as is commonly said.[61] He merely points out that the metaphysical effort should follow the religious experience, the personal intuition of values.[62] The metaphysician operates at a different level. He is attempting to "prove," and in so doing, he cannot help the unbeliever in his search for value.[63] To discover the *ens a se* is a different thing than to discover the Holy, even though the one reality attained is the same.[64]

The metaphysician falls into the hands of the scientist or the positivist, who must first beat reality into his own dimension, wherein he seeks to dominate and control it. Science seeks to make man the master, to rule the environment, to remove mystery; it does this by taking the given value of a thing and reducing it to a lifeless condition that permits experimentation and an orderly scientific arrangement.[65] The metaphysician, working at another level—the level of being—does much the same thing. Even though he would "prove" the existence of God, it would be a proof which finds him in control and follows the immediate intuition of the "holy" in a religious act.[66]

If man learns to approach the "things themselves," to go out to them, then the idea of the "holy," the highest value, will leap out to him. In this process, man does not dominate but is possessed by value, by the holy.[67] The particular process by which man approaches the "holy" is called the "religious act." It is the description of the religious act which occupies an important part of *On the Eternal in Man*.[68]

Scheler does not say that the idea of the "holy" thus attained (in the religious act) is outside the scope of metaphysics.[69] There is some controversy on this point, and, as was indicated, I. M. Bochenski does not think that Scheler was able to solve the problem he raised.[70] However, modern insights, especially a quite remarkable one proposed by Carlos Cirne-Lima, show the phenomenological dimension of St. Thomas himself.[71] What is more our concern is that Scheler restored this lost dimension to theology, specifically to the problem of faith. This fact has great bearing on the apologetic problem.[72] Whatever be the resolution of Scheler's metaphysics, his insight and the present influence of that insight—as well as its future development—is of outstanding significance.[73]

Scheler was never the sheltered idealist. He was ever conscious, not only of his deep, personal struggles, but of the circumstances of contemporary history. He saw the futility of the metaphysical approach to the fact of God's existence and the mystery of a

positive revelation. When one critic of Scheler attacks his distinction between "natural reason" and intuition,[74] he overlooks the
abstracted view of "natural reason" with which Scheler was dealing. It is one thing to argue endlessly about what St. Thomas really
meant and quite another to know what one's contemporaries
actually teach that he meant. Scheler's knowledge of Thomism was
that of his own day. Undoubtedly he was no expert, but he had
been exposed to it through Brentano, the Dominican mentor of
Husserl, and he was intelligently aware of what men thought of
it.[75] If the Kantians, positivists, and pantheists had no respect for
the mind's capacity to grasp essences and to know the truth, it did
little good to tell them, "Yes, the mind *can* know truth." The
abstractions of the contemporary Scholastics had rendered the
scholasticism irrelevant, and Scheler was determined to remedy the
situation. The world's problems were too pressing for him to
remain out of touch.[76]

It was with an awareness of all of these opponents—neo-
Kantians, positivists, pantheists, Scholastics, and sentimentalists—
that Scheler described the religious act. He was answering practical
questions: "How can we once again lead man to Christianity?"
"How can we bring Christ to the world to repair its carnage and
horror?" "How can Christianity enter into a dialogue with a world
that has found it wanting?" "How can we build a foundation for
the structure of a positive and supernatural revelation?" Kant,
Schleiermacher, the psychologists and pantheists, and certainly
the positivists have failed.[77] The metaphysical approach has
failed.[78] The fact of horror and destruction alone is not enough,
although it is an important beginning.[79] The answer—to Scheler
—began with the religious act, and although his description of it
was never ultimately complete, we have indications of what it is
essentially. We shall consider these now.

The Religious Act: The Application of Phenomenology
to the Religious Value, the "Holy"

Scheler began with man. He recognized, with Kant, that this was
the direction of modern thought. It was no longer, first, a question
of metaphysics, but metanthropology.[80] Man has the capacity to

find the ultimate value if he will look for it. When he finds it, then Christianity will appear to him as the only society which satisfies the evidence of his own search for the holy.[81] The search has become complicated because false values are everywhere.[82]

The Negative Aspect

Hence, Scheler began his discussion of the religious act with its negative aspect. There can be no serious consideration of religious values until we clear away the "idols":

This law stands: every finite spirit believes either in God or in idols. And from it there follows this pedagogic rule of religion: the correct way of dispelling "unbelief" is not that of guiding a man to the idea and reality of God by arguments external to his personal conviction (whether by "proofs" or by persuasion), but that of showing him invincibly . . . that within the objective sphere of the absolute, which he "has" at all events as a sphere, he has, in our sense, "deified" a particular good. . . . Hence, what I have called the "shattering of idols" is the principal (and only) way to prepare the religious development of the personality.[83]

Otherwise, we are left with the kind of "constructed" religion that permitted the holocaust of the Great War.[84] A man can remain very comfortable in what he thinks is religion, and it may well be what Nietzsche termed *Ressentiment*, or mere angry rationalization.[85] Actually, he will have adopted the values of his own society and will give them religious names. He will merely go along with the humanitarian principles of his own day in practice, and meanwhile, safely tucked in the compartment of his reason, he will frame his little religion, safely sheltered from having any true meaning. Such a religion will no longer endure in the modern world, and the irreligious man will have every right to ask: What value does your religion serve if it makes you no different? If it cannot justify its existence pragmatically, then it will pass into oblivion.[86] This is actually taking place, and it explains the cry for a "new religion."[87]

Scheler presumed that the "shattering of idols" must take place within a community, since he was extremely conscious of man's social dimension.[88] As we shall see, even though he centered his search for value in the experience of the individual, he saw man as so vitally a part of a community that he could not find or flee from value by himself *alone*. The religious act begins by clearing away the idols of "progress" and "humanitarianism" and "sensual pleasure." Although Nietzsche went too far in insisting that Christian love was in reality the hate of a resentful man who codified his own frustrations into law, yet there are numerous evidences in Christianity of a valid application of Nietzsche's insight.[89] Man must recognize the idols of his society and those that infect his personal life.[90] This is utterly essential, since it is not a question of whether or not man will make a religious act. He has to make it, he has no choice. The question is: Will the object be a true one or not?[91] Belief has no cause, only unbelief:

Once the cause [of unbelief] is uncovered . . . then it is that the religious act turns from its whoremongering in spontaneous quest of its proper object, the idea of God. Thus the right method for all religious initiation, the method which must precede any kind of instruction concerned with religion is not "proof," but the awakening and activation of the religious act, the guiding of the proper object and objective good.[92]

This will mean a battle with society, a prophetic role, and Scheler does not hesitate to assume it.

He is particularly hard on "scientism" and its desire to control reality. He says that it "bludgeons nature into a corpse, and . . . claims to have discovered the innermost secrets of life."[93] He does not question the validity of the scientific method for the scientific goal. He asks only that it not usurp the role of religion in explaining the real meaning of life. Man ends up not as the creature, the dependent being, the part longing for wholeness, but rather becomes the creator, the organizer, the producer of meaning. When Europe gazed around after the Great War and saw the condition of society, it should learn the futility of science, the horror of the mastery of man.[94]

Along with scientism goes the pantheistic worship of humanity, or a humanitarianism replacing the true community of love. It worships progress, and insists that the world is getting better all the time.[95] It was sparked by a theory of evolution, and it could explain away the phenomenon of religion in psychological terms. Religion was a state in man's development which he will outgrow,[96] but suddenly in the aftermath of the War, it has lost its grandiloquence and messianism.[97] Again, Scheler would not deny that there has been progress, nor would he ignore the capacity of one value to lead to another higher one.[98] He merely insists that religion cannot sit idly by while the idol of "progress" leads us to destruction.[99] This is the idol which has glorified work as the supreme value. Ridiculously enough, even the enjoyment of pleasure has become subordinated to useful work. "It is true," says Scheler, "the enjoyment can and should be subordinated to higher values . . . but subordinating it to utility is an absurdity.[100] His conclusion is interesting:

Here again, the propelling motive of the hard-working modern utilitarian is *Ressentiment* against a superior capacity and art of enjoyment, hatred and envy of a richer life that can enjoy pleasure more fully. . . . We ask "What is the use of the endless production of such objects if the type of man who consumes himself in producing them, and who owns them, is fundamentally incapable of enjoying them—while the man who could enjoy these objects is deprived of them?[101]

Even sports become mere recreation from work, and must serve the great god "utility."[102] Man's passage from the "estates" to the "classless society" caters to the "utility value" of struggle, and not to the prior good of man.[103] Such idols must be overturned before there can be a "religious act."

The Positive Side of the Religious Act

When he comes to the positive side of the religious act, Scheler is more labored in his approach. Our sources are not clear, and his promise to delineate its characteristics was never fulfilled.[104] He does tell us that there must be certain personal characteristics which accompany the religious act. If we are to escape our environment, there must be love, humility, and an attempt at self-mastery.[105] Love is required because we are not dealing with an idea, but with an active reality, a quest, ultimately a quest for a person, and love is the genuine source of such knowledge.[106] The fact that the person reveals himself in values is in itself a love, since

Scheler never tires of telling us that a person is not obliged to reveal himself.[107] We cannot pursue the "holy" as some detached ideal, but it must involve us as persons in quest of the life of true value and meaning. We are searching not merely for the true, but for *Summum Bonum*, the highest value, and this would have to be a person.[108]

Our search must take place within the community, since it is a mutual search in love, and such love is found only in the community.[109] The religious act will never be isolated, but the person who performs it will know that the lack of love he finds in the world is only a reflection of his own refusal to love in the first place.[110] This experience, too, is a community experience, where we stop talking about the love of humanity, and get down to a realistic love of neighbor.[111]

Humility is equally necessary as love of neighbor. And here, as with love and self-mastery, there is a growth toward the more perfect religious act. It is not a question of first loving, being humble and self-contained, and *then* performing the religious act. It is rather a continual process of interaction.[112] The humility will mean "subduing the Cartesian will to dominate being."[113] Since society will always try to make the relative into an absolute,[114] humility must make us aware of our dependence, our weakness, our insignificance apart from the wholeness which God gives.[115]

The emphasis on self-mastery, a constant indication of Scheler's personal struggle, highlights the battle between the animal instincts and the thrust of the spirit. His several marriages, the passionate power of his own drives made him increasingly conscious of his need, until ultimately he seemed to sink beneath it in a kind of cosmic despair.[116]

Since the religious act takes place at the very core of man's being,[117] the criticism that some made of Scheler's sentimentalism becomes inane.[118] Scheler was not creating value from religious feeling.[119] The value was already in the things of creation if only man would perceive them and their hierarchy, and not rest at the lesser values as if they were the ultimate.[120] This was the crime of the philosophic attempts at value-formation of the past century, which made religious sentiment or mere humanistic values the absolute. Christianity's failure to recognize this led it to meet the opponents on their own impossible grounds and produced an apologetic which gave an ultimate value to the naked intellect. Such attempts were doomed to failure.[121]

In the Middle Ages man did not have to be convinced of his own creatureliness; he took it for granted. He had "humility before being" because reminders of the divine were a part of his very culture. It was a creatureliness that was included in the very social deposit, and when there was talk of "proving" the existence of God, this was merely a proof of something that was already taken for granted.[122] This age of faith has passed away, and now we recognize that we cannot prove the real, we must experience it. We return to the dimension of Augustine, which was not a matter of proving the existence of God, but of "discovering" Him.[123] It is in the religious act that this takes place.

The religious act is not knowledge *of* God, but knowledge *through* God, who reveals Himself in things, or in the values that leap out of things. In performing the religious act we recognize that our experience does not come from ourselves, and it is no mere reflection of a created need which we seek to satisfy, but an actual contact with something that *is*, the fact of the "holy," "*the* Person" whom I experience when I perform the religious act.[124] "This act is *sui generis* and cannot be classified under the heading of either intellectual or volitional acts."[125] Hence, it is no mere social or psychological need, but an ontological one, the actual presence of the divine within man.

It is in the analysis of the qualities of the religious act that Scheler comes closest to defining it. First of all, "all things of a finite and contingent kind" must be grouped together into a "single whole." This is essential, for "without this preparatory operation a religious act cannot take place."[126] This "single whole" includes the subject himself and all that is of value to him, all that is a part of his experience. This would mean, of course, a paring away of idols. Even the agnostic is making the finite into an absolute, since "belief in nothingness is quite different from non-belief."[127]

After this primary grouping of all finite things into a single whole, the subject of the religious act discovers that nothing in the world can satisfy him. He experiences a kind of transcendence of the world. This is not something we can prove, though imaginative analogies help. It is something which the subject will experience in his performance of the religious act.[128] His "religious fear" will appear groundless; his "repentance" will have no finite object, and in "religious hope," he will hope for that which he has never experienced. His "mind oversteps the bounds, not only of this or that one finite thing, but the very sum and substance of all finite things."[129]

Finally, the subject of the religious act will expect an answer from the divine person he has thus contacted. If this were merely a metaphysical approach, it would leave man hopeless in the face of a kind of tortuous anxiety, which would be satisfied by a kind of extrinsic revelation of positive religion. But for Scheler, the phenomenologist, man has experienced not simply a need (for we cannot expect that our needs will necessarily be satisfied), but he has contacted the "divine" that is given in things, and the divine is no thing, but a person, who—*in love*—"must" answer.[130] Consequently, there must be a revelation, and the "essential difference between natural and positive religion lies in the *nature and manner* of revelation."[131] We expect revelation, since our contact with the a priori and "given" value of the holy that we find in things demands it. It does not demand Christ or a positive revelation which is "transmitted by the exceptional and sublime link with God enjoyed by certain persons."[132] Revelation is the very fulfillment of the religious act.[133]

Hence, we cannot expect that God must first be known before we can give a real place to the religious acts, since "God, by his very nature, is revealed only in them . . . as the basic cause which moved the subject to perform them."[134] Ultimately, Scheler is not denying the uniqueness of the Christian revelation, nor questioning its gratuity. He is a philosopher who studies what he sees and experiences, and attempts to describe it. He claims to make a clear distinction between that which "rests . . . on essential insight and what is a matter of positive faith."[135] However, it is not difficult to understand that the theologians of his own day would be extremely cautious in handling ideas which seemed to make of grace an expected help, and to make of revelation the necessary fulfillment of nature. We have already discussed his insistence that he did no violence to the boundaries between faith and intuition,[136] but it seems necessary at this time to say a word about his anticipation of the "supernatural existential."

The Anticipation of the Supernatural Existential

Scheler's insistence on the experiential dimension of man's knowledge was bound to create theological difficulties when dealing with
the God-man relationship. The "standard view of nature and grace
in post-Tridentine and neo-Scholastic theology"[137] is described by
Karl Rahner:

The supernatural grace through which man is justified and can do just
works was regarded as something in itself beyond consciousness. This is
a theological opinion which has always been in dispute. But it is the
prevalent one and has determined the standard view of the subject:
Supernatural grace is a reality which we know about from the teaching
of the Faith, but which is completely outside our experience. . . .
Grace is a superstructure above man's conscious spiritual and moral
life. . . . Once one has this view, then of course the sphere of our
spiritual and moral actions, within which we are present to ourselves,
seems to be identical with "nature" in the theological sense. . . .
Nature is what we experience of ourselves without revelation.[138]

Rahner goes on to point out that such a view cannot avoid the
"extrinsicity" label, and grace was seen merely as an "entitative
elevation."[139] This would explain the "modern lack of interest in
the supernatural."[140]

Then, gradually, "it began to be understood that the orienta-
tion of man as a spirit towards God is not an 'extra,' but it is what
makes him what he experiences himself to be."[141] With insights
such as this, the heart of Thomistic thought, obscured perhaps
after Trent and forgotten in textbooks, where "the manageable and
the simplified" too often become the "criterion of truth,"[142] could
be recaptured and developed. The emphasis on the divine indwell-
ing began to replace the somewhat exclusive development of "created grace."[143] The modern mind wants to view man as a unity,
or, as Rahner puts it:

We want a synthesis of all the different things we know about him. We
think "existentially." And so we want as far as possible to "experience"
the reality of grace in our own existence where we experience ourselves.[144]

Then Rahner goes to the very heart of the problem. What order are we actually in? Is there an order of nature and an order of grace in the present reality? (Or is there merely nature and grace?) And can we not say that the Incarnation has so changed things in the world that "by his free coming into the world, he makes the world's order of nature his nature?"[145] The Word would, in this view, be "*the* person in whom God communicates himself hypostatically to the world."[146] In this way we cannot think of grace without relating it to God's love, and we are in no danger of heresy as long as "grace is always the free act of God's love, which man can 'dispose' of *only* in the measure in which he himself is at this love's disposal."[147] There is a danger in thinking that "just because grace is free and unmerited" it must also be "rare." Rahner asserts that "theology has been led astray far too long already by the tacit assumption that grace would no longer be grace if God became too free with it."[148]

Thus, no matter what the state of man, "supernatural transcendence exists in every man who has reached the use of reason." Since, in his moral actions, man, as it were, takes a stand toward the "*totality* of his actual existence," then "every morally good act done by man is in the order of salvation."[149] Relying on such principles (which Rahner asserts have a basis in Scripture), we discover that any effort to bring man face to face with the meaning of life "is the awakening and making explicit of what is already there in the depths of man."[150] Consequently, the "question whether a metaphysical [that is, pretheological] argument has as its real starting point pure nature or historical nature is in the concrete case of no great importance."[151] This would not mean a denial of the gratuity of grace, since "spirit" (in the existential order) means an openness to "supernatural fulfillment," but "grace is not, therefore, an exigency of its nature."[152]

Of course, the problem of the "supernatural existential" is an involved and unsettled one.[153] Nevertheless, the direction of modern theology is indicated by Rahner, and Scheler was one of those to anticipate it by his refusal to divide up man, or for that matter, God. The relationship of man to God "is not utterly unlike the ordinary good faith which holds among human persons."[154] Consequently, Scheler did not make the clear distinctions which were required by the degree of theological development of his day.

When he spoke of "repentance" as a way to God, he was appealing to the "existential" man he knew and the God that he loved:

Even if there were nothing else in the world from which we might create the idea of God, repentance alone could draw our attention to God's existence. Repentance begins with an indictment. But before whom do we indict ourselves? . . . Where is the source of strength and where the idea for the construction of this new heart, and where the effective power for its making?[155]

Ultimately he reduces repentance to a manifestation of "God's love for us." He is not denying the unique reality of a positive revelation. To say that the various doctrines were merely the psychological expressions of man's inner yearning was the very thing he condemned in Schleiermacher and Otto.[156] But, for Scheler, as for Rahner, Christ is here, and the Christian event is a present reality. It was a part of the world which man experienced, and to admit this was not to deny the gratuity of grace nor the uniqueness of positive revelation. Scheler's critics—in his own day—were right in questioning his theology.[157] Scheler was equally right in being honest to the insights which were a "significant step in reawakening the problem of faith . . . the way in which faith displays itself in one's personal existence and in the interpersonal community of man."[158] When a man is ahead of his time, as Scheler was, we do not condemn his critics. We are as grateful for their loyal faith as we are for his new vision.

The Religious Act in Morality and in Liturgy

Scheler's approach to the "religious act" becomes clearer when he explains that it is not an isolated and individual performance, nor something that confines "itself within the human interior." It operates through the body in two ways: "purposive conduct and expressive action."[159] The "purposive conduct" means a pursuit of the "holy," which man actually undertakes between the religious act and its moral expression, so that "an identical component of value-cognition is present in both moral and religious act."[160] Nor can we isolate man in his performance of the religious act. Liturgy and its expression—in forms of worship—are essential, and a similar interplay between action and knowledge takes place. Man will perform the religious act in a community of love, and "religious knowledge is not wholly present *before* liturgical expression; ritual is an essential vehicle of its growth."[161] Scheler explains that the very position of people at prayer, whether they *stand* or *kneel*, is both an indication of their attitude toward God and a factor in the formation of this attitude. One cannot expect a man to reach the religious act first and then to express it in some liturgical form or moral action. Scheler sums up his views in this important passage:

Since religion is just as much practice as theoretical knowledge, and since theory and practice are here inseparable, it would be ridiculous to say to a man who has made some approach to a given religion or church, While you have still not accepted every one of this religion's tenets of divinity, you may not, for conscience's sake, perform any act of worship which this religion prescribes." One might as well tell a painter that before he begins to paint . . . he must see a landscape in the same way as that in which he gradually learns to see it as his picture takes shape. No! Pascal was right when he said, "Do thou but kneel and faith will come." And so we should thus advise our man: "Try to perform the moral acts and ritual which this religion lays down, then see whether or how far you have grown in religious understanding.[162]

To Scheler, religion was a life process, not an idea, and this was the burden of his quarrel with traditional apologetics. They borrowed the arguments of the Middle Ages without recognizing that the social datum, man's image of himself, had thoroughly changed.[163] Those who criticize his metaphysics and stop there, or those that claim he confused emotion and the intellect,[164] do not appreciate the force of his vision. He was standing in the ashes of the Great War and feeling the fire of its horror; as he wrote:

When therefore such an event as awakens the core of the human soul and unpinions this mainspring for great activity impinges not only on the individual soul . . . but on the community of men; when it impinges on the worldwide community, divided in peoples, which has nothing over it but its God; when its impact is greater than that of any event in the whole of history, when the event is in addition so unimaginably saturated with tears, suffering, lifeblood as the late war—*then* one may expect the call to a renewal of religion to resound through the world with such power and strength as has not been for centuries.[165]

He saw the opportunity of the hour and the futility of past methods of apologetics. He heard views of a universal Church and saw the mutual efforts of Christian countries to pin the blame for the war on one another.[166] In the period of reconstruction, religion had to be more than an idea, more than a reality on paper, more than a clear and cogent proof. It had to be a religious act, lived and experienced and expressed, founded in the very presence of God in things themselves, wherein man finds God before he even proves His existence:

For the *religious* consciousness, it is a composite axiom about the nature of things, that what is absolutely valuable must also exist. . . . For that reason, love of God, in a special sense, and fear of God, for that matter, *precedes* in the evolution of a given individual religious consciousness, even the religious act in which the existence of the "godly" thing is posited; here, love of God is understood *not* as love of a deity whose existence is already assumed, but as the qualitative character of the act of loving when addressed to "something" within the "value-modality" of holiness.[167]

Scheler took for granted that the false ideas and idols which perverted the true object of the religious act were communicated within society.[168] Consequently, anyone concerned about faith or value-formation had to work within this framework. This is the only way to prevent the deception whereby:

Men may be firmly convinced with their conscious judgment that they profess the Christian idea of God. . . . But at the same time, as to the actual form of their *Weltanschauung*, they may be ruled by an entirely different idea of God.[169]

Hence the religious act could take place only with a community which would form "one power of willing love and obligation, embracing all men in their work together, independently of mere communities of interest."[170] It is only in such a community that man truly becomes an individual, wherein he is not preyed upon by a variety of pressures which destroy his freedom,[171] wherein man finds the "true *individualism*, which is to say the Christian individualism implicit in the Christian ideal of Community."[172]

Within the community there will stand certain types of value-persons (the type depending on the kind of community), and the highest of these is the "holy" one.[173] Since persons determine in large measure the "predominant ethos" of an age, "the problem of 'exemplar and following' appears to Scheler to be of the greatest importance for ethics."[174] He was convinced that:

There is nothing on earth which prompts a person himself to become good as originally, immediately, and necessarily as the insightful and pure beholding [*Anschauung*] of a good person in his goodness.[175]

Religion is not a study, nor is it a speculative discussion, and it is easier in the religious community to decide what true religion is by a contact with a true saint.[176] For the *religiosus* or *saint* is thus described:

He is a person whose spiritual figure presents us to an extraordinary degree with a likeness, however inadequate, of God's own personality: this it does to such a good effect that his utterances, pronouncements and deeds are no longer measured against a norm of common application.[177]

Scheler recognizes the important place of such persons even in the most primitive religious societies, and *a fortiori* would expect them in the more perfect and developed forms.[178] Actually, he attempts to show that Christ, *the* "holy" one and the *perfect* exemplar, would be expected by a man who understands the religious act. The religious act reaches for the *Summum Bonum*, and, as we have seen,[179] recognizes that this must be a person. This beginning revelation of God would only be fulfilled in the revelation of the perfect God-man which Christ is.[180] Such talk troubles his contemporaries as we have seen,[181] although the general idea of "*Wertpersonen*" within the community was not exactly new. Scheler's thorough development in *Der Formalismus* was unique.[182]

It would be wrong to imply that Scheler did not recognize values apart from the "holy," as, for example, in the state or in science. He complains of the "depersonalization of science"[183] even as he asks the "deepest and richest possible harmony between the Christian and his culture.[184] What he opposes is the absorption of the religious experience by secular values and religion's refusal to recognize its own unique and autonomous role. He says:

If religion is once again to become the true guide and leading spirit of civilized humanity . . . then it is first and foremost on condition that it become aware of its autonomy; the religious consciousness must extricate itself from dense entanglement with the values and norms of secular "culture" which the Great War rendered all too questionable.[185]

At the same time the Christian must proceed with sympathy for his own society and an intimate experience of both real and artificial values. Scheler describes this in an interesting analogy of modern man's dance before the "idols":

Only one who does not dance in the depth of his soul, but who yet knows that his body is swayed by the rhythm, can discern the dance.[186]

The work of religion in the world is a death struggle with the purveyors of false values. In the past, religion has known its era of glory, but today its very existence is threatened by the idols that will accept nothing but complete homage.[187] Religion can not stand off and offer its proofs which convince no one. It must assert its autonomy and meet modern man head on:

The world's object is not the development of its own forces in the sense of a constant enhancement of value. If it is not raised up by Redemption, if higher powers do not freely condescend to it, to raise it ever anew, then—it falls into the void. Constant danger of death . . . constant sinking to his knees for weakness—walking only by virtue of a power descending in compassion to raise him ever and ever again; this . . . is a far truer picture of man than . . . [his] bounding . . . into a land of increasing splendour and limitless horizons.[188]

Max Scheler—Evaluation

Max Scheler understood clearly that the apologetic which had been suitable for a believing world had little effect on the unbeliever. The "metaphysical" approach of the past did not take man as he really was, even though metaphysics had its special and important place. It was, however, a secondary operation, and had to follow and appreciate the unique quality of the religious experience as a life-search rather than the defense of an idea. With the help of phenomenology, Scheler described the religious act as he perceived it. He established its validity as the guide to the highest of all values, the "holy." This value was not merely in the mind, nor was it merely the convenience of an orderly rational construct. The value rose up from the "thing itself," and through a rigorous rejection of false values and a consistent intuition of the true, the *Summum Bonum*, the highest and absolute value was seen to be a person, *the* Person. By the use of his intuitional method, Scheler could answer Kant and Schleiermacher, the positivists and the pantheists, the psychologists and even the Scholastics who ended up either destroying the foundation of values or establishing them on an unreal foundation.

His realization that love is an instrument of knowledge was perhaps his most important contribution. He saw the mutability between knowledge and love, and saw equally as well that such love could be found only in the Christian community. An impersonal society would not do, since it ended up overpowering, obscuring, and ultimately destroying man. It had to be a true community, wherein the individual was truly responsible, and where any lack of love was but a ripple flowing back from his own refusal to love. Along these lines he developed his famous insights into collective guilt and the true repentance, which did not merely blot out a memory but transformed one's being. He also insisted that the person must act—morally and liturgically—within the community if he is to grow in the capacity to perform the religious act. He could not view the thoughts and actions of man in separate categories.

He stressed the importance of the "persons of value" within the community, explaining that the experience of the Divine would best be seen in His counterparts. Scheler could not be merely a philosopher, or a theologian, nor could he be just a psychologist or a sociologist. He was dealing with man as he knew him, as he knew himself, and no dimension could be unimportant. The dynamics of the social group could not be put aside while he considered the pure concept of love. Nor could the frailty of man be overlooked, nor the cultural tensions which shaped his attitudes. The descriptions of the "religious act" could never be quiet and speculative; they must seek out man in the tangled and troubled world in which he lived.

For this reason, the community could not be above self-criticism. It had to face even the most violent analysis—such as Nietzsche's summation of Christian love as a hate-inspired *Ressentiment*. False values could creep into the community; the love for humanity could replace the love for neighbor. Hence, the community must ever seek to purify its religious institutions, its unyielding pursuit of the "holy."

Some see in Scheler a dangerous pessimism, but it strikes us that this impression flows more from the fury of his indictments than from his apologetic program. He saw a great goodness within man, a kind of divine spark, and this, ultimately, is the basis of all optimism. He believed in man, because he believed in God, and his passion to tear down idols was the result of his own deep involvement in the world. He was not preparing a program for the intellectually proud, or an outline for the university campus alone. He was envisioning the ordinary man, the man who bowed before industry and felt the chains of an economic system and the national struggle for power. He knew that at the core of man's being there was an ache that only the *Summum Bonum* could soothe, an emptiness that only the loving *ens a se* could fill. He had lived through the false optimism of the prewar years and had watched Europe dissolve into a horror of armed camps and suffering people. If Christianity were unique, if it were to mean anything to modern man, then it must begin to interpret life's meaning to a society that seemed increasingly pointless. And it must do this in terms and with methods that man could understand.

Max Scheler was a realist, torn by the awareness of problems facing his Church, his world, his Germany, his Europe, his own being. He saw the effort of the impersonal societies of "humanitarianism" and "scientism" to choke and dominate man and to establish themselves as the absolutely "valuable" under the banner of "progress." He reminded the world that such a philosophy had led to the ruin of the Great War. And he reminded Christianity that the horror of the war alone would not lead it to strength and relevance. It must be as violent as a fiery Moses in uprooting idols, and it must justify its existence before the world by the purity and pragmatic power of its communal love. Then would wisdom leap out from the revelation poured into things by their Creator, then would man be open to the revelation which explained his existence and made progress his servant, not his unfeeling master.

His attempt to show phenomenologically that Catholic Christianity was *the* revelation by its correspondence with man's discoveries in the practice of the religious act was not carefully developed, and seems to reveal his previous faith in Christ. But he envisaged the gradual entrance of man into the community of love, and who knows but that the gradual awareness of true value would creep in its Christian way into a man's heart, even as Scheler described it? He was quite obviously describing what had happened to him. In view of the meager development of this portion of his apologetic we can only guess what he ultimately envisioned. At any rate, we find his descriptions of the religious act most relevant and valid in our approach to an unbelieving world. If he does not give the apologete a complete system—and who could—he offers a *modus operandi* which is both valid and phenomenologically sound. It is real.

He tells the apologete to attack society's idols, to permit the unbeliever to know a place in the community, to have faith in the capacity of man to have faith. He would discourage any effort to convince a man merely intellectually, or to expect that he will believe without doing, or without experiencing love. Scheler would require any apologete to ask himself: What are your intentions? What are you trying to accomplish? To whom are you speaking? What world does he live in? How does a man come to truth and value? What are the obstacles to faith? Do you believe that this man may perhaps not believe because you have not loved? These questions reveal important apologetic principles which have not lost their relevance today.

At times Scheler contradicts himself, and at times his thoughts run too hastily for clarity. He was a man on fire, an active man who had a job to do, and everywhere he looked he saw more that needed to be done. Some say he did not resolve the metaphysical problem that he created. But there is a growing impression that his metaphysics may be supremely sound. Some say he had mere insights that were important, vastly important, and have become a permanent part of our contemporary philosophy. At any rate, interest in Scheler grows, and a world which was barely ready for him now begins to listen. With theology's advance, he does not have to answer the charges of "naturalism" and "fideism." These are words which have lost much of their sting. Nor need he fear being grouped with the "sentimentalists" in an age which is beginning to recognize the cognitive power of love. Even the Scholastics, who bore his attacks so poorly, have realized that the Thomism he knew was as impoverished as he said, and its revitalization can utilize many of his suggestions.

Max Scheler was a man ahead of his times, a disturbed and restless man whose prophetic insights about Europe's fall from faith have been realized in another war, in gas chambers and concentration camps, and in a second Vatican Council, which has taught us all to beat our breasts. Fortunately, today we are pre-pared to recognize the world of the unbeliever. We know that we cannot "prove" God or "Christ" or the "Church" to him. We know that he has values, and we know that we must show him the poverty of our own, as we ask him to join us—at least in a begin-ning way—in our search for God in a community of love. Max Scheler would have liked that.

THE APOLOGETIC OF
MAURICE BLONDEL (1861–1949)

Like Scheler, Maurice Blondel was painfully conscious of the Church's irrelevant apologetics which were offered to an unbelieving world. The methods of the theology manuals were outdated and ineffective.[1] They spoke to men who were already disposed to listen, for "only he who loves and is ready to give himself to love is able to see and interpret the signs of love."[2] It was futile to offer arguments which the modern philosophical spirit rejected in principle.[3]

Maurice Blondel was born in Dijon, France, in 1861, the fourth child of an old and successful Catholic family.[4] He was shy and sensitive, protected and curious, "slight, sinewy, with quick, deft movements and very prompt reactions."[5] He had the heart of an apostle and it was this that prompted him to enroll at the École Normale, where he would be exposed to the varieties of faiths and backgrounds of France, and thus be better prepared to teach philosophy at the university. It was at the École Normale that he recognized the unconcern of his fellow students with the Catholic faith, and their intense preoccupation with the varying ephemeral assertions of the new philosophies.[6] He himself found no satisfaction in these philosophies, which were to him "too intellectualist, too abstract, and too favorable to a spectator's attitude."[7]

It was also at the École Normale that he was exposed to the

thought of Léon Ollé-Laprune, who acted as director of studies, and whose great work, *La Certitude Morale,* emphasized the personalist approach in the search for truth.[8] Blondel had great difficulty in passing his *aggrégation,* owing to his poor background in the rationalist scholasticism offered by Dijon. This caused him untold anguish and humiliation. It was only in 1886 that he finally passed on his third attempt and began teaching at the university in Aix and working on his doctoral thesis. He had very little time for reading while working on his doctorate. The resultant *L'Action* is largely a reflection on his past learning and on his own experience.[9] He was to remain at Aix for the rest of his teaching years, having been named a professor—again with great difficulty—in 1897.[10]

He had difficulty pursuing his doctoral topic when he insisted that he wanted to write on *L'Action.* He was told that he probably meant that he wished to write on the *idea* of *L'Action,* but he replied very strongly that he meant what he said.[11] The dissertation itself was criticized for the difficulty of its language and the abstruseness of its thought. This irritated some of his professors and even aroused the complaints of a famous American admirer, William James.[12] In a classic reply, Blondel told the members of his examining board:

One can never hope to succeed in preventing impatient and presumptuous minds from wanting to grasp and believing they have penetrated everything without competence. . . . If I wrote certain parts of my work six or seven times, it was not for the pleasure of remaining obscure: I sincerely tried to reduce the difficulties which come from the imperfection of the expression, and I am distressed that I was not more successful. And yet I did not hope . . . to make all the obstacles disappear. Style is not only a passage open to others, giving them access to our thoughts; it is also a protection against hasty judgments. The right thing would be to be understood neither too soon nor too late.[13]

For all of Blondel's shyness and reserve, there was a bold courage that marked his work. Very early in his professional life, he was aware that he had a unique and unavoidable task, "to conciliate the claims of modern thought."[14] He could not ignore the cultural trends in an age which had "every right to be regarded as one of the richest in the history of French culture."[15] In the Introduction to *L'Action,* he insists that there is partial truth everywhere, and expresses his utter contempt for the man who will make a single aspect of truth the whole.[16] This particular kind of narrowness seemed to arouse the ire of this shy and perceptive man. He wrote to his beloved disciple, Auguste Valensin, later a professor on the Catholic faculty at Lyons, reflecting the whole spirit of *L'Action*: "I have a horror of unilateralism."[17] Only an idealist, cut off from life's important contacts, could ignore the legitimate objections to Christianity in contemporary society.[18]

L'Action was more than a doctoral thesis. It was the vision that would accompany Blondel through his life, a vocation that demanded he try "to open up a scientific passage amid so many barriers, to understand equally the legitimate demands of the modern mind and the unassailable permanence of Christian truth . . . and to throw into the chasm between them . . . the whole of oneself."[19] This single vision possessed him early in his career and would not leave him alone. His letters from 1886 until early in the 1890's show how he struggled with this "intuition" to make it ever clearer. To Émile Boutroux he wrote in 1886:

I have not chosen it: it simply appears, but still I am afraid of it, and I would not dare follow it alone. I need students; I need the active life. I want to study *L'Action* and to clarify it. I want to discover the nuances which will make it clear and guarantee its sincerity. Between Aristotelianism, which reduces practice to thought, and Kantianism, which separates them and exalts the practical order to the detriment of speculation, there is something to define, and I want to accomplish this in a very concrete way by an analysis of action.[20]

In another letter, written to M. le Doven for the approval of his doctoral topic, he also spoke of a mysterious "something to define." This "something" was the fruit of his reflection for "several years," and he felt certain that *L'Action* was the way in which to coordinate the "ancient doctrine, according to which the will acts in accord with an object" and "Kantianism, which places the will outside and above reason." As important as thought is, "it is yet truer, perhaps, to say that to think well, it is necessary to act well."[21]

Even the vocation to the priesthood, to which he gave a considerable consideration, could not interfere with his abiding vision. In his *Carnets Intimes*, he wrote:

To devote oneself to others is the role common to all men, just as Christianity is the universal remedy—but how? Is it to be in intellectual conflicts, in the melee of ideas? Or in hand-to-hand fights, in the political and social fray? There the cassock is a scarecrow. It compromises one and one compromises it. One's personal action is incommoded and restricted.[22]

Blondel decided against the priesthood and married Rose Royer in 1894. Three children were born of the marriage, and his wife died in 1919.[23]

As strongly as Blondel knew that he must engage in hand-to-hand fights, he also knew that his work must be that of the "thinker" rather than the "doer." But it would be the thought of a man who struggled with the practical religious questions of his society. This was his concern at the very beginning of his *L'Action:* "Does human life have any meaning, and does man have a destiny? Yes, or no?"[24] Mere speculative thought could not answer such questions as these. Speculation permitted self-deception and the egotism of the dilettante.[25] Man must enter into the "brutality of daily experience"[26] and realize that "there is a living laboratory" where he will find the "science of life" in the "flesh, appetites, desires, and thoughts, whose hidden struggle I feel perpetually."[27] It will be a restless search, but a real one, not "governing myself only by my ideas," but engaging in "practical action, which will not tolerate respite, nor even bring complete clarity."[28]

It was this practical concern of Blondel that led him to discourage his friend, Victor Delbos, from undertaking a merely historical type of thesis in his doctoral work. In a letter written in 1889, in the midst of Blondel's own struggles, he tells Delbos to choose a subject "which rises up spontaneously from one's constant meditations and expresses the free movement of the spirit." He found no point in a purely historical effort, since history should help us "draw from the past that which still lives, and to collect therein the seeds of personal thought." In order to do this "one begins by taking root in the spirit of another and nourishing therein his substance."[29]

This was the very advice that Blondel himself followed. He was concerned with speaking to the men he knew, his contemporaries. He saw the Church closed in upon itself, speaking the idiom of another day. And he saw the men of his own society grasping at straws in their need and frustration.[30] He could not isolate himself in the security of an ancient and institutional Church. If Chris-

tianity and society continued to move along straight lines at
different latitudes, nothing could be done to bridge the chasm. As
Blondel put it in *La Semaine Sociale*, written in 1909:

Formerly the Saviour left the ninety-nine faithful sheep on [sic] their
pasture to go in search of the one that was lost; there are some,
nowadays, who would remain behind with the one faithful old ewe to
secure it more firmly.[31]

If the Church insisted on cutting itself off from its own culture, if it did not speak to men in a dialogue which they could
understand, if it did not rid itself of the trappings of medieval
society, then "only a patent and glorified constraint, or the coercion of visible power" would be able to "guarantee the unity and
efficacious links of the religious body."[32]

As Blondel struggled with his life-idea, he welcomed criticism,[33] shunning the life of the lonely scholar who thought independently of students and experience. In a letter of 1893 he spoke
of the many editions of *L'Action*,[34] and his daily dictations to a
fifteen-year-old scribe. He continued to amend and revise as the
struggle with other minds made his own vision clearer. Each time
he had to admit that "paper is a mirror which humbles one
exceedingly."[35] But he accepted this struggle between doubt and
certitude, clarity and obscurity, with an awareness that this was the
real state of man in the present life. In a passage of exceptional
insight, he writes to Frederick Rauh in 1892:

To answer your frankness with equal frankness, I confess that we should
never sacrifice certitude for tension nor tension for certitude; it is indeed
idolatry to believe, in that gross and withered way, that we have *arrived*
and are in possession of the object of faith; but equally is it idolatry to
have that kind of conscience which is satisfied never to find. . . . Did
not Pascal say . . . that in truth the proof of heart and good will was
the mingling of shadows and fleeting light? . . . There is only true
certitude, deserved and honest, where there is from the start and at the
same time tension.[36]

It is in a letter to his former director of studies at the École
Normale, M. Ollé-Laprune, that Blondel characterizes his unique
calling as that of the "apostle of the unbelievers."[37] In order to do
this he insisted humbly but emphatically that he must understand
the unbeliever's frame of reference, and approach him with a
method that he will accept as worthy of honest dialogue. He

clarifies this in a letter to A. Georges Perrot, the director of the École Normale in 1893:

My goal has been to accept the differences of human consciences, without discouraging good will, without questioning sincerity. And if at times I have appeared to support closed minds or weak and sluggish consciences, it is only to lead them where I think their secret will is taking them, and to give them more when they were satisfied with less.[38]

It was his theory of *L'Action* that would serve as the"permanent connection"[39] between *"la croyance et la science."* He does not propose to be a theologian, but "in intention and method, [his] work is exclusively philosophical."[40] But this does not mean that he cannot speak of the supernatural, since it is a phenomenon that can be observed. If, as is sure, philosophy cannot produce the supernatural, with equal certainty it cannot deny its existence. In the same lengthy letter to Perrot he says:

If I speak of the supernatural, it is still a cry of nature, a call of the moral conscience and a demand of reason as I understand it. . . . So, when I speak of that which surpasses knowledge and reason, I do so in the name of reason and by a need of nature.[41]

He does not look for understanding from those he seeks to help, but they have moved his heart from early student days, since "they maintain a true generosity in their rejection of the truths in which I believe, and in their very appearance of misrepresenting these truths, they do not cease to share in them invisibly."[42] They are moved toward those very truths by an inner determinism which they do not recognize. Blondel seeks to expose this present dynamism.[43]

In searching out the early influences on the life and thought of Blondel, an impossible task in any case, his own testimony points to a pair of outstanding masters at the École Normale:

If the choice of my subject, the nature of my approach, and the very meaning of my conclusions were imposed upon me gradually, without an intermediary or external interventions, yet I owe a great deal to two of my masters at the École Normale, M. Émile Boutroux and M. Ollé-Laprune. The latter has provided me with some of the material, the former with some of the form of my philosophical convictions.[44]

Gradually, during the years of work on the thesis, Blondel became aware of the efforts of the Möhler and the Tübingen school, almost a century before, in Germany. He considers himself in this "romantic tradition."[45]

After completing his dissertation, and finally being established as a professor at Aix, he continued to reflect, to correspond faithfully, and to stay free of the intellectual riot which followed upon his ideas.[46] He wanted the debates to rage, and made no apology in his own behalf, save to answer carefully the letters of his critics and intimates. On occasions he was ingloriously lumped with the Modernists.[47] Valensin tells us of the ignorance of such a charge and of the pain that this caused Blondel.[48]

He had, however, a great sympathy for the Modernists, and he saw them as a reaction against the ultra-traditionalism of the Church, the closed kind of thinking that admitted of no change, and thought that old answers were adequate to answer totally new questions.[49] The *Letter on Apologetics*, which will be our chief concern in the treatment of Blondel, was written in 1896 for the *Annales de Philosophie Chrétienne*, three years after the dissertation, *L'Action*, was accepted and published.[50] It was an effort to apply the principles established in *L'Action* to the apologetics of his own society. The Modernists were certainly extreme, but their refusal to accept an unfair apologetic was well taken. Blondel, in the *Letter*, attempts a more effective, honest, and truly philosophical approach.[51]

For the years following the publication of his doctoral thesis, most of the work of Blondel which was written for periodicals centered around the Modernist controversy. This work, as was already indicated in regard to the *Letter on Apologetics*, was largely an application of the theory of *L'Action* to current controversies. Some of his more important apologetic efforts were:

1. A series of articles published under the signature of L'Abbé Mallet, treating the apologetic work of Cardinal Dechamps. These appeared in the *Annales* from 1905 to 1907, and were later gathered together and modified and published under the title *Le Problème de la philosophie catholique*.
2. *La notion et le rôle du miracle* also appeared in the *Annales* in July of 1907 under the pseudonym of Bernard de Sailly.
3. A brief work, *Qu'est-ce que la foi?* also appeared under the name of L'Abbé Mallet in 1908, and was published by Bloud of Paris.
4. *La Semaine Sociale de Bordeaux et le Monophorisme*, written under

the name of Testis, was also published by Bloud in 1910. It had originally appeared in article form in the *Annales* from 1909 through 1910.

5. Another series of articles, appearing in *Annales* in 1912 to 1913, was published by Bloud in 1913 under the title of *Comment réaliser l'apologétique intégrale.*[52]

During this period, the letters of Blondel were rich in apologetical insights. Unfortunately, these, and his most important work, *L'Action*, have not been translated. In fact, only the *Letter on Apologetics* and *History and Dogma* have appeared in English, and this only in a single volume, in 1964.

Blondel lost his sight in 1927 and discontinued his teaching.[53] The rest of his life he dictated his works, though he found this most tedious. He even found it almost impossible to listen to someone else read to him.[54] The bulk of his apologetic work was accomplished before 1913. In that year the editions of the *Annales* were put on the Index, retroactively to 1905. Even though the articles of Blondel himself were exempt from the condemnation, and the sentence was aimed principally at Laberthonnière, yet Blondel proceeded with great caution from that time on.[55] Most of his later work was an expansion or emendation of his original thought, and as has been indicated, the authorities are divided upon the results of the revisions.[56] The great trilogy which absorbed his declining years, *La Pensée* (two volumes), the second *L'Action* (two volumes), and *L'Être et les Êtres* contain over 2500 pages. We do not presume to make an exhaustive evaluation of Maurice Blondel, but will concentrate our efforts on the first *L'Action* and his apologetic writings.

Since Blondel's death in 1949, interest in his work has gradually grown. Actually, however, the important place of Maurice Blondel is just becoming clear. He was the target of "traditionalist attacks" in his own lifetime after the appearance of *L'Action* and the *Letter on Apologetics.* However, the prominence of Loisy and Blondel's refusal to be linked with the Modernists toned down his critics.[57] Yet, even in our own day it is not uncommon to hear the name of Blondel mentioned pejoratively, as if he still lived under a shadow.[58] A closer look at the times in which he lived may help us to understand why.

Historical Background: Modernism

The rise of the Modernist crisis was the historical setting in which Blondel thought and wrote. It is necessary to understand something of the philosophical, theological, and historical background of this age if we are to understand the significance of *L'Action* and the *Letter on Apologetics*. We are not concerned here with a universal view of the Church at the turn of the century, but more particularly with the Church in France.[59] In his classic study of "religious sentiment" in France, Henri Bremond takes us back to the world of Jansenism and the Bossuet–Fenelon struggle as the starting point of the Modernist crisis.[60] The spirit of mysticism suffered an irreparable loss when "Bossuet, despite himself, by his attacks against the false mystics, had thrown suspicion and ridicule on the true mystics themselves."[61] Dru follows the same line of thought in pinpointing the origin of France's *fin de siècle* crisis at the revocation of the Edict of Nantes and the Jansenist struggle. Then he indicates that "the consequences of these two episodes might not have been lasting had it not been for the paradigmatic conflict between Bossuet and Fenelon which followed."[62]

In support of his thesis, Bremond asks us to compare the work of Francis DeSales at the beginning of the century with the influence of Arnauld's *Frequent Communion* at the end, and insists that the Church had moved from "conciliating the world" to a "remembrance of severity and justice."[63] The Jansenist spirit endured, he was convinced; "Its defeat has never been a complete one." Bremond, writing in the midst of the crisis, could ask: "When shall we find again that youthful ardor in well-doing, that filial confidence in divine love, that joy in living the Christian life, that goodness linked with so little moroseness and with so much wit and freshness?"[64]

Claudel, too, was aware of the lasting effect of the Jansenist spirit and its tendency to despise "the noble faculties of imagination and sensibility," and blamed Jansenism for the "long crisis from which religion is just beginning to emerge."[65] This distortion of Christianity, made firm by the victory of Bossuet over Fenelon,[66] led to what Blondel was to call extrinsicism, "an utter contempt for *le fait intérieur,* to a fear and suspicion of Pascal himself, to the double divorce between thought and feeling and will, which explains the impotent rationalism of the 19th century scholasticism."[67]

A serious attempt had been made in the nineteenth century by Abbé Louis Bautain (1796–1867), professor at Strasbourg, to introduce a "Platonic-type philosophy, which makes light of abstract reason to highlight the intuitive intelligence," but his quarrels with his bishop left his work in suspicion.[68] His work was actually an anticipation of Blondel. Others had also made attempts to stem the growth of irreligion, and to make Christianity speak to the culture of the day. But, as Aubert sums it up:

In spite of the renewed hopes at the end of the century through the work of Chateaubriand, de Maistre, Lamennais and their disciples, irreligion had only grown in France during the 19th century, promoted as it was by politics, literature, and especially by the scientific and philosophical movement. The chasm separating the Catholic faith from contemporary thought—represented by such as Comte, Littre, Tain, Renan, Berthelot, Husley, J. S. Mill—seemed to grow each day.[69]

Even though the "chasm broadened, it became increasingly clear that the philosophies of the day could not deal with the key problems of life and its meaning.[70] Neo-Kantianism had become the dominant philosophy of the university after the Franco-Prussian War, "thanks to Renouvier and especially Lachelier, who formed, at the École Normale, so many generations of professors." Efforts were made to adapt Kantian philosophy to support the Catholic faith, but it allowed only a kind of "nonrational" faith, outside the scope of reason.[71]

At the turn of the century, there were numerous efforts to show that the act of faith was a combined effort of "reason, sentiment, and will."[72] But there was no synthesis which combined the demands of traditional faith and the rising current of modern thought.[73] To add to the confusion, the work of the American, William James, had been translated into French in 1898 and in 1906, and his denial of transcendance was of course unacceptable to Catholics.[74] Similarly, the work of the renowned Auguste Sabatier, who fought fiercely against arid intellectualism, had ultimately to be rejected because it reduced dogmas to mere symbols.[75] It was Ollé-Laprune, the former teacher of Blondel, who made a serious attempt to bridge the chasm. Blondel describes his effort:

[To believe] is to bring to life the intrinsic reasons, demonstrable and demonstrative, by the adherence of our whole being; it is to join the fulfillment of a heartfelt consent, voluntary and practical, to the rational assent; it is . . . to treat truth as a living thing, or even as a person, who gives up his secret only to one who is deserving, not as something knowable from without by saying "yes," nor as an obscure tendency with concealed roots or obscure origins; rather, it is to realize that the living truth is not merely an object of science or of curious belief (*croyance*), but that it demands the giving of self in trust, and that, being itself essentially an interiority, it is accessible more from within . . . than from without or by a simple vision of logical coutours.[76]

Ollé-Laprune would never be able to mold a philosophy which would catch the attention of contemporary minds and still remain within the scope of the neglected traditions of the Church. It would be his most famous disciple, Maurice Blondel, who would struggle with such a task. It is hard to improve upon Aubert's summary of the age which would produce the *L'Action* of Maurice Blondel:

Philosophic anti-intellectualism, protestant mysticism, psychology of the subconscious—many disconcerting elements were in the air at the end of the 19th century which would make perilous any effort to rethink the problem of faith in the framework of modern thought. One can scarcely wonder that the initial attempts were at times lacking in balance and that serious deviations, like modernism, should occur. Summarily, the crisis, like every crisis of faith, and in spite of its enormous price, would bear fruit, and the most able theologians, little by little, would succeed in filtering out the portion of truth contained in the one-sided and exaggerated contemporary efforts, and integrate the *nova et vetera* into a harmonious synthesis.[77]

L'Action Française

It would leave an incomplete picture were we to ignore the Church's "official" support not only of a philosophy grown irrele-vant,[78] but also its adherence to a vanished monarchy in France. This latter problem also was of serious concern to Blondel, since there was a strange connection between "traditionalism" in the

Church and this nostalgic longing for the days of kings. Dru traces this "political" error in judgment also to the days of Bossuet and the Quietists:

The quietist controversy, in the course of which Bossuet wrote that he had "God, the King and Madame de Maintenon on his side," marks the great *caesura* and is at the origin of the divorce between Catholicism and living thought, genuine art and honest scholarship, which Blondel and his generation (who rediscovered the spiritual tradition) were the first to recognize, understand, and reverse.[79]

Dru sees this as the other side of the Modernist coin, a reaction on the part of popes and churchmen to the immanentist philosophies and the growing irreligion of France. In other words, the Church was reactionary not only in regard to the currents of philosophic thought (granted that they were dangerous), but also in rejecting the current liberal trends in politics.[80] Blondel was conscious of this, and viewed the rise of Charles Maurras and the L'Action Française party with horror.[81] We add here a few remarks about the rise of this party, which provided the politico-religious background of Blondel's work.

It is easy to understand the Church's fear of the Republic. Conditions under the monarchy, politically at least, had made for serenity and protection. Democracy seems to mean liberalism, which might bring chaos and persecution.[82] Leo XIII had made his pleas for "*ralliement*," and urged Catholics not to fight the Republic.[83] But the appearance of *Graves de communi* (1901) meant that "the encouragement to the Christian Democrats and the Social Catholics had been muted, and *Rerum Novarum* was played down."[84] Religious conditions in France at the turn of the century were far from favorable for the Church. The Associations Act of 1901, rigorously enforced by the premiership of Émile Combes, meant the expulsion of the religious orders and the consequent inability to staff the religious schools. It also led to the Separation Act of 1905, which denounced the Concordat of 1901. The newly elected Pope Pius X had much to fear.[85]

The Action Française itself, founded by Charles Maurras at the time of the Dreyfus incident, "was at first without a precise ideology. . . . It was neither Catholic nor royalist, but a political and moral reaction to the decadence of public life, to the scandals and affairs which threatened the Third Republic."[86] Maurras, a

disciple of Comte and an avowed unbeliever, had strong royalist
leanings from his background, and sought to "convert" people to
the idea of the monarchy. The loss of the Franco-Prussian War had
increased the desire for royalism among great numbers.[87] It attracted the "men and women who wanted to go on living in the
past."[88] Charles Maurras saw in the Catholic Church not a religious way of life, but a champion of "reason" and "order." The
Church was the only hope of preserving the classical treasures
which were threatened by the romanticists and other forms of
barbarous impulses.[89] The French Revolution had destroyed all
the wonders of Greece and Rome, and "was responsible in his eyes
for the decay and corruption of the moral and political fiber of
every people it had touched."[90] The only way to proceed against
the ravages of the nineteenth century, according to Maurras, was to
adhere to every form which would secure the ancient traditions. In
literature, he stood for a simplicity of style; in politics he urged the
restoration of the monarchy. And he saw the Church and its law as
the essential ally in the accomplishment of his goals. Freemasons,
Protestants, foreigners, and Jews must be expelled or kept under
severe regulations.[91] The Church as a source of order was not
heralded by Maurras alone. He struck a responsive chord in those
who approved the "trend in favor of authority, hierarchy and
discipline, rather than a search for ultimate truth." More and more
people, "tired of religious strife and parliamentary finagling, were
looking for a force that could heal social and intellectual rifts
[and] discipline the national energies."[92] This spirit was forming
even during the early school days of Maurice Blondel.

With the rise of Modernism, the Church was looking for any
support it could get. And "the campaigns of the Action Française
against liberalism and democracy, and against all tendencies to
compromise with them, coincided with the anti-Modernist campaigns."[93] Gradually, under the impact of fast-moving threats to
the Catholic position, "the leaders of the neo-Thomist revival . . .
gravitated toward the Action Française. Unworldly men, great
scholars like Billot . . . saw only its single-minded opposition to
the worldly forces of modernism."[94] Admirers of Maurras were on
Catholic faculties everywhere, and his supporters read like a theological "Who's Who" at the *fin de siècle*: Billot, Peguès, Garrigou-
Lagrange, Clérissac, Besse, Bernanos, Maritain. A key figure was

Umberto Benigni, "a close aide of Cardinal Merry del Val, who was Secretary of State to Pope Pius X."[95] Billot himself, who had the ear of Pius X, was responsible for the Church's support of the movement long after its more widespread influence began to wane.[96] The World War delayed its condemnation, and it was not finally condemned until 1926, even though seven books by Maurras had been put on the Index in 1914.

It was actually the theologians' support of Maurras that led Blondel to battle with the Action Française.[97] We mention only in passing Blondel's decision to involve himself in social and political action to some degree, since he knew that the Church's identification with decadent forms and its refusal to recognize the possibilities of a purification of "liberals" and "integrists" could only steep her more deeply in irrelevance and lack of contact with the world.[98] Our concern is rather to show that the philosophic and apologetic efforts of Blondel were blocked and misrepresented by a neo-Thomism which had consummated a strange marriage, and by an authoritarian Church which permitted the "persecution of ecclesiastical scholars seeking to interpret Christian doctrine in the light of modern social and scientific developments."[99] Blondel entered the fray, knowing that the answer to Modernism was not veterism. Yet, his attack on the Action Française was never an end in itself, as it seemed to be with Laberthonnière, but only the removal of a barrier for establishing the Church in the world, a barrier which *had* to be removed. Much of the Blondel-Laberthonnière correspondence is an effort on Blondel's part to produce balance in his friend's views.[100]

It is hard to imagine a Catholic world which accepted "a declared atheist as its intellectual leader for twenty-five years."[101] What Blondel saw so clearly in an early intuition, it took him years to develop and defend in the right language to be heard.[102] His early battles with the Thomists centered around the Thomism he knew. His critics, who ridicule his ignorance of "true" Thomism,[103] seem themselves ignorant of the impoverished Scholasticism which he learned. It had been a painful experience, and had almost cost him his doctor's degree in philosophy.[104] His contact with Rousselot opened him to the prospects of Thomistic thought, and he gradually altered his opinion of the work of the Angelic Doctor.[105] In fact, his insistence on looking at the work of the neo-

Thomists honestly and openly may well have been a deciding factor in his gradual break with the beloved Laberthonnière.[106] And the very hesitation to reprint *L'Action*, and his insistence on revising all of his original thoughts, was largely based upon his refusal to be satisfied with inaccuracies of any kind.[107]

We offer this brief summary of the training and the cultural surroundings of Maurice Blondel. We proceed now to examine his *Letter on Apologetics* to discover what significance it has for us today.

Letter on Apologetics: Background

Hardly had the tumult raised by *L'Action* of 1893 time to quiet down when there appeared a series of articles in the *Annales de Philosophie Chrétienne* which provoked another explosion. These letters form the *Letter on Apologetics* by Maurice Blondel. He had written to Abbé Denis, the director of the *Annales*, thanking him for his discussion of *L'Action* and requesting a chance to write out "some of my ideas on the actual role of Christian philosophy, on the demands of contemporary thought in matters of religion, and on the very conditions of apologetics."[108] Though he was accused of abandoning the traditional apologetics, he insisted after publication that he considered the *Letter* a mere outline, and was hoping to find a way of "reestablishing contact with the impenitent rationalists."[109] He was not prepared for all the attacks raised by the neo-Thomists and the professional apologetes. He realized that the title of his articles had been too general, since it made the readers think that he would treat "*ex professo* apologetics in all of its aspects."[110] He had no intention of denying the validity of historical proofs, but wanted to establish apologetics on a unified basis.[111] He was concerned with a narrower and more technical question: "Is there a lodestone in man himself, perhaps in reason itself, comprised by the primitive and antecedent destination of man to the supernatural?"[112] This is the key philosophical question, and it is a question of common interest to all men.

Actually, the *Letter* treated the acceptable "method" of apologetics and presumed a grasp of *L'Action*.[113] Blondel saw that the apologetes had not recognized the changes that had taken place in society, with the general acceptance of the scientific method. To think that age-old arguments would have the same validity that they had in the days of faith and before the progress of scientific knowledge was to put new patches on old clothes.[114] Blondel realized that many Catholic theologians, typically represented by an article in the *Revue Thomiste*, had ignored the difference between theology and philosophy, and had brought dogmatic convictions into the domain of philosophy.[115] It really made little difference whether one spoke of Scholastic theology or Scholastic philosophy, since in reality they dealt with the same areas. Blondel admitted that such a union had its advantages, but among its disadvantages was its disregard of the modern unbeliever. No one could ignore the fact that Kant had lived and that important changes had taken place which prohibited the naïve "conjoining of historical, scientific, metaphysical, and theological truths."[116] To act thus was to ignore the need for a "subjective preparation," which was not merely "prepedagogical," but "essential."[117] Blondel did not mean that former arguments had no value at all, but as he clearly stated:

Far from discrediting or denying the many methods that apologetics uses, I wanted to purge them of all corrupting alloys, to separate them from all ruinous compromise, to assure them of the role and relative value which they should have, by putting them in their rightful place, without allowing them to be overrated or distorted at the risk of ruining them.[118]

Some too readily called an argument "scientific" or a fact "historical," but Blondel was extremely suspicious of too great a sympathy for the idealistic phenomenology of the period.[119] Eventually, this epistemology would be turned against the Church, and when science and history were discredited the "scientific" basis of Christianity would be subverted as well.

Blondel understood that the crisis facing the Church demanded a philosophy that could meet modern man on his own ground. "Modernism, in his view, was not the cause, but the effect of the crisis: a recoil from veterism, from a philosophy incapable of dealing with new questions."[120] The Church was allying itself with positivism and the conservatism of Charles Maurras. Such an alliance was deadly.[121] The argument from miracles, for example, became a "scientific proof," rather than the use of illustrative signs that spoke to the well-disposed.[122] As Blondel's ideas began to take hold, and the influence of Maurras grew dim, Blondel wrote in the *Mercure de France* of 1907 that there was occurring "a purification, because what succumbs or dissolves in the present struggles, the decaying institutions, the petrified forms, are either dying or dead . . . the laborious parturition of modern consciousness will not end in some sort of symbolism (modernism) detached from dogma, or in literal, mechanical practice (veterism), but with a more precise definition of dogmatic facts and truths."[123] There had been too much emphasis on the purity of ideas, as if the problems of the day would be resolved by clearer philosophical definitions. Actually, the Church had to realize that "it is the whole man who is in question; so that it is not thought alone which must look for him. The center of philosophy must be transposed into action, because it is there that the core of life is to be found."[124] In a later correspondence with Teilhard de Chardin, he would utterly reject "the mediocre explanations and limited views which make of Christ an historical accident, which isolate Him in the Cosmos as a superadded episode, and which seem to make of Him an intruder or a displaced person in the crushing and hostile immensity of the universe."[125] Blondel insisted that we must go out and meet the world, and admit its progress, since "in the measure the world and mankind grow greater in man's eyes, Christ likewise grows greater in our eyes and in our hearts."[126] From such a framework, "the perpetual task of philosophy and apologetics (for me, isn't it all one at the roots?) is to discover that He is the greatest, the incomparable."[127]

It would be wrong to think that Blondel anticipated his conclusions in his philosophical efforts. He was not merely amassing apologetic arguments to prove the truths of the Catholic faith, he was immersing himself in the world, knowing full well that Christ can be found, but not anticipating his conclusions by unworthy preconceptions. Hence, a modern author can say that Blondel's importance lies "in the attitude he adopts and the method he employs," since he involves the whole of man—not merely his mind or will alone—in the search of life's meaning.[128] He will not play the theologian; he insists on remaining a philosopher. But the area of philosophy must be extended to all of observable reality, even the apparent entrance of grace into human psychology.[129] In this way, "supernatural revelation no longer appears as a gift imposed on the human spirit by strange arguments and a totally intellectual and purely extrinsic apologetics, but . . . comes to satisfy man's most profound tendencies."[130]

Blondel had a chance to revise his *Letter on Apologetics* in 1932 in *Le Problème de la Philosophie Catholique*. He admitted certain excesses in his treatment of Catholic theologians, and regrets that he did not admit the theological category of "pure nature." But essentially, as Duméry insists, the thought of Blondel is here, and it may well be proclaimed his masterpiece.[131] Even though he emended it, "the substance of the *Letter* was very far from being repudiated by Blondel."[132] True, "the *Letter* was delated to the Holy Office; it was rescued thence by Leo XIII at the insistence of Cardinal Perraud."[133] "It has been the subject of protracted debate on the continent; it is high time for us to discuss it here."[134]

Letter on Apologetics: Its Argument

Blondel made clear at the outset of the *Letter on Apologetics* that he wanted to do justice to the demands of both reason and faith.[135] His position as a philosopher gave him a freedom that he required in such an investigation, an investigation that hoped to say "something which counts in the eyes of unbelievers."[136] In the past, "bad arguments" had been used for the best of reasons, to lead men to the faith, but in the end the Church suffered from such methods. True it is that men are sometimes more readily moved by insufficient arguments, but we ought to be harder on ourselves than our critics are—evaluating our arguments with unfailing rigor.[137]

At times our weak arguments were proposed with a kind of infallibility, and in a passage of rare fury, Blondel says:

I hate the infatuation of people who are tough-minded with the tough-minded, who see too clearly to see properly, who are proud of their myopic certainty, who are foolishly indignant at the folly or the intellectual perversity of unbelievers, and who . . . have neither due respect for souls who are still seeking the light, nor a sense of the mysterious profundities of our destiny.[138]

In a letter written after the publication of the *Letter on Apologetics*, Blondel wrote that we enforced our bad apologetics with such vigor that frequently we looked upon the unbelievers as if they were either ignorant or insincere. Such an approach would lead to "an intolerance founded on a foolishness which is not Christian."[139] There could be no contact between Christians and the world until we recognized that the Christian call was in some way present in every philosophical effort that led man to seek true meaning.[140] If Christianity is essential for salvation, it is only reasonable to presume that there will be some trace of it in the man who is only man, "purely human."[141] There is a legitimate presumption that a Christian philosopher can make.

False and Incomplete Methods of Apologetics

Blondel then proceeded to discuss current apologetic methods. He rejected utterly those apologetes "who attach themselves to the findings of the positive sciences as though they were the expression of absolute reality. . . . It is no business of theirs to attain or to reveal the final ground of things."[142] Other methods had some validity, but Blondel was insistent that such methods "must be condemned root and branch as both trivial and dangerous."[143] His criticism here of science and the scientific arguments was much like that of Max Scheler.[144] Similarly, Blondel sees science and philosophy at different levels, and insists that this method has no value.

Another method of apologetic argument was the historical one, in which the apologists "consider Christianity chiefly as an historical fact to which all the rules for assessing testimony are to be applied."[145] He rejected this as an unsound philosophical approach. There are so many contingent facts in history "which I can legitimately disregard. How far am I responsible for a voluntary abstention in their regard?"[146] There is no inner necessity compelling me to take these facts seriously, and consequently "the proofs are valid only for those who are thoroughly prepared to accept and understand them; that is why miracles which enlighten some, also blind others."[147] To establish revelation by miracles "is therefore asking too much of philosophy . . . to make it ratify or confirm . . . the autonomous conclusions of historical apologetics."[148]

Blondel, like Scheler, insists that the "wonder" aspect of the miracle is not what convinces, but that "miracles are truly miraculous only for those who are already prepared to recognize the divine action in the most usual events."[149]

His critics accused him of denying the historical fact of revelation, and the essential historical arguments which support it. [150] He replied:

I have never dreamed of suppressing the necessity of the fact of revelation, nor of weakening the value of the historical proofs of the *divine fact*. . . . I have merely tried to protect them against their proper inconsistency . . . and to show that they have their convincing power . . . only when rejoined to the foundation of the method I have described.[151]

His critics continued to believe that he was dismissing all of the past apologetics, whereas actually he was only trying to give them a philosophic validity. As Bouillard puts it: "He was not concerned with proposing new arguments but with the preparation of the unbeliever to grasp the old."[152] Many of the arguments, most effective in ages past, have little advantage today. "When metaphysical and theological ideas had what one might call their normal and almost automatic sway over men's minds," such methods could be effective. The Thomistic system can be effective "once a man has entered this system," but "the Thomist starts from principles which, for the most part, are disputed in our time." We must meet people on their own ground, and not just regret that times have changed. We have a battle on our hands, and "we must not exhaust ourselves refurbishing old arguments and presenting an *object* for acceptance while the *subject* is not disposed to listen."[153]

The third method of apologetics was more suitable to Blondel. He describes it in this way:

If an analysis of our innermost needs and a thorough consideration of our powers of thinking and loving leads us to find, in the dogmas proposed for our belief, the harmonious counterpart to them, it must be agreed that this affords a strong presumption in favor of this Christian religion. . . . Many of those whom we wish to reach are not capable of having, perhaps not even of understanding, any further requirements. It is possible to show, as Chateaubriand did, that the Catholic spirit is a source of beauty superior to any other . . . to find . . . that every upright and developed soul contains an aspiration towards Christianity.[154]

As valuable as this argument is for many in the portrayal of the moral and intellectual fittingness of Christianity, "the danger lies in putting it forward as the one properly philosophical argument for the truth of Christianity." This can be a most effective argument, but it presumes that a man "has already tested [his] faith in the crucible of rational criticism and preserved it intact." But it will have no effect on the man "who proposes to take philosophy for his guide and who feels the need to dig down or climb up wherever reason will take him."[155] To a man like this, the modern unbeliever, Christianity becomes something imposed from the outside, and "we must not claim to take hold of our adversary when we are in fact out of touch with him."[156]

There is, of course, a danger that this apologetic may abandon orthodoxy. We can make the Christian revelation sound as if it is a mere extension of natural morality, and "the very notion of the supernatural remains vague and ambiguous." We have to distinguish between the use of reason before and after the act of faith. Hence, Ollé-Laprune has true merit for believers, but "the great need of apologetics today is to start from the fact of a theoretical and practical incredulity."[157] It is for this reason that Blondel spoke of his attempt to crawl into the mind of the unbeliever. He asked the believer first to be aware of his own unbelief, the unbelief he shares with an unbelieving age:

It is not a question of a theoretical adhesion to a dogma which is external to us, but of the practical insertion into our hearts and our conduct of a lifegiving truth. . . . So it is ourselves whom we should interrogate when we inquire into the nature of conversion and of the obstacles to conversion. . . . There is no doubt about the preference of our contemporaries for those who, in Pascal's phrase, seek with groanings in the sincerity of their hearts rather than those who dogmatize and condemn, triumphing in the assurance of their superiority.[158]

Another method of apologetics is similar to the one just treated. It maintains that "Christianity alone satisfied all the artistic, intellectual, moral and social requirements of mankind."[159] This argument maintains that the laws of Christianity "are the very same laws of human life, neither more nor less." There is a

danger here, as in the previous argument, of ignoring the supernatural quality of Christianity, for "we must not forget that if
Christianity claims to satisfy man's natural needs, it also claims to
arouse and fulfill new ones." This apologetic can end up in a too-
scattered and individualistic approach, so that we are looking for
what is missing in people, rather than "looking only at what is, in
fact, there." Thus, we have no science of apologetics which is
universally applicable, but we "confine the need of modern apologetics to mere makeshifts."[160] In his evaluation of this method, as
before, Blondel is not discrediting it, or questioning its usefulness,
but attempting to mold an argument that is scientifically and
philosophically sound. Thus the criticism of Amedée de Margerie,
dean of the philosophy faculty at Lille in 1896, is not accurate,
when he accuses Blondel of taking the foundation away from all
arguments but his own.[161] He wants to unify and coordinate all
apologetics by establishing its real foundation.

Then Blondel deals with the so-called "scientific apologetics,"[162] which was, from his descriptions, quite similar to the methods taught in most seminaries and colleges until very recently. First
we prove the existence of God, then admit the possibility of revelation. After that we use history to show that there has been a revelation, and we establish the historical value of scriptures and the
authority of the Catholic Church. "Catholicism is thus established
upon a scientific basis." We might add to this the complete
harmony of Christianity with all that is human and good (thus
bringing in other proofs), so that when Christianity is "perfectly
understood, it is its own proof."[163]

Such an apologetic could have been most effective in a world
which accepted without argument the authentic value of Christian
revelation. Now man stands outside. We can continue to perfect
our system for the satisfaction of the members of the Church, or
we can take an honest look at ourselves and the rest of mankind.[164] Blondel reiterated the idea which had inspired his *L'Action*:

There are two ways of looking at the history of philosophical ideas.
Either we remain outside the main stream which sweeps through the
world of thought and radically exclude everything which is opposed to
the system we have adopted . . . and that is to cut ourselves off from
the only sort of life which is really fruitful. Or else we try to perceive

that stirring of parturition with which humanity is always in labour; we set ourselves to profit by this vast effort, to enlighten it, to bring it to fruition . . . to be less ready to suppose that there is nothing of value for ourselves even in those doctrines which seem most opposed to our own, to go to others so that they may come to us—and that is to find the source of intellectual fruitfulness.[165]

When we operate within a closed system, we tend to make continual judgments about the rest of mankind. We feel ourselves apart from them, and do not appreciate their struggles for truth, their sacrifices for the discovery of meaning. We can make Christianity seem so obvious that we ignore the struggles that we ourselves undergo to live it. These struggles do not become apparent when Christianity remains a well-structured and scientifically supported idea, but only when it is seen as a life to be lived. Such an apologetic can mean something as the reflection of a believer; it will remain completely outside the experience of the unbeliever.[166]

The world that knew the wedding of faith and reason is over. Faith and reason seemed to go their separate ways. What we called "reason" was usually faith's reflection, and the unbeliever's faith was only in reason. Consequently, "when reason, left sole mistress of the knowable world, claimed to find immanent in herself all the truths needed for the life of man, the world of faith found itself totally excluded."[167] Consequently, there is only one course left for us in the face of the immanentists, to discover if "in the only order which remains [reason], there does not reappear an imperious need for the other one [faith].[168]

This was a key point with Blondel, this bridge or connection between the order of philosophy and Christianity. If we did not center our apologetic efforts in this common area between the disciplines, there could be no way of reaching modern man. Christianity would always appear to him as an external and imposed discipline. We must look for the signs in man that there is another order that he cannot reach by himself, but that he must reach if he is to be made whole. "There must be some trace of this insufficiency, this impotence, this demand in man simply as man, and an echo of it even in the most autonomous philosophy."[169]

This trace is inevitable because man recognizes in his own struggle both a need for a "transcendant something" and the incapacity to attain it by his own powers. "As soon as the poverty of our limited being can contract a debt which must be paid for in eternity, then the encounter takes place, the difficulty stares us in the face, and the problem is set."[170]

For this reason, Blondel insisted that there must be a new way of reaching man apologetically, *his* way. He called it the "method of immanence," and it consisted ultimately, not in avoiding the current issues facing the Church, but in "forcing philosophy, like orthodoxy, to remain faithful to itself."[171] Philosophy has been able to escape the important questions. It has been able to stop the discussion short with partial answers and partial explanations, since the discussion has been at the level of ideas and not of the reality behind the ideas. The "method of immanence," which we will now explain, adds another dimension, and forces the philosopher to move into the real world.

The Method of Immanence

Blondel described the method of immanence very simply, returning to his description of the will in the philosophy of *L'Action:*[172]

The method of immanence, then, can consist in nothing else than in trying to equate, in our own consciousness, what we appear to think and to will and to do with what we do and will and think in actual fact—so that behind factitious negations and ends which are not genuinely willed may be discovered our innermost affirmations and the implacable needs which they imply.[173]

The "innermost affirmations" are simply affirmations of the transcendent, even of the supernatural, though we must not prejudge the object of our affirmations if we are to remain true to philosophy, something which "no one has done, perhaps, with complete consistency."[174] Blondel sees a twofold will within man, the *volonté voulante* and the *volonté voulue.*[175] (This is the terminology used in *L'Action*, whereas the "way of immanence" is used in the *Letter.*) This discussion is at the very heart of Blondel's original thesis, *L'Action*. Macquarrie offers a good explanation of the method:

The basis of the dialectic is the contrast between action and its realization. This contrast constitutes the *permanent dissatisfaction* of human life, and provides the incentive to further action. In the endeavor to close the gap, as it were, action may be seen as expanding in ever widening circles from self-regarding action which has regard to all humanity . . . it becomes clear that the contrast (between action and its realization) cannot be overcome within the natural order. Thus man is directed from the natural to the supernatural by the demands of action itself.[176]

In other words, the *volonté voulante* is the persistent, permanent, willing-faculty of man. He cannot *not* will.[177] This will "is at the heart of every free decision."[178] Each free decision is the product of the *volonté voulue* which continues to will and continues to sense the "inadequation" between itself and the *volonté voulante*. In the second edition of *L'Action* (1937), Blondel compares the twofold will with the Scholastic distinction between the *voluntas ut natura* and the *elicited will*.[179] It would be wrong to think of them as two wills. Bouillard, perhaps, describes the relationship best of all when he says: "It [*volonté voulante*] does not stand at the side of the *volonté voulue*—it operates within it as its principle and as the rule which allows it to judge."[180] Man must pass "option" by "option" to the *unique nécessaire*, the absolute, the transcendent. We reach a certain point where "the idea strikes us that another would be able to furnish from outside what we are incapable of providing. . . . It will come to satisfy the imperious demands of our profound will."[181] Hence, Blondel can speak of a kind of "determinism" that operates. We are not able to stop willing; we are not able to remain satisfied with that which does not satisfy.[182] For this reason, the "nihilist," who attempts to stop at nothingness, is fighting his very nature, and is doomed to defeat. So it is with the "pessimist." The "dilettante," who is attracted by partial answers and mere baubles, will also face disillusionment, since "the problem of destiny cannot be escaped."[183] If man denies this "élan" within his makeup, and refuses to pass on from option to ever higher option, "his desire perishes; it will have ever wished for what never was; that will be eternally present which it wishes eternally to avoid."[184] His own egoism cuts him off from the movement of universal life, and everything worth seeking escapes him. He will become "as one alive who is tied to a corpse, . . . his dead idol."[185]

This struggle will not affect all men in the same way. But all will sense their own inner failure when they struggle alone. They will sense that "something must be done with one's life"; they will demand meaning, and they will not find it short of the *unique nécessaire*. Man will not know necessarily what is there outside of him, but he will learn that something must be.[186]

The way of immanence, or the method of *L'Action*, does not preclude thought. It is not action without reflection, nor is it will without intellect. "Action for him means—in the transcendental sense—all human activity and includes thought."[187] As Blondel himself puts it: "*L'Action* [is that] in which is realized the harmony of knowing, willing, and being."[188] Or in another place he says: "All thought is at the same time act and knowledge. . . . Born of activity already realized in us, thought conserves its vitality and worth only in becoming light and force in the service of the activity which will make it real.[189] He was searching for an apologetic which would try "to remain in the philosophical terrain which is human and common to all . . . to place the religious, supernatural, mystical, heavenly problem, from a rational point of view which reclaims all spirits, to free in this way Christianity from artificial barriers, stifling prejudices, so as to put it in circulation among the rank of humanity."[190] All men could be made conscious of this struggle that lurked within their own soul. They would begin to recognize it if their attention were called to it. But they would never be moved by the abstract thought which was convenient for making distinctions, but did not show realistically the joining of natural and supernatural, the very demand for something beyond. Only *L'Action*, the way of immanence, could do this.[191]

Blondel often spoke of the "inadequation" that man experienced within himself. This is another way of approaching the same idea, the *volonté voulante* and the *volonté voulue*, the tension between what a man is and what he aspires to be.[192] This was the so-called "logic" or "dialectic" of *L'Action*, whereby a man sought to resolve the conflicts he experienced in life's struggle. This "logic" should lead to the *unique nécessaire* by the steady process of moving from one option to a higher one, retaining within it "the absolute that is in them,"[193] and sacrificing the "phenomena." And so the "logic of action" will "determine the chain of necessities that compose the drama of life and lead it inevitably to the denouement."[194]

Actually, the entire third part of *L'Action* is devoted to

showing that the *élan* of the will cannot stop short at any merely
human or natural goal. He reviews past philosophies of action and
shows their inadequacies.[195] In a note, reedited by Blondel, to be
inserted in *L'Action*, he sums up his views, a description of the
"inadequation" between the *volonté voulante* and any natural
object which is freely chosen by the *volonté voulue*:

Man cannot restrict his destiny to sensual joys, nor to conquests of the
positive sciences, nor to the development of individual life, nor to the
expansion of family or society, nor to concepts of metaphysics of
independent morality, nor to superstition that he invents in order to
complete or to make sacred his life.[196]

In effect, he was saying that the "immanentists" who refused to go
beyond the natural were not truly immanent at all, for "the very
notion of immanence is realized in our consciousness only by the
effective presence of the notion of the transcendent."[197] Actually,
the immanentists stopped short, and they made into a system, or
built into a dogma, that which was never meant to be such. This
was a violation of the true way of immanence, which can "never do
anything more than indicate blank spaces which cannot be filled or
established in their reality by any resource of ours."[198] These
blank spaces indicate the presence of the supernatural, but they do
not deny its gratuity. The method of immanence considers "the
supernatural not as an historic reality, not as simply possible, like
an arbitrary hypothesis, not as optional, like a gift which is proposed but not imposed . . . but . . . as *indispensable* and at the
same time *inaccessible* for man."[199]

   Of course, Blondel's words evoked the complaint that he had
denied the gratuity of the supernatural. He was accused of confusion, of Modernism, of real arrogance. He anticipated the difficulty
in his *Letter*, and when he spoke of the supernatural as "indispensable," he said that he might seem "to bring the freedom of the
divine gift within the system of human action in such a way which
is illegitimate."[200] He explains that each of us reaches a position
that he must "pronounce upon his destiny." In this process of
L'Action, which no man can avoid, "we must reach the point
implicitly at which the option becomes possible . . . between the
solicitations of the hidden God and those of an egoism which is
always evident enough."[201] Man, in other words, can say "Yes" or

"No." If he says "No," this will not alter the *élan* of his whole being toward the *unique nécessaire;* "he will endlessly perish because all that he has loved will in some manner be devoured or annihilated by the magnitude of his desire."[202] To say "Yes" means that man "opens" to the transcendent, but Blondel believes that the philosopher can "in no way determine what this transcendent will be."[203] The discussions at the time of Blondel's work were, of course, loud and long,[204] but for the most part today,[205] Blondel has been vindicated.

It is the common opinion today that Blondel was speaking of "the observable man," and it was not required that he think of man in the state of "pure nature."[206] He could write to Father Semeria:

Thus I operate neither from the structure of a supernatural imposed on our nature by divine decree, nor from that of a human nature, absolutely taken, which would require a supernatural order. . . . For my whole effort has been to establish satisfactorily that philosophy, properly taken, has no pronouncement to make for or against the dogmas which are the exclusive property of theology.[207]

As Aubert has pointed out, Blondel is not reducing the supernatural to the natural, but is dealing with "observable nature," and consequently the origin of man's need could well be supernatural.[208] He goes on to say that "the theologian who knows the doctrine of God's universal and salvific will and the necessity of actual and prevenient graces, that raise fallen man to meet his obligations, will have no trouble recognizing in the unsatisfied desires . . . the concrete manner of God's action in him."[209] Thus it was Blondel who called the attention of the theologians "to the subjective side of faith," and insisted that it is not enough to point out that faith is "a gift of God and an activity of man." But it must be shown how "the divine action enters the web of human psychology." This is a true theological breakthrough, whereby "the action of grace is transferred to human psychology and contributes to the creation of the subjective dispositions which make faith possible."[210] In this way the prime rationalist objection to faith is overcome, whereby "supernatural revelation no longer appears as a gift imposed on the human spirit by strange arguments and a totally intellectual and purely extrinsic apologetic.[211] Revelation becomes the lodestone (*pierre d'attente*), the "germ" that Blondel spoke of in his letters:

There is at the core of our being or at least at the core of certain of our decisive actions a power unformed by grace, a germ which *should* find in the gifts of Revelation and in the life of the Church the necessary nourishment for faith—a germ without which we would be able to assimilate nothing from without, and which reveals itself in our conscience not merely in the form of a vague, undetermined need, a natural weakness or lack, but under the form of an aptitude for the recognition of the objective credibility of revealed truth.[212]

To Blondel, a theology which maintained that grace gave an "ability" but not a "facility" in action did not come to grips with the vital question. Such would have to be classed with the "mediocre explanations and limited views which make of Christ an historical accident."[213] Modern theology has come to recognize this important contribution of Maurice Blondel. Karl Rahner, in his treatment of the "supernatural existential," gives explicit credit to Blondel (via Malevez) for the development of his own thought.[214] It is easy to understand how Blondel could be misunderstood in his own day, and it would be easy to chastise his critics unreasonably for their failure to see what we have only lately begun to realize. The error of his critics is far less believable than the amazing insight of Blondel himself, an insight which was rather carefully developed sixty years before Vatican II.

Such an insight could come when philosophy was "not a submissive slave, simply providing notions or an arsenal of arguments . . . but a human activity, solid and autonomous."[215] He did not look upon nature as something static and fixed, nor would he fix speculative limits for supernature.[216] He was well aware that his problem as an "action" philosopher was different from that of the idealist, since "in theoretical thought there is no problem with the supernatural properly so-called. . . . The problem is posed only in the concrete in a philosophy of action and life."[217] He would struggle with this idea, dissatisfied to the end with the expressions that aspired to contain his thought. Again and again he would try to make clear that "the Christian supernatural corresponds to the inner aspiration of man," and "the God of Jesus Christ is no stranger to the God of the philosophers."[218]

Only if man engaged in the demands of "action," only if he followed the upward chase of option upon option could he become what he already is, "so as to make real the absolute in ourselves and ourselves in the absolute."[219] For "we apprehend God not by thought but by action,"[220] and "at the moment when we seem to touch God by a stroke of thought, He escapes, unless we hold Him and seek Him in action. Wherever we stop, He is not, wherever we move, He is. To think of God is an action."[221]

This followed from the root principle of his philosophy, namely, that "even the complete knowledge of thought and life does not supply or suffice for the activity of thinking and living."[222] For "to know is to be what one knows; it is to produce it, to have it, to become it in itself. *Sumus quod videmus.*"[223] This "being" was the real test of the validity of his philosophic method. He offered no other justification.[224] Blondel makes this clear in *L'Action:*

Likewise, without being supported by any theoretical justification, action carries its own sufficient certitude; it constitutes a conclusive method; it is experimentation in the most scientific sense of the word, a rigorous and demonstrative experimentation which supplies the speculative study, and which is in itself in no way supplied.[225]

Thus, if we were to ask Blondel precisely how he knows that a life of action would mean the experience of emptiness and "blank spaces," he would answer that the "reasons for affirmation are found in the very experience; that is why education knows how to communicate it, by docile practice, as an experimental truth."[226] The very process of living will naturally include "reflection," but "it is not so much reflection *on* action as reflection *of* action on itself."[227]

Blondel resembles Scheler here, in suggesting that the unbeliever must be involved in some sort of practice, or "experimentation" as he calls it. If he will enter into the community "and act as if he already had the faith," then he will be assured of the validity of his effort, since "the convert has only to become aware of what is accomplished in him . . . and he will discover in the increase of life that results the best guarantee that he is not wrong, the certitude of the reality of the supernatural gift."[228] Some accused Blondel of extending his "experimental action" even to the sacraments, so that the prospective convert should try everything. But he replied that he meant only "to pray, to consult, to purify the conscience, to kneel at the feet of a confessor."[229]

Of course, there was the danger in such a method of "subjectivism," that is, that the dogmas themselves would seem to rise up from the needs of men. Thus, Aubert says:

It was not less dangerous . . . to insist on the necessity of experimentation without making precise its object; to make use of certain expressions which seem to indicate that the needs expressed in us bear not only on the idea of supernatural revelation in general, but on the content of different dogmas—as towards a subjective discovery of them independently of an external revelation.[230]

But this was precisely where Blondel abandoned the thought of Loisy[231] and the extreme tendencies of Laberthonnière.[232] He saw, however, the problem that the Modernists faced, and he recognized the danger of making religious truth so extrinsic that it seemed to invade our planet from space. Yet, he knew that he must walk the narrow line, and "not supernaturalize nature, nor naturalize the supernatural."[233] He describes in *L'Action* the relation of dogmatic truths to man's need:

It is legitimate to consider those dogmas not from the start as revealed, but as revealers; that is to say, to confront them with the profound demands of the will, and to see if can be found in them the image of our real needs and the attendant response. Perhaps, were they thus considered, we would be surprised at the human meaning of a dogma which many consider unworthy of a more careful consideration, and which they confuse . . . with a dry formalism of practices, with a torrent of mystical emotions, with a routine of visible ceremonies, with a casuistic legalism, with a mechanical discipline.[234]

It becomes clear that Blondel is concerned not with the source of revealed truth, since that belongs to theology, but with "a certain attitude of the subject, . . . less a problem than a problematic."[235] He wanted the theologians to recognize that philosophy had its own domain, apart from acting as the *ancilla theologiae*, and that many of the Churchmen "are still in the same position in regard to philosophy as people were in the seventeenth century in regard to science."[236] Yet Blondel was too realistic to expect much of a hearing either from the Scholastic theologians or from the unbelieving philosophers. He says rather pessimistically at the conclusion of his *Letter on Apologetics:*

For those who are perhaps already disposed to approve the method, or capable of grasping the necessity of it, will reject the conclusions, and those whom the conclusions might attract will reject the method.[237]

This "need" in man, even though all men have it and move toward the *unique nécessaire*,[238] must be aroused.[239] He proposes to do this, not by mere psychological tricks—which could in no way be formed into a scientific system[240]—but by encouraging men at every level to abandon their idols, to push on in a search for the satisfaction of needs, a push which will lead to the *unique nécessaire*.[241] He is looking for the tension of the struggle for meaning which is common to all men. As Wehrle says so well:

We cannot repeat too much that the subjective factors are neither arbitrary, nor individual, but universal. That has been the great merit of the metaphysical analyses of the subject pursued by M. Blondel to eliminate ceaselessly the so-called variable and to retain, for the building of a demonstrative apologetic, only the element susceptible of being scientifically organized. Hence the place of reason in the act of faith is increased, and the intelligible elements which enter into that act are equal to their very rich complexity.[242]

Blondel, however, warns that in applying this program of action, he does not intend that we should make judgments about our fellow men. It is not up to us to decide in particular circumstances what is or is not required, or "what the sufficient substitutes may be in each case."[243] The best place to begin is within our own lives, since we are not dealing with a mere dogma to be accepted in thought, but "the practical insertion into our hearts and our conduct of a lifegiving truth—a truth which is the better known the better it is practiced." This leads him to conclude: "So it is first of all ourselves whom we should interrogate when we inquire into the nature of conversion and of the obstacles to conversion."[244] Then we can look at the atheist and see that even he, in his way, "implicitly affirms God."[245]

Philosophy itself is an apologetic,[246] as long as it remains autonomous and recognizes that "one no longer has the right, if one wants to be both a philosopher and a Christian at the same time, to start off covertly on the basis of one's faith, and then

pretend to reach it for the first time."[247] But a philosophy of
action is truly an apologetic, and will convince a man that he "can
never legitimately or in reality confine himself to the human level,
that even when he appears to do so, this appearance conceals . . .
a real participation in what he fails to recognize, and that . . . no
natural solution is a solution at all."[248] Blondel's views on Christian philosophy are generally well known and have been discussed
perhaps more frequently than his apologetic views—at least here in
America.

It seems, however, that the truths of his faith certainly sup-
plemented his philosophy, and actually permitted him to have
great confidence in his action hypothesis than otherwise would
have been the case. This is the impression one gets in reading his
correspondence with Chardin in 1919.[249] It was in this correspondence, initiated by Valensin, that Blondel gave his own views
on the meaning of the Incarnation, and the consequent divinization of the world.[250] We do not mean to imply that he did not
remain true to the principles of his autonomous philosophy, but his
faith permitted him much larger horizons than otherwise would
have been the case. He admits to Chardin that "the problem of the
Incarnation has appeared to me from then on [1892] (and perhaps
likewise before every other philosophic question) as the touchstone
of a true cosmology, of an integral metaphysics."[251] He agrees
wholeheartedly with the positive views of Chardin about the world
and the place of Christ in the world, and insists that we must not
fear progress. He warns him that it is dangerous to attempt to
represent such mysteries as the Incarnation in physical symbols,
since even the mystics were dissatisfied with their own symbols,
and "with greater reason we do not stop at the symbols of our own
invention."[252] He insists, too, in a passage that has exceptional
value in the light of the present interest in Chardin:

We must not forget that we do not have to conquer the universe to find
Christ in nature; we have to give up all creation for the precious pearl,
to die to the world, to live by a new life. We do not deny the beauty
and wonder of the world, but we must not forget the place of self-
denial, even as John of the Cross spoke of passing through the "dark
night," not out of scorn of esthetic beauty, denying the needs of our
heart. . . .[253]

After a beautiful exchange of letters, wherein each began to see
more clearly the thought of the other, Blondel felt that Chardin

was less concerned than he was with recalling "the divine incommensurability" and with making clear that there is "no divinization without supernaturalization, and no supernaturalization without death and rebirth."[254]

Through his philosophy, Blondel had made a large point of stressing self-denial, suffering, humility, and sacrifice as the necessary dispositions to prepare for the *unique nécessaire*. We must not even give the impression to the unbeliever that our struggle has been without a terrible cost,[255] or that we could be open to revelation without a "moral attitude . . . a great humility, a great self-denial."[256] "Pure detachment," he wrote to Chardin, "reunites us effectively to all; it is not by the *pleins* that we arrive at the *vide salutaire*. It is in emptiness that we find plenitude, God, and the rest by increase."[257] Chardin wrote that there would be adequate self-denial in the "passive purifications which Christ has appointed for us in order to transform into Himself all those qualities of our personality that we strive to develop for His sake."[258] Despite this difference, they were basically of one mind, especially in their positive view of the world and in their remarkable awareness of and concern for the unbeliever.[259] Blondel, "the Apostle of the unbeliever," saw in Chardin a kindred soul, and would have rejoiced at the explosion of interest in him. He would have appreciated the very important fact that Chardin knew what was in the minds of contemporary men, and to know this is the prerequisite for any solution to the problem of religious indifference and unbelief. More than anything else, Blondel was the opponent of the closed mind, born of an idealism which would walk through crowded streets, look everywhere, amass data for defense, and return home without having seen any people. Blondel saw people, listened to them, and this caused both his suffering and his success.

Evaluation

The author of a recent dissertation on Blondel insists that the "use of this method will never replace the traditional apologetics of the Church." He says that it *"might* [emphasis ours] render very valuable service to the psychological and moral preparation of the subjects." He concludes his analysis with the astonishing assertion that "in apologetic work one should take [*sic*] recourse to this formula only when he foresees that the traditional apologetic offers no chance of success on the minds which are completely closed to it, yet intellectually capable and disposed to receive the internal arguments."[260]

The apologetics which Maurice Blondel offered was neither a last-ditch type of approach to isolated intellectuals, nor was it a psychological effort suitable for a special few. Furthermore, he never intended that it should replace the traditional apologetics. It should provide a foundation and give a direction to any and every apologetic. Gélinas does not seem to recognize that Blondel was telling a closed Church that it had to become an open Church. Otherwise, even to speak of an apologetic was futile. He was not speculating, he was announcing an empirical fact. He saw the Church cut off from its own culture. He recognized the widespread apostasy which would lead a later generation to attempt a priest-worker movement.

And the reason that the Church did not recognize the tragedy of a Europe fallen faithless at its feet was the very narrowness and abstract idealism which Blondel castigated. It was a peculiar kind of narrowness, arrogantly asserting that it had the whole truth and man must humbly obey the demand of God, which His Church clearly echoed. Blondel was describing a Church which most of us know very well, a Church which told us that we had the truth, and all around us the world hovered in darkness. Consequently, we became suspicious of every form of thought which was not our own. Sociological surveys, polls of public opinion, even the atrocities committed in the world called Christian did not convince us that something was wrong. A man who does not listen cannot be convinced, and our idealism made us suspicious and defensive. We did not even hear the objections, as Blondel pointed out, because we hid behind a wall of ideas. Scheler had insisted that we must return from ideas to things. Blondel described far more clearly the narrowness that would make us irrelevant to modern man. In an age of liberalism, we were closed and conservative. In an age of positivism, we were deductive and aprioristic. The "image" we presented to the world was at odds with our culture, and we would never be heard.

Scheler had spoken more clearly of the need for love, and the reciprocal waves of love which beget love. But Blondel, recognizing the protests of a Comte, could see clearly that the Church stood so emphatically on the side of the past that a man of the present (to say nothing of the future) could not seriously consider her message. He grew up with a deep sympathy for the Modernists. He reminds us of Pope John and his overtures to the Communists. Like John, he knew that his opponents recognized the problems of society, even if the answer were partial and imperfect. Blondel asked that we listen to others, that we respect their sincere efforts to resolve real problems. Since the Church was not providing answers, it was important for the Church to observe carefully the successful social, philosophical, and religious movements. Condemnations should come slowly, and very likely they would not have to come if we would draw from our contemporaries the valid facets of their insights. Instead, Blondel saw the Church standing apart from the rest of mankind, pharisaically judging, timidly fleeing, and dully repeating answers to questions that were not being asked.

Blondel's confidence in man, his relentless optimism anticipated the spirit of Vatican II. As Bouillard points out in the Introduction to *Blondel et le Christianisme,* the apologetic which made Christianity a kind of extrinsic obligation, to which man must submit in obedience, was replaced by a dynamic way of life which responded to a need buried deep within man's heart. Blondel was well aware that history does strange things and that what is often called "tradition" is merely a reaction to circumstances, a reaction canonized long after the occasioning circumstances have died. Times change and so does man, and the world which accepted revelation—merely questioning its content—was gone. So was the world that bowed to an institution which did its thinking and made its decisions. It had been replaced by a world which started with man (even as Scheler had recognized in his metanthropology) and had to find in religion something which echoed in man's breast.

This was uncharted theological ground. So Blondel entered in as a philosopher, a phenomenologist, who knew nothing of "pure nature," but only of the man he observed and *loved.* His confidence in man was only exceeded by his confidence in God, a God Who had scattered Himself in creation and in the inner life of His chief creature. He insisted that grace had made its way into human psychology; he could see history as a growing development of Christ's presence in the world. The religious needs of the unbeliever grew greater, since the present memories of past faith reminded him of what life should be. Blondel saw man moving toward the very truths which he denied in the partial answers he gave. He was not speaking of a clever psychological approach to religion, he was not telling us how to approach the intelligentsia, or the contemplatives, he was offering a philosophical groundwork, a preevangelization, necessary for the unbeliever and the unbelieving part of every believer.

He asked the believer to stop judging his world, his society, until he had examined the obstacles to conversion in his own life. It was not the study of miracles that had convinced him, nor a scientific and an historical apologetics which had forced his assent under grace. It was the validity of the experience, the personal and objectively indefensible assurance that this was true because it was right. And once the unbeliever had been compelled—lovingly and openly—to reject solutions which provided no ultimate meaning to life, these very truths would respond to the void in his being. But he had to be moved from the world of ideas to the world of action. This was not an irrational world, but it was a world in which reason meant not rationalization, but contact with reality. It was a world in which a man could not rest in the complacent assurance that he *was* what he *thought* he was, but that he was *not* what he knew he *wanted* to be. Faith in such a world was not a body of truths to be believed, but a life to be lived. And there were as many obstacles as there were people, and as many struggles as there were "options." The believer and the unbeliever would share the experience of the void, and the believer, knowing well the cost of the climb, would have love and encouragement for his fellow struggler, his fellow seeker of the light.

This was not to deny the place of history, but it was to put one's mind into the mind of the unbeliever and to understand that the Christian fact was but one contingent fact among many, until man had entered the Christian door. Nor was it to deny the importance of the miracle, but it was to recognize that there was nothing wonderful about a miracle until it clearly became a sign. Man was within history and each man was Paul riding to Damascus. Man was surrounded by more marvels than he could digest, and the past miracles of Christ would not interest him until his own eyes were opened and his own ears were unstopped. We cannot, Blondel insisted, present the object until we have disposed of the subject. This will begin when we recognize that the "world is divinized," that God is here, knocking at every heart if man is but made to hear.

It is our job to make man hear, to arouse in him the need that will come when he recognizes that he has been satisfied with the "nothingness" of pessimism or the unsatisfying trinkets of dilettantism. Blondel was not as outspoken as Scheler, who insisted that we must tear down the idols. But he was equally as aggressive, and said the same thing in his systematic pursuit of *L'Action*. Blondel did not offer methods, but knew himself to be the "thinker." If he created the spirit of Christianity, then the methods would come. He did say, as Scheler did more clearly, that the unbeliever must have some place within the community, where he can struggle with the believer to find meaning, where he can know that he will get a hearing and not a pat answer and a smug judgment.

Once Blondel brings man to the need for the *unique nécessaire*, the transcendent, the supernatural, he goes no further. He believes that this will lead man to try Christianity, and only the Christian way in all its fullness will satisfy him. He leaves this to God. He believes that all we can do is help man to face himself, and if God wants him to go further, He will lead him. One cannot imagine him counting the number of converts, but that is not to suggest the number was unimportant. He saw that man would be moved toward the Christian message when he saw in it not a "legalistic casuistry," not a "mechanical discipline," not a "dry formalism of practices," not a "routine of visible ceremonies," but a way of life whose dogmas had "human meaning." This would mean, of course, an open Church; it would mean that the accoutrements of the day of kings would disappear; it would mean that Christianity would be the most divine because it was the most superbly human. The attitude that he engendered, far more than any involved and complicated system, will be his lasting heritage.

He remains the apostle of the open Church, the patron of the open but responsible mind, and the champion of a faith that wants answers, that will ask the world important questions, and that will love the men with whom he enters into dialogue. He will engage in such a dialogue not to judge any motives but his own, not to predetermine the results, but to seek truth no matter what it may cost him in sacrifice or swallowed pride. Such a quest can achieve nothing without a moral attitude which stands respectfully before the will of God, which echoes in the *élan* of man himself. The writings of Maurice Blondel reveal more than a philosopher. They reveal a chosen soul, whose vocation seems almost uniquely from on high. One wonders, in the strange events of history, whether Blondel may not one day join, in the ranks of the officially canonized, Pope Pius X, whose policies he opposed in the struggle for the same Church.

The beautiful words he wrote in the final chapter of *L'Action* seem to echo his own heart, even as they portray the heart of his thought:

We recognize that He does all in us, but by us and with us. . . . We share freely in His necessary liberty, in accepting that He may be in us what He is in Himself, the *Ens a Se*.[261]

IV

JOHN HENRY CARDINAL NEWMAN

A serious work, *Cardinal Newman and Apologetics*, published in 1952 attempts a rather elaborate defense of Newman's orthodoxy.[1] It is well known that Newman was under heavy suspicion during his lifetime, and that the conferral of the cardinal's hat was a rather late and much criticized honor. After his death, the storm increased. The confusion centering around Newman came from the distortions of his thought at the hands of such French scholars as Abbé Dimnet and Henri Bremond.[2] Newman was painted as an antiintellectual and a philosopher of the heart, and some saw in him a new hero in the cause of subjectivity. His defense of personalism, so popular in the age of Vatican II, was called a plea for relativism; his attack on the rationalists was seen as an assault on the intellect. Although Cardinal Newman preceded Blondel and Scheler chronologically, his place in the theological sun is actually of rather recent origin.

On the Continent, the Germans, under the guiding hand of Erich Przywara, S.J., were the best at understanding the mind of Newman.[3] They saw in him a philosopher who was deeply committed to the place of the intellect, but who had no place for the caricature that made of man only a mind. They recognized that he was not willing to sacrifice doctrinal integrity to relevance. Przywara especially opposed any interpretation of Newman which denied the need for an examination of rational evidence in approaching Christianity.

The acceptance of Newman in the English-speaking world was cautious. His fellow countryman, Martin D'Arcy, accuses him of a kind of nominalism, which makes invalid the comfortable universal ideas of ordered thought.[4] Most American seminarians had some contact with his *Idea of a University* and a few of his sermons, quite carefully selected. But it is only in the last decade or so that the true power of Newman has been allowed to flower, and the magnitude of his prophetic vision has been seen. It may be due far more to the Germans[5] than to the English-speaking peoples that Newman has come into his own. The works of Newman, careful commentaries and reflections on his thought, and efforts to determine the sources scanned by his creative mind flow from the presses of Germany.[6]

In examining the apologetic of John Henry Newman, we discover that his vision was often similar to that of Scheler and Blondel, though born of a different intellectual milieu. Our study includes a brief investigation of his intellectual background and the philosophic framework in which he constructed his apologetic. Since it is not our purpose to write a biography, we will stress only those facts in Newman's career which have bearing on our apologetic interest. Our discussion of Newman's apologetic centers largely on his mature work, the *Grammar of Assent*.[7] At the end of this chapter we offer a brief evaluation of Newman, concluding this section of the study with a crystallization of the thought of our three major sources as it has relevance today.

The Intellectual World of John Henry Newman

The life of Newman spans the nineteenth century, from 1801 to 1890. His early religious training was not exceptional, and he attributes his "first conversion" to an important contact at the age of fifteen with a Reverend Walter Mayers.[8] This youth experience was Calvinist in tone and was likely a direct source of Newman's early concern with conscience, salvation, and Providence. He was extremely sensitive and shy, and his shyness persisted in an extreme form throughout his entire formal education. It was only as an Oxford fellow at Oriel that Newman, under the encouragement of Whately, began to break from the prison of his own thoughts.[9] He always required time alone for meditative restoration, and his autobiographical memoirs reveal a tortuous introspection and examination of personal motives. On several occasions, at important crises in his life, he suffered a peculiar kind of nervous collapse, which he attributed to a deep-rooted pride. Culler describes him as sanguine and optimistic, and at times he became so excited with new ideas or projects that he was emotionally overwhelmed with the results before he had even begun.[10] At the same time, there is a shadow of pessimism in Newman,[11] but not in the categorical dimension in which Chadwick describes it. H. Francis Davis' observation seems more satisfactory. Davis sees Newman marked by a kind of eschatological direction in his early years and writings, a sense of foreboding and a preoccupation with judgment and the end of life. Later in his development, Newman has a more incarnational approach, which sees the world as redeemed and reaching out for God.[12] Consequently, the *Grammar of Assent* and the *Idea of a University*, products of a mature Newman, achieve an exceptional balance between Pollyanna and the pessimists.

His early reading was typical of the Oxford gentleman.[13] He read deeply in the Latin and Greek classics, not always with a sense of their meaning and historical significance, but more often in preparation for the strenuous examinations characteristic of the tutorial system. He read Aristotle extensively, but it was only in the common room at Oriel that the *Organon* of Aristotle would become a kind of temporary Bible. He read Gibbon's *Decline and Fall of the Roman Empire* several times in his youth, and he refers to it in an important place in the *Grammar of Assent*.[14] He read and enjoyed the virulence of Paine's *Common Sense* and Hume's attack on miracles, and studied deeply the work of Locke while yet in his teens. Chadwick's insistence that Newman did not seem to be aware of how deeply he had been affected by the skepticism of Hume seems to be another oversimplification.[15] Granted that few men pick apart an idea as Newman did and dissect its every shadowy detail, the intellectual tone of his age and his contact with the liberals of Oriel is quite sufficient to explain his "skeptic's" approach. Unquestionably, Newman saw value in Hume's discussion of the miraculous. Even in the *Grammar of Assent* he disagrees less with Hume's observations than with his preconceived attitude.[16] Newman's emphasis on the sign value of the miracle rather than on its element of wonder, an anticipation of modern theology, could well have been nourished in dialogue with Hume, as well as with Milman and others.[17] It was the mark of Newman's mind, as is clearly seen in the *Grammar*, to give every man a hearing.

Newman read omnivorously all his life, but his exposure to the liberals of Oxford taught him to reflect more than he read. It was Copleston, an important influence in Newman's days as a fellow, who insisted on *"multum non multa."* Hawkins was the one who insisted that Newman weigh the value and meaning of words, and who corrected his early sermons and essays. And Whately, perhaps the most influential of the noetics on the young Newman, was a man who prided himself on reading only a few books. Whately picked the minds of other men and venerated the powers of logical analysis. Later Newman reacted violently to Whately's way of logic. *The Grammar of Assent* stands as its most careful indictment. Yet, the influence of Whately on young Newman, who had assisted Whately in the preparation of his essays in logic, was important.[18]

The intellectual world of Newman's England was a curious one. Politically, the English stood aghast at the horrors of the French Revolution that were whispered across the Channel. Burke stood for a special kind of conservatism in thought. The English prided themselves on their traditional balance which could achieve the noble ends of *liberté, fraternité,* and *égalité* without the passion and the pathos of the French. Newman himself prophesied dangerous times ahead in England, alarmed by his awareness of a monarch massacred by the guillotine, an emperor who wanted the world, and recurring revolutions in thought and action. Consequently, England must move cautiously, traditions must be safeguarded, and Oxford must not fall to the demands of the intemperate and the irreligious.[19]

Despite this political conservatism, the world of ideas was exceptionally turbulent. It is impossible to capture the many melodies of its moods, but we will attempt a general overview, hoping to understand the attitudes of the audience to whom Newman addressed his *Grammar of Assent*. Gunter Rumbold has attempted to list and evaluate the minds to which Newman reacted in his personalist anthropology. He lists Descartes, Francis Bacon, Locke,

Hume, Shaftesbury, Paley, and Joseph Butler.[20] We will also consider the influence of Newton and Samuel Taylor Coleridge, and the evangelical dimension of religious thought. These varied currents of thought were felt at Oxford, and Newman reacted to them in the formation of his own ideas. The influence of Pascal is hard to trace, although Newman refers to him frequently.[21] The long hours spent with the Fathers of the Church, the unique sense of the historical, and the fervor of exchange in the Oriel common room each had its part to play. But first we shall consider the general world of thought in which Newman lived.

It might be well to begin with Descartes, as Rumbold does, since all Englishmen owe much to his emphasis on the place of self-knowledge and the force of the logical idea.[22] This, however, is a debt which Newman shares with the entire world, a debt which has made unwarranted assumptions as unacceptable as it has made Hegelian idealism possible. We prefer to begin, however, more modernly with the place of John Locke. Chronologically, Locke belongs to the seventeenth century, but he can rightfully claim the eighteenth century as his own.[23] It was Descartes, indeed, who provided a new and important spark of European thought with his *Cogito*. There could be proofs of God, proofs of freedom and immortality, and proofs that made use of a different kind of reason than the Scholastics had known. The scientific reason of Francis Bacon had found in Descartes its theorist, and doubt would become a new and exciting virtue. Reason would be the new-found hero, the vigorous defender and discoverer of God and morality.[24]

But it was John Locke's *Essay Concerning Human Understanding* which:

epitomized the intellectual outlook of his own age and shaped that of the next. For over a century he dominated European thought. His work in conjunction with that of Newton created a new mentality among intelligent people and instantly affected religious thought. . . . The spirit in which he dealt with Christianity is more important than what he actually said about it. He made a certain attitude toward religious faith almost universal.[25]

That attitude did not underestimate the importance of religion or belief. In fact, he insisted that God's existence could be demonstrated with a mathematical certainty, and that "belief is the consequence of rational proof."[26] But the God of John Locke was an impersonal God, and revelation was the reason's purest religious tone. Theology became largely unimportant, and doctrine could be reduced to pragmatic simplicity. It was a religion of action, a religion of morality and right conduct, with little need for complicated structures of fine theoretical distinctions. It was the kerygma of deism, a religion wherein man worshipped an inverted incarnation, whereby man and reason became God. Miracles and mysteries were no more. Religion became as clear as geometry and far less occult and sophisticated.[27]

The success of Locke's *Essay* was due to more than the power of his ideas. The world must be ready for an idea, circumstances must provide the right soil and air. Unquestionably, the growing success of Newtonian physics and the scientific method helped. Man could see the progress, the marvels of his own creation. Natural mysteries fell before the precision blade of reason and scientific investigation. New horizons, closed by religious narrowness and superstition, were unveiled. Organized religion of a traditional kind had meanwhile become embroiled in petty quarrels and brutal wars. The infinite tolerance of the latitudinarians, later to become a quite narrow intolerance, spoke of God's universal fatherhood, a simple Bible, a clear and wholesome morality free from casuistry. Clarke and Tillson brought religion to reason's court and were certain they had won a unanimous victory.[28]

The deists maintained that nature's designer had achieved a perfect work. Evil was explained away, nature's laws held all the revelation that man needed, and reason would unlock all of nature's pages. Even the Christian apologists of the more traditional creeds resorted to Locke's methods to quiet the very attacks on revealed religion that his *Essay* had unleashed. William Paley's *Evidences of Christianity* (1794), the most popular apologetic textbook of Newman's day, spoke of the clear and unequivocal proofs for God's existence and the certain evidence for Christianity contained in signs. He gave comfort to a Christianity threatened by deism,[29] but the deists were winning the battle. Their answers were so simple, their explanations so uninvolved, that the ordinary man could follow them. Elaborate proofs of the Resurrection did not have the appeal and the social impact of the new-found simplicity. Even the deists, however, were not destined for success in their effort to capture the religious enthusiasm of the public.

Their religion, stripped of creed and cult, ceremony and symbol, was so simple that it became dull once the impact of its iconoclastic arrogance had become commonplace. As Gerald Cragg puts it, there could be no satisfactory solution to the religious problem as long as both deists and Christians remained in "the restricted orbit in which eighteenth century rationalism moved."[30]

It was Bishop Joseph Butler's *Analogy of Religion Natural and Revealed* (1736) which most clearly saw the solution to the religious problem. His work was an important and acknowledged antecedent of Newman's thought. Butler was not tied to a dishonest rationalism. He faced the fact of evil in the world and the sufferings and silence born of nature. The nature he saw was not predictable and omnipotent, not minutely measurable and beneficent. It was at times a monster and at times largely mysterious. It could not explain away evil and misery and human tragedy. Life was frequently a gamble, in which man was not certain which way he must move. The mystery of nature, its unexplainable quality, was analogous to the obscurity and difficulty of religious truth. This analogy is omnipresent. What we experience in nature is only to be expected in religion.[31]

Faced with the darkness and mystery of life, we must be guided by probability in our decisions, not by a lucid and mathematical power of reasoning. We seek only a balance of probability when we decide upon the right course to take. This is true both in matters of ordinary life and in religious decisions. The ultimate authority in religious matters, once the various probabilities have been balanced, is conscience, which "by its nature claims to rule man's life."[32]

The impact of Butler's thought did not significantly quiet the thrust of Locke's attack. It was David Hume who answered Locke more tellingly in the eighteenth century, though his rebuttal created as many problems as it solved. In his *Treatise of Human Nature* he showed that Locke's philosophy led nowhere when pushed to its ultimate conclusions. Hume was the apostle of skepticism who "demolished all the traditional certainties: God, the soul, nature and matter, causation and miracles." In his *Natural History of Religion* he explained that the phenomenon of religious belief originates along lines much different from the theoretical arguments which lent it support. Perhaps, as Cragg says,

Hume's importance was not so much in what he said as in what he made it impossible for others to say. "Rationalism had attacked superstition, only to be attacked in turn by skepticism."[33] The eighteenth century leaned heavily on William Paley's apologetic as some kind of answer to the rationalists and skeptics, and the book was used as a prescribed textbook at Cambridge. It was another century, however, before Newman provided a more complete and satisfying answer.

Newman's exposure to the philosophic currents of his own day was not restricted to a careful reading of its most eloquent exponents. It was in the involved discussions of the faculty at Oriel College, Oxford, where he watched, and for a time admired, the liberal mind at work. Here the twenty-one-year-old Newman sat among the noetics during their interminable discussions. Here he studied the sophisticated mind of his own day, a mind which accorded dialectic the only validity in approaching truth. He sat shyly by and watched the audacious Copleston, the precise Hawkins, and the colorful Whately tear traditions apart with the hungry blade of Aristotle's *Organon*. In one sense, as Culler points out, Aristotle was not an authority but merely an important precedent permitting them to abandon all authority.[34] Only gradually did Newman become comfortable in the group. Religious problems were gnawing at him, a deep concern for the moral good of students was under the surface. Largely, he was examining his own experience as a student, and secretly recognized the futility of enduring tense examinations and poring over the Greek and Latin classics if these efforts led only to confusion and semantic displays. As time went on he became disenchanted with logic and word games, and turned his attention to the improvement of the educational system of his own school.[35]

Newman was well aware of the religious indifference that was growing at Oxford. He had experienced sadly the champagne feasts among the students that preceded the formal Communion service. His efforts at reform were met with blasé amusement or unconcern. When he was appointed tutor at Oriel in 1826 his formal education was over, and he became more consciously concerned with his religious mission and his responsibility to his fellow men. No longer was his mind "an instrument being fashioned, but an instrument at work." Holy Orders meant to him a life of service, and the service could not be a comfortable life and a token effort to help Oriel students place significantly in the University examinations. Gradually, in the 1820's, we see his attitude change from that of a logician and man of letters to a determined and outspoken man of God. It was his reaction to the noetics and his intimate concern for the students that set him upon the course of a modern apologete.[36]

He insisted on spending time with the students to develop and form them. He began to recognize, as he would later spell out in his *Idea of a University*, that his own ideas of education ran counter to the spirit of his day. Education was becoming secularized and he believed in the place of theology and religious formation. Education was becoming pragmatic and he stood for the "man of the philosophic habit." Gradually, he recognized that he stood apart from Copleston and Whately, and felt a kindred pulse with new faces at Oriel, such as Froude, Keble, and Wilberforce. It was this association that led to the Oxford movement, which resisted the state encroachment on education and struggled for traditional religion against the liberals and evangelicals.[37]

It would give a wrong impression of Newman to intimate that his battles were fought in the narrow world of the Oriel common room or even in the university milieu of Oxford. When the religious dissenters began to gather force and to threaten the hold of the established religion on the educational philosophy of Oxford, Newman was a fiery leader in the parliamentary struggle.[38] At a later date, when he had been received into the Roman Church and had been appointed rector of the Catholic University in Dublin, he was willing to fight the battle openly and vigorously with layman and hierarchy.[39]

During his tutorship at Oriel, Newman recognized the need to impress the few, and not to be concerned with the many. He was out to challenge the intellectual, sensing that the people moved the way their leaders did.[40] His view of the tutor's responsibility at Oxford was one of personal contact, a molding but not a forcing influence. He sought the challenge of other minds, and he knew that isolation was only profitable if it followed upon a vibrant and personal exchange. This, of course, was his view of the value of a university, wherein a freedom mingled with personal contact would inhibit the eccentricity of isolation and the frozen formalism of uniformity.[41] At Oxford and at Littlemore, Newman labored with the little flock. His *Oxford University Sermons,* preached at St. Mary's shortly before his reception into the Roman Church in 1845, were aimed at the few, the important few who would determine the intellectual and religious direction of the masses.

There was another important dimension of religious and philosophic thought in Newman's England. It was the evangelical strain that Newman had personally experienced in his first conversion. It owed much to John Wesley's genius, but cannot be equated with Methodism.[42] It had an element of radical Calvinism that was foreign to Wesley's gentler touch. It spoke of man's corruption, had little time for dogmas, insisted on an emotional and enduring conversion, and offered the simple beauty of an unadorned Christianity to a world reeking with religious strife. The formal cult had as little place in its repertoire as the complicated doctrine. It was concerned with the needy and the neglected and the socially deprived, and it sponsored a vigorous missionary movement. Charles Simeon was an important luminary in its rapid growth at the close of the eighteenth century.[43] Although its origins were bathed in a plea for tolerance, the evangelical movement became bitterly anti-Catholic with the rise of the Oxford movement. Newman was not only aware of its power from his youthful experience, but saw its rising influence among the masses, who turned from the logistics and skepticism bred of liberalism. The first part of the *Grammar of Assent* was a direct effort to refute the evangelical cry: "Jesus, yes; dogma and theology, no!"[44]

Newman would not accept the picture of man that was offered to him by his society, and it is in his anthropology that we find the key to his apologetics.[45] The English philosophers had distorted the image of man, and because of this initial mistake their entire system came tumbling down. Bacon had seen man as the discoverer and master of nature. Locke and his followers had been blind to anything in man but a cold and mathematical reason. The apologetic of William Paley, which had formed the mind of the English clergy, tried unsuccessfully to meet Locke on this impossible battlefield. Hume had taken away man's unity and left in its stead a bundle of impressions and notions quite accidentally assembled. The religious liberals, quoting an Aristotle dipped in Locke and Hume, seemed indifferent somehow to what really happened to man. The evangelicals insulted man's mind and made his Creator quite merciless and despotic. Butler alone had a total picture of man and can be claimed the "conqueror of the century in which he lived."[46] Newman was able to unite with him, to improve upon him in reassembling man into a balanced whole. Only then could he begin to wage his twofold war: the war against the religion of pure feeling, and the war against the religion that dissolved faith into a series of logical derivatives. We must agree with Rumbold's conclusion in *Das Wesen der Person nach John Henry Newman:* Newman stands in most questions against the English philosophers of the seventeenth through the nineteenth centuries, particularly against the chief streams of rationalism and liberalism.[47]

Newman nonetheless listened to his opponents and saw the value in the distorted figure that each one called man. He did not care about the quality of the source in which he found truth. Hence, Culler can assert that Newman seemed to admire most the intellect of those whose character was questionable. When he sought to describe the ideal philosopher, he went to Aristotle's "magnanimous man," whose shortcomings Newman recognized clearly. He makes similar use of Cicero and Cato, Gibbon and Goethe.[48] He extolled reason as did Locke, questioned everything with vigor as did Hume, respected science as did Newton, loved and learned from history as did Gibbon, and stressed experience and feeling as did the evangelicals. Newman wanted to see man, to understand man, and to describe man in his total dimension.

Ultimately, however, it would be wrong to think of Newman as an eclectic. He himself insisted that each generation rides on the shoulders of the previous age.[49] The conclusions of one generation became the certainties of the next. Yet, as Chadwick asserts, Newman was "a man of exceptional independence of mind."[50] The death of Newman's sister Mary had a tremendous impact on his life and direction, somehow turning him inward and toward God.[51] We can stress his intellectual contacts with the noetics, but we cannot neglect the impact of his brother's conversion to Unitarianism. Newman never lost the sense of reflection that was instilled in his dialogues with Whately, and the torture with which he wrote tells us something of the torture with which he thought.[52]

Another important factor of Newman's intellectual formation

and experience was his study of the Fathers. It was very likely here that he absorbed something of his Platonist approach, especially from his perusal of the Alexandrians in preparation for his work on the Arian controversy.[53] It was the same Platonist spirit he admired in Butler and in Pascal, the spirit which so attracted him in Samuel Taylor Coleridge.[54] It was Coleridge's insistence that "there is something in the human mind which makes it know that in all finite quantity, there is an infinite," which Newman would quote approvingly in the Grammar of Assent. It was also in Coleridge that Newman would have likely discovered the world of Tübingen's Möhler or Konigsberg's Immanuel Kant. England was well isolated from German thought, and Newman did not read German. Coleridge could well have been a bond between the world of Newman and that of Möhler. Coleridge had written:

Evidences of Christianity! I am weary of the word. Make a man feel the want of it; rouse him, if you can, to the self-knowledge of his need of it; and you may safely trust to its own evidence.[55]

Coleridge also insisted that men are largely right in what they affirm and wrong in what they deny, a sentiment developed by Newman throughout his writings. At any rate, the personalism of Newman's thought, which sought out kindred sentiments from varied and intertwined sources, was undoubtedly nourished at the fount of the Fathers he drank in so fervently.

It was from the Fathers, too, that Newman derived an historical sense of Christianity, which is the genius of his Essay on the Development of Doctrine. Unlike Ward, who took his theories to history, Newman found his theory there.[56] He had read Gibbon's account of Christian history several times. In his Grammar of Assent, he makes much of Gibbon's faulty preconceptions. Newman went to history objectively and opened to Christian theology the important sense of historical growth and development which is the key to much of modern theological renewal. Theology had looked to history for confirmation of its dogmas, had attempted to assemble an arsenal of defensive and justifying testimony, but had considered doctrinal development to mean a clarification or a logical unfolding. Newman displayed the organic growth of the Christian revelation within history.[57] He saw a striking parallel in the dynamic growth of Christ in history and in the life of the individual. He saw the same parallel in historical heresies and in personal prejudices, and described this parallel in the *Grammar*. Butler's concept of the analogy might have helped him in his vision, but his view was vastly more panoramic than anything Butler envisioned.[58]

Ultimately, Newman was Newman. Although he read widely, it was not in books that Newman found the exciting spark of creative thought, but in living minds,[59] and in his own unique person. Newman loved his fellow men and suffered deeply from their slights. His change of religious allegiance brought him few friends and lost him many. Whereas his own sister rejected him, Rome did not receive him with a brother's arms.[60] His life is a history of attacks by enemies and former friends. But this sensitive and suffering man had something to say, and he had to say it. The honesty and integrity which he considered so essential in a man's search for faith was the clearest quality of his own life. His writings carefully reflect, as the writings of any personalist or existentialist must, his own life. Both Blondel and Scheler insisted that the Christian who would be concerned about the conversion of an unbelieving world must understand the obstacles to conversion within himself, the "idols" before which he dances. Newman's own conversion, its growth and perseverance, was the thread he wove through everything he wrote.

Conscience plays such an important role in his work because it played such an important part in his life. It led him to renounce all for the treasure in the field, a treasure which brought him suffering and tears. There is a sense of foreboding about Newman, a sense of alienation, a horror of sin. It creeps through his works and permits Chadwick to call him a pessimist. But that is to see only one side of Newman. There is about him a sense of peace, the secure sense of a man who has found himself, the certitude that comes when a man believes and knows why.

Newman is a man who opposed his own generation because he loved. He knew that he lived in a "novel era," in which men were growing independent of judgment and shaking off the traditions of the past.[61] Newman became the most independent of all because he became the most personal. He could not accept Locke's reason because it did not exist in his own life. Nor could he adopt the skepticism of Hume, since he knew that his own life demanded certainties. He could not accept the liberals because they took away the faith that his conscience demanded. Nor could he accept the evangelicals, who despised the very mind that made him man. He sought truth within himself no matter its cost, and he knew he found it when "it follows on investigation and truth, . . . it is accompanied by a specific sense of intellectual satisfaction and repose, and . . . it is irreversible."[62]

Newman's Apologetic

Newman's own struggle to find the repose of a certain faith and his awareness of the growth of unbelief in his society stamped the mark of an apologete on everything he wrote. He was not the detached idealist, and consequently his experiences constantly invaded his writing. Our concern in this section centers around Newman's *Grammar of Assent* (1870), which is his chief and most mature apologetic work.[63] Although we have not ignored the several commentaries on the *Grammar*, we follow the advice of Stephen Dessain and go to Newman himself.[64]

The *Grammar* is a difficult work, perhaps the most involved and abstruse that Newman ever wrote. Once we have mastered its main line of argument, our difficulties do not cease. His powerful asides, strewn almost casually throughout this work, are quite as important as the work itself. This is especially true for our study, since we are equally concerned with the apologetic insights Newman offers. Newman wrote for a specific audience and some of that audience, the rationalist and the skeptic, is with us still. The larger part of Newman's audience, however, those who accepted the fact of revelation but not its Catholic form, has dwindled and has been replaced by a mounting army of unbelievers. Similarly, that portion of Newman's apologetic which appeals to the historical will not have the relevance today that it had a century ago. Man's sense of history has been largely replaced by a sense of present value. It is our impression, based largely on personal and vicarious experience, that modern man is not much impressed with the miracle of Catholicism's historical continuity.[65] This is a supplementary argument that will have persuading power only after modern man sees Christianity's unique value in his present life.

Consequently, the breadth of Newman's apologetic forces us

to limit our scope according to our present purpose. He offers a threefold apologetic, which follows the accepted pattern of the nineteenth century: 1) the religious demonstration, 2) the Christian demonstration, and 3) the Catholic demonstration.[66] The Catholic demonstration was a reaction to the Protestant Reformation. The Reformation split Christendom into many churches, each claiming to present authentic Christianity. Today, the World Council of Churches acts on the assumption that no single church possesses the plenitude of Christ. A growing opinion contends that each Church is but a feeble expression of the great Christian mystery, and any body which claims to be unique or catholic is idolatrous and egotistical. Newman was well aware of this mentality, and he emphasized the need of an infallible Church, lest men be led into learned skepticism or unlearned superstition. Today, Newman's *"demonstratio catholica"* is obsolete because Protestant ecclesiology is no longer what it was in his time; the ecumenical movement has no counterpart in nineteenth century England. We are not concerned in our study with *"demonstratio catholica."*

We are concerned with the *modern apologetic problem,* and later in this study, we will make clear that this is the problem of the unbeliever. This is not to say that there is no place for a *"demonstratio catholica."* That, however, is another project.

In his Christian demonstration, Newman comes very close to the position of Scheler and Blondel. They did not distinguish between the Catholic and the Christian demonstration. They believed that if they could help lead man to Christianity, then the power of Catholicity would have to speak for itself, and man would be led to it only when he discovered that it alone satisfied his needs.[67] All three saw the need for a Christian demonstration, since all were confronted with different forms of a very similar "Enlightenment." The enlightened (to Scheler, the prophets of the *Aufklarung;* to Blondel, *les philosophies;* to Newman, the rationalists) were not opposed to religion; they saw its value in giving purpose to personal life and order to social life. Some even held on to a personal God, but largely they looked for the God of reason and order.

It was in the religious demonstration that Blondel and Scheler, and Newman as well, centered the real force of the apologetic. It was an answer to those who saw no need for religion at all, to those who said that man stood all alone, and any talk of God was mere projection or transference. Newman replied to such an argument that he would be an atheist if it were not for the sounds of his conscience.[68] Scheler, and especially Blondel, saw the same "enlightened" thought reach new and sophisticated forms of development along evolutionary and psychological lines. All three realized that the "enlightened" rejected any revelation, and that is why they began their apologetic with man as he was. If there was to be dialogue with an unbelieving world, if Christians were not to end up arguing among themselves, then the apologete had to begin with man without God. The "God-is-dead" proclamation was first announced in the nineteenth century.[69] Newman heard it in the common room at Oriel and in the cynicism of his fellow students at Oxford; Scheler heard it in the words of Nietzsche; Blondel saw it in the extremes of Modernism. Apologetics had to begin with a man without God if Christians were to begin on a common ground with the nonbeliever.

Newman inherited an apologetic which did not speak to his world.[70] It offered proofs for God's existence which did not prove God to him. The God of the proofs was an impersonal God, the God of the deists and not the God of Newman. It offered proofs for the revelation from signs and prophecies, and while Newman saw value in such an approach, he knew it demanded a preliminary preparedness which could not be taken for granted. Revelation might be "demonstrably true in itself," but it was not "irresistibly true."[71] An apologetic had to start not with ideas but with men, not with abstractions but with reality. So Newman began with what Przywara calls the "Glaubensbegrundung," what Fries calls more accurately the "Religionsbegrundung," what we will call the preevangelization.[72]

Newman saw upon man the mark of God and knew that the "experience of existence is united with and given together with the experience of God."[73] Newman began with conscience, the key to his apologetic, the contact with the eternal that all men shared, and, without its testimony, all arguments were just so many words.[74] But before treating Newman's argument from conscience, we must first examine the method which Newman employs in the *Grammar of Assent*. It is in this method, as well as in what he says, that Newman ushered in a new era.

The Phenomenological Method of Newman

The *Grammar of Assent* had a twofold purpose, according to a note recorded by Edward Caswall on the flyleaf of a copy of the *Grammar* presented by Newman himself:

Object of the book twofold: In the first part [it] shows that you can believe what you cannot understand. In the second part [it shows] that you can believe what you cannot absolutely prove.[75]

Dessain, commenting on this quotation, explains that the *Grammar of Assent* is really two books. Part one, "Assent and Apprehension," was written to show the "importance and value of dogmatic formularies" in dialectic with the evangelical and liberal Protestants. This part is of far less importance than the second, which is entitled "Assent and Inference," and is directed at the rationalists. Since this latter group, whether we call them rationalists or secular humanists, is of far more concern today, we center our attention on the second part of the *Grammar of Assent*. This is the modern apologetic problem, the dialogue with the unbeliever. The past methods, both in Newman's day and in our own, have generally provided a believer's apologetic for the unbeliever, and have argued from a kind of reasoning which the unbeliever did not recognize or from conclusions he could not honestly accept.

Newman did not start with the mathematical reasoning of Locke or the faith-laden reasoning of the orthodox Christian. He insisted that one must admit of various kinds of proof for various kinds of reality. Hence he offered his now famous distinction between real and notional assent.[76] If we deal with ideas alone and want to reach a merely logical conclusion, a notional assent, then abstract reasoning is quite sufficient. This would be true in mathematics or in mere assent to propositions. Such notional assent can be as weak as a simple profession, which is "little more than an assertion," or as strong as speculation, which is "the most direct, explicit, and perfect" of its kind.[77] But if we are dealing with the concrete and the personal decisions of life, then we must speak of a real assent. Real assents "are sometimes called beliefs, convictions, certitudes; and as given to moral objects, they are perhaps as rare as they are powerful."[78] In a celebrated passage, Newman shows the futility of logic in concrete matters:

Logic makes but sorry rhetoric with the multitude; first shoot round corners, and you may not despair of converting by a syllogism. Tell men to gain notions of a Creator from His works, and, if they were to set about it (which nobody does) they would be jaded and wearied by the labyrinth they were tracing. Their minds would be gorged and surfeited by the logical operation. Logicians are more set upon concluding rightly, than on right conclusions. They cannot see the end for the process. Few men have that power of mind which holds fast and firmly a variety of thoughts. . . . To most men argument makes the point in hand only more doubtful and considerably less impressive.[79]

Newman was not dispensing with logic, nor was he scorning reason. He did distinguish between theology and religion, however, and said that we could not expect theological conclusions to precipitate religious decisions.[80] Religion had to do with the personal and the real, and theology waged its important battles in the world of the notional. In the first part of the *Grammar*, which concerns us only as it lays the logical groundwork for the second part, Newman showed that the religious man needed the protection of theology. If the theologian were not on hand to separate the notion of truth from heresy, soon the religious life of the individual would be confused and superstitious. Theological notions could and would have concrete applications, but the mode of assent in theology and religion was different. In the *Grammar*, Newman proceeded to show how men reached certitude in concrete matters, such as belief.

He did this, not by a theory of epistemology, but by a careful and minute description of the process. He did not set out to prove that men reached certitude in the real and personal areas of life. He took it for granted. It happened, and he was interested in describing precisely how it happened. Although Michael d'Elizalde had proposed a similar argument in seventeenth century Naples, and although Amort and Butler had carried the idea forward, it was Newman who was "the first to venture a strict analysis and defense of this complex procedure."[81] He approached the problem as a phenomenologist, with common-sense observation and personal introspection as his most effective tools. Newman was rejecting the epistemology of Locke and the Locke-inspired apologetic of Paley. Locke insisted that certitude usually came from logic and Newman observed that, whereas certitude was common enough, the logic of which Locke spoke was quite uncommon.[82] Locke would admit that on occasions "sufficient probabilities" could lead to a quasi-certainty. But what Locke considered an anomaly, Newman called usual, and it was not merely an apparent certainty but the real thing. Basically, Newman had a different vision of man, a new anthropology, based on his own experience of reality. He chastised those who forced man into some preconceived mold and only accepted the mental operation that acted according to their theories.[83] They studied the mind in one mode of operation, in mathematics or in formal logic, and they applied this narrow vision to the whole richness of human experience. The scientific mind, too, which attempts to impose its method on a more involved reality, must recognize that "in its very perfection lies its incompetency to settle particulars and details."[84] Man was reaching all kinds of concrete certitudes at the very moment that the rationalists or scientists were insisting that it could not happen. Newman refused to stray far from the practical experience of life. Here he could study living minds, and here he could see the divine nature operating in man, man not as theorists said he should be, but as reality revealed that he was.[85] If God wanted man to reach certitude in some other way, then it should have been apparent. As it was, man went right on living and even dying for the certitudes which the rationalists said he could not possibly have.

Newman knew that man often seemed to be certain when he actually was only prejudiced or temporarily convinced. At times he seems ambivalent on this point, on one occasion seeing certitude on every side and on another stressing how frequently apparent certitude masquerades for other mental states.[86] Real certitude fulfills three conditions, and even these conditions are typical of Newman's method of describing the phenomenon rather than defining it:

It seems then that on the whole there are three conditions of certitude: that it follows on investigation and proof, that it is accompanied by a specific sense of intellectual satisfaction and repose, and that it is irreversible.[87]

When it comes to the ultimate justification of such certitudes, Newman merely insists that this is the way man is. The only ultimate justification of our capacity to reach certitude in concrete and personal matters is the incontrovertible fact that we do. This is true in numerous areas of life, even though much of life is guided by probabilities. Newman points out that:

They [our probabilities] are probabilities founded on certainties. It is on no probability that we are constantly receiving the informations and dictates of sense and memory, of our intellectual instincts, of the moral sense of the logical faculty.[88]

We cannot, however, prove that our senses grasp their objects, nor that the mind reasons or conscience is operative, nor that we reach certitude in concrete matters. These are primary truths that we accept. Newman is not interested in such proofs. Referring explicitly to the question of certitude in concrete matters, he says: "How it comes about that we can be certain is not my business to determine; for me it is sufficient that certitude is felt."[89] He censures Locke for his "unreal and theoretical" approach to man, whereby "he consults his own ideal of how the mind ought to act, instead of interrogating human nature, as an existing thing, as it is found in the world."[90] When Newman requires proof, he cites the "common voice of mankind." Life is too short to await the logical proofs that never come. Mankind moves on and Newman is too much of a realist to scoff at men as they hurry by. He rushes to join them.

Newman's Vision of Analogy

Newman's awareness of the world of concrete reality is reflected in his application of the principle of analogy. Butler was obviously the source of the idea, as we indicated above, but Butler never envisioned the applications that Newman would make of this idea.[91] Butler had stressed the analogy between the world of nature and the life of man, insisting to the scientists that the uncertainties of nature paralleled the doubts and difficulties man would experience in his search for God. Newman applies this analogy to the relationship between the awareness that we have of individuals through the sense and the knowledge of God that comes to us through conscience:

The evidence that we have of their presence [individual things] lies in the phenomena which address our senses, and our warrant for taking

these for evidence is our instinctive certitude that they are evidence.
. . . Now certainly the thought of God, as theists entertain it, is not
gained by an instinctive association of His presence with any sensible
phenomena; but the office which the senses directly fulfill as regards
creation that devolves indirectly on certain of our mental phenomena as
regards the Creator. Those phenomena are found in the sense of moral
obligation. As from a multitude of instinctive perceptions, . . . we
generalize the notion of an external world, . . . so from the perceptive
power which identifies the intimations of conscience . . . we proceed
on to the notion of a Supreme Ruler and Judge.[92]

When Newman talks about our quest for certainty in the concrete
matters of religion, he asks: Why should this be any different from
a judge's search for rectitude in handing down his decision from a
variety of evidence? Or from a critic's attempt to determine au-
thorship of a literary work?[93] Newman sees life as a whole, and the
evidences of one part of life tell us a great deal about another part.
When Newman refers to the "common opinion of mankind," he
does so not merely to heap up evidence but from a profound
awareness of the divine hand working analogously in all the events
of human life. The one God does not have many methods of
operation, and if we observe carefully we find the similarity beneath the differences. The reason that Newman saw analogies
everywhere is that he saw the one God everywhere. Thus, he could
never maintain that men reached different conclusions in their
reasoning as a result of faulty reasoning. As a rule men reason
rather well, but they start with different presumptions and their
conclusions are already reflected in their beginnings.[94]

The principle of analogy is the heart of his theory on doctrinal
development, and thus he explores the development of any idea in
history or literature and begins from this point. Both Chadwick
and Walgrave see in his *Essay on Development* a description of the
Church's growing awareness of the revelation of Christ analogous
to a description of the individual's dynamic growth in belief as
contained in the *Grammar*.[95] Analogy is ever the basis of his
argument. What at first seems to be a mere descriptive example
turns out to be another application of the rhythm of analogy.

It is this same principle, sincerely applied, that enables
Newman to begin his apologetics with man. It gave him his sense
of community; it permitted him to see the value of Locke and to
praise the talents of Hume.[96] The apologete must stress similari-

ties, and Newman found them everywhere. He did not feel himself apart from his fellowman. Even as he could call upon the common opinion of men in establishing the phenomenon of conscience or the sense of alienation and sin,[97] so he could point to the solid orthodoxy of the ordinary faithful when even their bishops were led astray.[98]

In the *Grammar of Assent* or in the *Apologia,* he could be certain of the futility of logical argument[99] because he saw how inconsequential it was in the ordinary dealings of men. Nor did he hesitate in both these works to cite evidence from his own conversion, since he realized that there were thousands of men who would share his experience.[100] He was confidently aware that the God of Revelation must have left His mark on the nature of man, and if man were observed minutely and patiently, the voice of God would be heard consistently, calling man to himself. Newman's principle of analogy, anticipating the supernatural existential and the incarnational emphasis of a later age, saw that the final end of man must somehow be anticipated in his beginnings, since the one God was both the beginning and the end.

This is the principle that sparked Newman's vision of man, a vision actually centered in God. It is the principle of wholeness that underlies Newman's anthropology, as we pointed out in our introduction to this chapter. The philosophers saw but one part of man and called it the whole. Newman saw the unity in every part and the analogous touch of God's hand in all creation. Some think that Newman borrowed the evolutionary insights of his age, but it seems that his vision came from his own creative genius.[101] When Chadwick calls Newman pessimistic, it makes us think that he has not understood this key principle in Newman's thought. It was the principle of analogy that kept Newman from the twin evils of extreme optimism and despair.

Converging Probabilities and the Illative Sense: The Way to Certitude

Once having established the fact that man does reach certitude in matters of concrete fact, as is evidenced by personal experience and the testimony of mankind, Newman proceeds to show how this takes place. The way of logic or formal inference cannot explain it, since logic does not deal with the personal and the concrete. We can reach certitude without such evidence, and when we have it we are not always certain.[102] Newman says: "Inference, considered in the sense of verbal argumentation, determines neither our principles, nor our ultimate judgments—that it is neither the test of truth, nor the adequate basis of assent."[103] He goes on to say that the "real and necessary method" of arriving at concrete fact is:

the cumulation of probabilities, independent of each other, arising out of the nature and circumstances of the particular case which is under review; probabilities too fine to avail separately, too subtle and circuitous to be convertible into syllogisms, too numerous and various for such conversion, even were they convertible. As a man's portrait differs from a sketch of him, . . . such is the multiform and intricate process of ratiocination, necessary for our reaching him as a concrete fact, compared with the rude operation of syllogistic treatment.[104]

These probabilities can come from a variety of sources, and the determining factor in what evidence a man accepts and what he rejects is largely determined by the makeup of the man himself and the "intellectual and moral character" of the person who attempts to convince him. There are myriad influences that shape the mind and heart of man, and Newman's awareness of these influences was far in advance of the psychological insights of his own day.[105] What ultimately determines how a man will view the probable evidence that is presented to him is his illative sense, which Newman defines as "right judgment in ratiocination."[106] It is the illative sense which shapes a man's presumptions or self-evident principles. The principles do not simply appear, but they are formed mysteriously, wonderfully from the variety of concrete events that make up a man's experience. They will accompany him in all of his efforts to reach conclusions. Thus, Gibbon looked at history in a certain way and Hume viewed miracles in a special light because each had a personal reasoning power which shaped his life. Newman does not presume to analyze every element of the illative sense or to chart the rules of its development.[107] He merely describes its mode of operation and recognizes its influence in every concrete judgment that a man makes. Locke's influence caused many of Newman's contemporaries to see reason, or ratiocination, as one thing in all men, and to see also that all would reach the same conclusions if they reasoned properly with the right evidence. Newman says that there are similarities, but the reasoning power of every man is a unique and personal thing. Just as there are a variety of tastes or numerous kinds of memory, such as a memory for names or colorful details, so it is with ratiocination. There is a reasoning process in history and theology and business judgments, and the illative sense is the perfection of the concrete reasoning power in any given area, the perfection that enables man to reach certitude. Even within a given area of concrete facts, it will be an individual thing.[108] A man must be concerned about directing and strengthening the illative sense, but Newman was well aware that men are deeply formed and shaped by the circumstances of life and that they move slowly.

The important thing to Newman was that man could and did reach certitude in concrete matters, and that the ultimate test of certitude was man's sense of being sure. There is no reason to persist with idealistic theories, but we are obliged "to confess that there is no ultimate test of truth besides the testimony born of truth by the mind itself, and that this phenomenon, perplexing as we may find it, is a normal and inevitable characteristic of the mental constitution of a being like man on a stage such as the world."[109] The individual took on an importance that he did not have in the anthropology of Newman's contemporaries. Man reached certitude by the evidence that he chose to accept, and the illative sense of man decided precisely when this mound of converging probabilities was high enough to produce certitude. It was operative in the very self-evident principles that guided man, principles which are self-evident, Newman insisted, because they are evident in no other way.[110] It was operative as man sifted the evidence that attacked his senses on every side, and as he decided whom he would listen to and whom he would ignore. And finally, it was operative in the very conclusions that he reached, since the first principles were present in the conclusions and had shaped every halting step along the way.[111]

When the illative sense is operating perfectly, it consists of both implicit and explicit elements. Implicitly, it judges in a kind of sweeping together of all evidence at once, acting almost instinctively or intuitively.[112] Yet, this instinct is actually a gathering together, in an imperceptible way, of all sorts of evidence, and it embraces a variety of implicit selections and rejections. Explicitly, the illative sense examines the evidence that leads to the conclusions, and it becomes aware not only that it is certain, but why it is certain. This was the perfection of judgment that Newman called the illative sense, whereby the man assents almost intuitively and then reflects upon the probabilities that preceded certitude. It results in subjective and objective certitude.[113] Newman was realistic enough to recognize that many men reached certitude without this explicit reflection, and he called their certitude interpretative or material.[114] They never had the real challenge to their certitude, and only if some event occurred to threaten the repose of their minds would they discover whether or not they had real certitude. Some individuals might withdraw their assent, others might only fortify it.

Newman also recognized that many people go through life without real doubts or certitudes. This is true in matters of religion, where a great many men do not inquire at all. They refuse to discuss religious questions: either they are afraid to challenge their beliefs, or they do not have the kind of mind for it; in some cases they simply lack the capacity.[115] Every man, however, has this illative sense in general, whereby he can reach certitude on concrete matters, but ultimately he will reach certitude on his own personal grounds. This does not mean to say that there is no similarity or common ground in the illative sense. This would be to deny objective truth. Newman, in fact, appeals to his own illative sense as a guideline to thousands of others, who may well see things as he does. Or, at least, his description of the operation of his illative sense in matters of religion will be a help to others who examine their own lives.[116]

His best descriptions of the illative sense rely on his principle of analogy. It can be called a sense because it arouses a feeling, just like a sense of beauty or a sense of accomplishment. It is personal, like taste or memory or the *phronesis* of Aristotle. It is a rational faculty, even as a particular kind of genius is, and yet it is not merely reason. A man may have it in the area of history and lack it in the area of religion. He may have it in the field of business and may have no capacity for it in the region of philosophy. It can be directed and cultivated, but only to a point. In fact, Newman points to a man's lack of it in religious matters as a strong argument for the necessity of revealed religion.[117] In his descriptions of conscience, Newman shows that conscience is in moral areas analogous to the illative sense in matters of certitude about the concrete.

Perhaps the most original aspects of Newman's development of the illative sense are the emphasis on its personal quality and the description of the feeling that accompanies it. This again takes us into the area of Newman's anthropology. Man's feelings are important, and the ordinary individual knows that he is certain when he feels that he is. What passed for certitude would prove many times to be mere conviction, and it could be recognized as such if it failed to endure. Certitude must be indefectible.[118] Newman does not hesitate to use this same criterion of personal feeling in validating the individual conscience. He was not afraid of feeling, since feeling was an important and a providential part of the man he knew. His emphasis on the personal quality of the illative sense was also a challenge to his time, both within and without the Church. The Catholic theologian would call him a nominalist, because to Newman the individual could not quite fit any genus or species, nor could a word quite capture the concrete reality.[119] It was this theory of the individual that played an important part in his *Essay on Development*, allowing him to see the personal and verbally incommunicable part of revelation.

Newman's Apologetic for the Unbeliever

John Henry Newman was a realist. Since he recognized that God was not of interest to many of his contemporaries, he knew that revelation and the Church were of even less interest.[120] He wanted to approach "rationalistic infidelity" with an apologetic that would begin with man. He knew that the scientific proofs for the existence of God, as, for example, those offered by Paley and his disciples, did not lead man to a personal God. The arguments for the divine character of revelation and the Church, which pointed to miracles and prophecies, relied on presuppositions that Hume and Montaigne would not accept.[121] The ordinary man would be much more impressed by "religious" coincidences in the present than by historical miracles in the past.[122]

Newman was not denying the value of the arguments for the existence of God or the traditional apologetics of the divine sign. But he saw in them only a supplementary value, and Gundersen distorts the spirit of Newman when he attempts to show that Newman actually had three of St. Thomas' five arguments for God's existence.[123] Newman was facing a generation that had a much different opinion of reason and proof than did the world of Aquinas. Attempts to relate Newman to traditional Thomism are only relevant when they situate each man in his historical frame-work.[124] The Thomism Newman knew was not the enlightened variety of Congar or Chenu. Newman was not simply saying the same old thing in another way, he was approaching a new genera-tion with a new system. He was enough of a child of his own day, as Scheler insisted the apologete must be, to recognize that the traditional proofs meant very little to his own mind.[125]

He wanted to look into the mind of another man and to study his presumptions.[126] He wanted to start with some common denominator that all would admit. He was almost obsessively aware of the presence of God's Providence, and he looked for its reflection in the nature of man. A study of man himself, in history and in contemporary life, would reveal the common call of God that reached each man in the privacy of his own person. This call was a man's own conscience, and Newman describes its funda-mental role:

What I am directly aiming at, is to explain how we gain an image of God and give real assent to the proposition that He exists. And next, in order to do this, of course I must start from some first principle;—and that first principle, which I assume and shall not attempt to prove, is that which I should also use as a foundation in those two other inquiries (God's attributes and character), viz. that we have by nature a con-science.[127]

It was a personal conscience to which he appealed, analogous in moral matters to the illative sense in concrete, intellectual certi-tude. In reality, Newman was describing his own conscience, just as he described the operation of his own illative sense. It was a case in which "egotism is true modesty," since in being true to his own conscience, man is calling attention to the one God Who equipped him with that conscience. It is important to understand that Newman was not saying that Christianity was justified on intrinsic evidence. This was the faulty approach of the Modernists, and

Newman has been finally and thoroughly rescued from their company.[128] Conscience to Newman was not mere intrinsic evidence, it was extrinsic and authoritative. It was the mark of a personal judge upon man, and it took man outside and beyond himself.[129] He knew that some would reject the analysis of conscience that he offered, but he knew that there were thousands like himself, who would appreciate the validity of his confession.[130]

He began with conscience because all men had one, though he knew that it would be ignored.[131] Frequently in his sermons he described the devious ways in which men seek to escape the sanction of conscience.[132] In his mind, there could be no talk of revealed religion until man accepted the power of his personal conscience. This was the foundation upon which all else was built. Here Newman applied his principle of analogy with all of its force. He began with man at his most personal point, the point of moral decision.

Newman said that conscience was distinct from mere esthetic taste or personal preference, because, like the illative sense, it was accompanied by a unique feeling. This feeling was a kind of fear, a fear reaching beyond man to the notion of a personal judge. Man feared because he was not his own. He knew that he lived in the presence of a Person, a Person to whom he was responsible. He did not need the evidence of Sacred Scripture or the authority of the Church to establish this; it was obvious from personal experience and the voice of history and literature.[133] Newman did not argue, he merely described, and his description is the best argument of all:

Conscience has an intimate bearing on our affections and emotions, leading us to reverence and awe, hope and fear, especially fear, a feeling which is foreign for the most part, not only to Taste, but even to the Moral Sense, except in consequence of accidental associations. No fear is felt by any one who recognizes that his conduct has not been beautiful, though he may be mortified at himself, if perhaps he has thereby forfeited some advantage; but if he has been betrayed into any kind of immorality, he has a lively sense of responsibility and guilt, though the act be no offense against society,—of distress and apprehension, even though it may be of present service to him,—of compunction and regret, though in itself it be most pleasureable,—of confusion of face, though it may have no witnesses.[134]

Scientific proofs might lead some men to God, but if the proofs were not merely supplementary to a faith already possessed, the God would be the impersonal Being of the deists.[135] Conscience is the way to a personal God, because conscience tells us of a Judge outside ourselves, a Judge that is not merely the collected conscience of society. Even the child responds to lessons in morality, because conscience stirs deep within him. Primitive peoples, heavy with superstitions, attest to its existence and so does the whole history of mankind.[136] When the voice has been stilled in man, it is an evident case of social corruption and not of dynamic growth. Conscience is a kind of instinct, again comparable to the illative sense, and seems to pass through a maze of circumstances to a personal decision in a single and rapid act. But when Newman analyzed the nature of conscience, he saw its two-sided life. On the one hand, conscience is a "moral sense," a "critical office," a "judgment of the reason." On the other, it is a "sense of duty," a "judicial office," a "magisterial dictate."[137] On the one side, it tells us that "there is a right and wrong," and on the other, it offers "its sanction to that testimony conveyed in the feelings which attend on right or wrong conduct." It is in this latter sense that we discover "its primary and most authoritative aspect." But it is one act in its normal operation, and Newman was not concerned with any more analysis than was necessary to make his point. He did not even presume to determine to what extent our conscience relies on outside help in its formation. He simply asserted that man does not live in isolation, and he moves on to show how conscience leads us to God and then to Christ.[138]

Man recognizes the force of conscience in his life. He senses its approval; he squirms under its reproof. In its operation he recognizes a personal God, and little by little he discovers His attributes. The dark side of conscience is most obvious.[139] Man senses his own sinfulness and the sinfulness of the world. He is overwhelmed by it. He feels a peculiar kind of alienation and is actually cut off from himself—because he is cut off from God. He begins to see God as his Judge, angry at him because he does not do what his nature says he should. He senses God's justice and the need for atonement, and he recognizes that he cannot shift the blame for his life onto someone else. True, some will ignore the testimony of the conscience, but Newman has no time for such "perversions."[140] The ordinary man begins to feel cut off from the world, separated from God, and actually severed from himself. Everywhere he looks, suffering and evil greet him. Man can feel that, "Not only is the Creator far off, but some being of malignant nature seems . . . to be making us his sport."

Fortunately, there is another side to conscience, the *fascinans* (*attracting*) to balance the *tremendum* (*repelling*). Newman began with the "severe aspect" of sin and guilt because that seemed most obvious,[141] and that is the way man first encounters conscience. But as he observes life, man senses the "recurring blessings of life, the enjoyment of the gifts of the earth and of domestic affection and social intercourse," and he knows in his innermost being that "he is not utterly cast off." These human symbols are promises of another side of the Creator. Man senses an order, a "Divine Supervision," and conscience leads him to hope and to pray. He senses that he can expect benefits from God, that there is an answer to sin and guilt. When man begins to pray, he begins to expect a revelation, since "as prayer is the voice of man to God, so Revelation is the voice of God to man."[142]

All of this Newman discovered in his study of the primitive man of Greece and Rome, and also he pointed to the expectation of some revelation. All of this Newman sensed in himself and in the people of his society. This is the heart of natural religion, beginning with conscience and leading to revelation. Society may seek ways of silencing this eloquent substratum of nature, but nature will not change. The evidence of conscience will still speak to the man who will listen. Even the idea of a vicarious atonement will occur to the natural man, and the signs of the times will be as so many miracles to the unsophisticated. "And should it be objected that this is an illogical exercise of reason, . . . if logic finds fault with it, so much the worse for logic."[143]

Man must first see the action of his own conscience and believe what he sees before he can move forward to a possible revelation. "Belief generates belief," for the "habits of thought and the reasonings which lead us on to a higher state of belief than our present are the very same which we already profess in connection with the lower state."[144] If there is no common ground, and conscience is that common ground, then we cannot begin to offer an apologetic.

Newman's apologetic begins with conscience. His own illative sense notes carefully how conscience operates in the history of mankind and in the conduct of his own personal life. Conscience, seen in the light of the illative sense, would be the initial and most important of the converging probabilities leading to religious assent. Newman, like any other man, cannot accept any conclusions that go contrary to conscience. Yet, life is too short for a man to seek endlessly without finding.[145] His own struggle for unity, upset by sin and guilt, will cause him to quiet conscience with palliatives, or to examine the religious answers that are proposed. For Newman, Christianity alone satisfied the needs of his searching soul.[146] He did not say that every man's illative sense would interpret the evidence as he did. Others did not always start from his presuppositions, nor did they have his sense of history. But many would see in his struggle the reflection or the inspiration of their own. To bombard men with rational arguments that did not reach them was futile.

Some would object that Newman was raised in Christianity, and for that reason he had been taught to find it satisfying. But his argument from analogy, examining the major tenets of natural religion, insisted that Christianity alone "tends to fulfill the aspirations, needs, and foreshadowings of natural faith and devotion."[147] If man did not see his own natural needs met in the experience of revealed religion, he would not bother to consider its arguments. Most men are not concerned with a judicial examination of religious evidence. This was the unreality of Paley's approach. Such arguments as Paley's "allow men to forget that revelation is a boon, not a debt on the part of the Giver."[148] They allow a man to approach conclusions dispassionately and uninvolved. Newman would have men really concerned about the conclusions of their search, because the conclusions would enter into the conduct of life. Nor is he afraid to admit that his more human way, the way of inquiry rather than disputation, may lead men practically to reject Christianity, since "the fear of error is simply necessary to the genuine love of truth." Disputation will only involve man's reason; inquiry is the involvement of his whole concrete existence. Man's decisions become life decisions in an inquiry, and the quest is of necessity a personal one.

Newman found it hard to approach men in groups. He was so

insistent on the uniqueness of every human being that he was accused of nominalism. Actually, he restored to the concept of the universal that dimension which the idealists had ignored. In a sense, he reopened the problem of the nominalists when he said that "there is no such thing as one and the same nature; they are each of them itself, not identical, but like."[149] Elias was an apparent exception to the general rule of mortality, and "what is true of Elias is true of every one in his own place and degree." No single apologetic argument would reach all men because the reasoning power of each man was immersed in a life's experience and in a personal character that made it largely unchartable. It would be impossible to say precisely what arguments would reach a man. But every man would hear the voice of his personal conscience and would look for the light that would lead him from the darkness of sin and guilt.

When Newman spoke to the unbeliever, he was honest enough to admit that many unbelievers were living within the framework of traditional religious bodies.[150] Their views had never been challenged by life. In the case of educated minds, Newman finds it reprehensible that they have not conducted "investigations into the argumentative proof of the things to which they have given their consent." He does not admire the man who fears the risk of faith. Much passes for faith which is merely prejudice, and Newman wants the believer to be a man who has a right to think that his opinions or beliefs bear examining. The true believer does not doubt, but neither does he fear the challenge of his beliefs, for "to incur a risk is not to expect a reverse." But there are many who are listed as believers who do not truly believe. They are not merely *investigating*, since only a firm believer can investigate. They are *inquiring*, for an inquirer is searching for faith. "They who would forbid him to inquire, would in that case be shutting the stable-door after the steed is stolen. . . . Not to inquire is in his case to be satisfied with unbelief."[151]

Newman recognizes that there are various kinds of minds both within and without the Church, and an appreciation of the sanctity of the individual is the essential requisite of the apologete.[152] There must be freedom within a balanced framework, and we must be unafraid of the natural risk involved. The goal of Newman's apologetic was not a fearful forcing of all men into the walls of the

Church, nor was it an apprehensive effort to keep inside every nominal believer. The goal was to encourage a man to be true to his own conscience and to the personal demands of his illative sense. His apologetics is a service to mankind in its search for wholeness. He recognizes that to encourage questioning is to endanger faith. He was, however, living in an age of questions, since the skepticism of Hume and the methods of scientific investigation encouraged such procedures. Questioning can produce an unsettled mind, but questioning is also for many the condition of faith. Newman had enough confidence in the nature that God had made to encourage the risk.[153] He also notes that there may be an undercurrent of skepticism in certain minds that has nothing to do with the problem of belief or unbelief. Such minds could well be children of their own day. They possess a simple and deep faith, and yet are harassed by temptations "robbing Certitude of its normal peacefulness."[154]

Newman's insistence on freedom for the mind of the individual was a paramount reflection of his trust in Providence.[155] It marked his efforts in establishing the University of Dublin.[156] He knew that the human person needed some disciplined framework, but he could not operate without the freedom that made him a unique person. Faith, if possessed, could not be thrown aside. But there must be a freedom of thought in which the mind could expand:

Great minds need elbow room, not indeed in the domain of faith, but of thought. And so indeed do lesser minds, and all minds. . . . Yet, if you insist that in their speculations, researches, or conclusions in their particular science, it is enough that they should submit to the Church generally, and acknowledge its dogmas, but that they must get up all that divines have said or the multitude believed upon religious matters, you simply crush and stamp out the frame within them, and they can do nothing at all.[157]

This principle of freedom in investigation, so eloquently expressed, flows from Newman's knowledge of and respect for the individual. It is the principle that he continually applies, *mutatis mutandis*, in his apologetics.

It is this esteem for freedom that will prevent the apologete from prejudging a man. Newman could not force men into simple categories, and for this reason he could only have been a phenome-

nologist in approach. He described what he saw and only offered
apologetic insights, not a closed and narrow system. He had great
confidence in men, insisting that they were generally right in what
they believed and wrong in what they denied. He spoke of the
convert who could come from unbelief to faith without sacrificing
any of the certitudes of his lifetime. Conversion would not mean
the shedding of anything that he had, but only the enrichment of
what he already possessed.[158] He looked for the truth in men
outside the Church, and he described the "power of assimilation"
as a characteristic of true doctrinal development, whereby every
particle of truth could be drawn into the unity of the Church's
life.[159] He insisted that religion is a system and not a proposition,
and, therefore, there are various kinds of assent within its single
framework, from mere opinions to dogmas.[160] It would be a
violation of freedom to ignore truth outside of the Church, but it
would be irresponsible to be tolerant of false views. Every man must
be patient with the falsehoods of others, but to tolerate them would
be a mark of disrespect to the guiding hand of Providence.[161] A man
finds his meaning in his search for truth, and when he discovers it,
he cannot tolerate a view which says his position has no meaning.

Although Newman was a capable historian and his knowledge
of history gave an historical bent to his personal illative sense, he
did not expect this of others. He well knew that the key to Christianity's impact was not the historical evidence which supported it,
but the value that it had in the present.[162] Newman's apologetic
for Catholic Christianity is largely historical, but this does not
mean that an historical apologetic would necessarily recapture the
spirit of Newman. He well knew that the majority of men did not
have his sense of history, nor did they have a need to examine
Christianity minutely before history's tribunal. This could be a
never-ending procedure.[163] History would have its place in the
Christian apologetic because Christ was an historical event, an
event marked by supporting signs of His worth. But the real signs
would be in the present, and the historical reflections would be
measured at a contemporary court. The study of history, which
played such an essential part in Newman's conversion, was determined by the frame of his mind and the circumstances of his
life.[164] This would not be the case with the majority. With them,
Newman would begin with the common values that all men

shared, and these values were discovered on the plane of conscience. Until Newman could get a man to acknowledge his
conscience, the providential voice attesting to his personal worth
and responsibility, the dialogue of apologetics could not begin.

Evaluation of Newman's Apologetics

We have already indicated that Scheler was well aware of the work
of Newman. The similarities are striking, especially the treatment
of conscience, which is the key idea in Newman's apologetics and
has such an important place in the first part of *On the Eternal in
Man*. We have seen Scheler's apologetic efforts as a reaction to the
rational defense of the faith. Newman's apologetic was a similar
reaction to the mathematical reasoning which so poorly answered
Locke and Hume and their liberal disciples. Newman and Scheler
were both convinced that God had left a mark in nature that could
only lead to Christ. Both were well aware of the horrors of
suffering; both were accused of pessimism, and yet each in his own
way believed deeply and unequivocally in man. Even in their
epistemology, the similarity continues, since the Newman of the
Grammar of Assent is vigorously phenomenological.[165]

While it is difficult to establish a direct line of thought
between Newman and Blondel,[166] the similarity in their thought
and approach is obvious. Walgrave admits the similarity in vision,
but finds Blondel much the more profound and metaphysical.[167]
It is not hard to agree with his assertion that Blondel had completed the essential lines of his *L'Action* before he was aware of the
thought of Newman. But we cannot agree with his bold opinion
that "the central idea of the 'apologetic of the threshold' is not to
be found in Newman." He insists that there is a clear distinction
between the "dialectic of conscience" in Newman and the tension
of the twofold will (*volonté voulante* and *volonté voulue*) in
Blondel. His point seems to be that in Blondel the tension creates
a need for the supernatural (*unique nécessaire*), whereas in Newman the need, bred of conscience, is for a revelation, whether
"natural or supernatural." This is a refined and unimportant distinction as we see it. Newman well knew that this revelation was
the presence of Jesus Christ in the world. He may well have, as did

Scheler, prescinded from the fact of whether or not this revelation was natural or supernatural, but in reality the only revelation that would fulfill the demand of conscience, in the present economy, was the supernatural revelation of Christ. The tension which Blondel experienced and described was the strain created by what a man knew himself to be and what he aspired to be. This aspiration, the *volonté voulante*, was even described by Blondel, in a letter we have quoted, as God's providential hold on man, the eternal stamp marking the finite for the infinite. The same vision of Providence possessed Newman in his descriptions of the tension of conscience, faced with sin and suffering, and pulled him toward the redemptive plan of Christ. The need was produced by an awareness of sin in both Blondel and Newman, and the need could only be satisfied when man discovered the mystery of Christ's healing.

Both Blondel and Scheler were accused of obscuring grace and of making heretical concessions to the immanentists. Newman, too, was classed among the Modernists by some. In the light of present theological discussions on grace and nature, their orthodoxy is unquestioned. It was only to be expected that as they reacted against a closed idealism with a living phenomenology, the idealists would try to judge them by the very thought-patterns from which Blondel and Newman, as well as Scheler, were trying to escape. Today, however, the phenomenological method and the personalist metaphysic have been vindicated.

The outstanding quality of Newman's apologetic is its realism. He knew that the age in which he lived was a man-centered world, and any search for God would have to begin with man. The man with whom Newman began was not the preconceived variety of any system of philosophy, but the man he knew, whether scholar or charcoal burner. He knew that the frozen and rationalistic apologetics of the past would not do. He recognized that unbelief was a growing problem and would grow still greater. So, if he were going to work with man, he would have to break into the world of secular values and discover the mark of God upon man. If there were not a divine spark within man, then man could do little to remind his fellowman of God. There could be no apologetic, all faith would depend upon the action of God alone. Man would have nothing to contribute.

But Newman saw a unity in all of creation. There is a conscience operating in every man which calls him to a Person beyond the world. Here Newman found the common ground, the common value-making dialogue possible between believer and unbeliever. Man has a sense of guilt, an awareness of sin, and despite his efforts to run away and hide, he longs for redemption and wholeness. This was the man to whom Newman appealed, knowing that the needs of man would be fulfilled in the God-man. He was not naïve enough to think that he could reach all men, but he could appeal to those who felt responsible for themselves, those whose sense of sin and guilt sought a reasonable answer. Though Newman does not spell out the manifestations of sin and guilt as it appears in human consciousness, it seems probable that he would look for it both in its traditional religious forms and in the secular forms of fear and anxiety.

Newman had much sympathy for the struggle of the honest unbeliever; he knew by experience the tortuous routes of question and doubt. He admitted the validity of the unbeliever's values and asserted that he was often right as far as he went. The unbeliever just did not go far enough; he did not seek deeply enough. He did not push his questions that went beyond the scope of reason. But, in the values that the rationalist recognized, Newman found his hope of dialogue.

He saw the unbeliever both within and without the Church. He was not looking for a cautious program which would lead the nonconformist to the organizational Church.[168] He saw life growing from life, belief from belief, and he wanted to challenge the apathy or complacency of unbelievers everywhere. He asked a man to be egotistical to the point of personal responsibility. He needed an atmosphere of freedom for his dialogue, wherein a man could pursue his conclusions to their practical consequences. He did not want a growing mass of uncommitted believers, but he asked a man to risk his faith in open and honest challenge. He did not seek to unsettle the simpleminded and ignorant, but he wanted to shake up the proud and the indifferent. The battle of apologetics had to go from the classroom to the open market of personal conscience. What passed for faith was often superstition among the simple, but superstition at least was a closer correlative to faith than rationalism. Superstition, at least, had a sense of the sacred, an awareness of a transcendent Person beyond self. Rationalism doomed man to the deafness of his own logical displays.

He was confident of God's loving Providence, confident

enough to demand that man have enough freedom to find himself. In an age of doubts and questions, there was room for questions of faith, as long as they were the questions of a man who sought an answer to the problem of his own alienation. Newman knew in his personal life the suffering born of honest search, and he could meet any man in honest dialogue, except the indifferent man. This meant that he had to ponder the mind of his opponent; he had to enter that mind in sympathy and to discover its presuppositions. To engage in apologetic without knowing this was to offer irrelevant arguments and to build a higher wall between believer and unbeliever.

Christianity would fill a need in man's life, but first of all man had to have a need. He could tirelessly tell a thirsting man that the fountain at which he drank would never slake his thirst. But he could not meet a man who did not thirst. He distinguished carefully between theology and religion and between notional and real assent. And in his apologetics he did not seek to offer a philosophy, an ethic, or a religious sentiment. He sought to offer a hungry man the food that God held out, the food that he longed for and needed, the only food that could satisfy, because the one God Who had made man to hunger had also sent His Son to fill that hunger. This was not Modernism; this was a relevant apologetic.

There would be signs to indicate that Christianity was the right food. But the signs would be largely personal ones, and they would come in largely personal ways. The apologete could not be indifferent or out of touch, but must love the man he sought to feed, and must win his respect and confidence. Newman would not ignore the traditional arguments, but he would put them in a framework, without which they would have no meaning. He could not lead man by logical steps to Christianity, because man was not the logical creature that Newman's century painted him. Ultimately, under God, man would move from unbelief to faith when he was ready, and humanly speaking, he could only point to a host of probabilities that led him to assent. The apologete could only look carefully at his own world and offer it to man in a most probable way. To do that, he had to know his world, know his faith, and know the heart of the man to whom he spoke.

CHAPTER

CONCLUSION

Scheler, Blondel, and Newman recognized that the apologetic of the past did not reach the unbeliever. They pointed out that unbelief, in varying forms, had become ever more widespread.[1] When the unbeliever heard the standard apologetic arguments from reason, it was a different reason than he knew. It was a reason directed by faith. When he read the historical arguments for Christianity, his indifference indicated that he read history in another way. When he listened to the proving power of miracles and prophecies, he spoke of nature's laws, superstition, and naïveté. When he read about the wonder of Christ, he questioned the objectivity and reliability of the sources. When he was told of Christianity's marvelous growth, he noted the divisions within Christianity, its unchristian quarrels, and its opposition to human progress. The discussions with the unbeliever were interesting, but our apologetic did not seem to reach him. In the face of such an irrelevant apologetic, Scheler, Blondel, and Newman saw the wisdom of a new approach. As Blondel said:

We must not exhaust ourselves, refurbishing old arguments and presenting an object for acceptance while the subject is not disposed to listen. It is not divine truth which is at fault, but human preparation, and it is here that our efforts should be concentrated. It is not just a matter of adaptation or temporary expediency.[2]

The traditional apologetic had been of some benefit to the believer. For this reason, he often failed to appreciate the sincere difficulty which the unbeliever had in accepting such an apologetic. Even some of the more balanced attempts in modern times implied that only an unreasonable man, or a sinful man, could ignore the force of the arguments for Christianity.[3] Only since Vatican II have we begun to recognize practically the insights which Blondel and Scheler offered half a century ago.[4] Now we are seriously concerned with saying "something which counts in the eyes of unbelievers."[5] This is our understanding of the modern apologetic problem.

In this final chapter we propose:

1. To describe briefly the modern problem of unbelief.
2. To list the more important apologetic principles that were revealed in our historical research and to show an awareness of them in the words of Vatican II.
3. To propose, in an epilogue, an apologetic program for the unbeliever which develops the principles found in research and follows the spirit of Vatican II.

Historical Problem of Unbelief

Newman had recognized the growth of agnosticism and religious indifference. He insisted that even apparent faith might actually be a kind of meaningless conformism.[6] Blondel had seen the problem of unbelief among his classmates at the university, and, very early in his career, had decided to be the "apostle of the unbelievers."[7] Scheler saw a lack of faith and love as the real cause of the First World War, and insisted that neo-Kantianism and sentimentalism were undermining the possibility of genuine belief.[8] The problem that these men recognized in its infancy only grew more widespread and more pronounced in our own day. The cult of unbelief began to take new forms. Some forms were as apparent as Communism, others were as stealthy and mysterious as early French existentialism. Yves Congar describes the new developments:

The Church's task is largely unprecedented, for, in our opinion, there has been a secular world and fully lay life since the time that social and political life was fully laicized, and especially since the inauguration of a mechanized civilization, which, born outside the Church, has never been consecrated and regulated by her. . . . We know well enough that men are turning away from God and that the contemporary world is a world of unbelief. . . . For the first time, the Church is really confronted by a secular world.[9]

In reality, we were faced with a new man. Scheler had seen him being absorbed by science and humanitarian goals. Blondel had seen him turn from the Church and seek to face the problems of the world with his own best insights. Newman had seen him torn between sophisms and emotion, and had insisted that logic would never attract or win him. Gradually, the new man became more than a shadow, more than a future threat, more than an occasional intellectual. He was our next-door neighbor, the man we worked with, the fellow whose parents had been active in the Church. Gerard Philips describes his emergence from history's womb:

Since the end of World War II we have with us a new man, profoundly affected by the latest scientific and technical advances. As a result of the discovery of atomic energy and the conquest of space, he has not simply acquired a new way of feeling, thinking and living; he has literally become someone else and he scarcely recognizes himself. . . . An atheism does exist, one that is not only lived, but preached, organized, and militant.[10]

Strangely enough, it was often difficult to distinguish the unbeliever from the Christian. He was not a man without values, nor was he always restless and unhappy. Society made it easier for him to be accepted. At times he could appear the more sophisticated, the more liberated: the man "on top of things." Frequently he seemed able to live comfortably without ultimate answers, to be able to ignore God and the transcendental. He might even have a sense of freedom that the believer lacked. We found it hard to categorize him as empty and searching. As Charles Davis puts it:

We are too facile in attributing a sense of emptiness, frustration and restlessness to unbelievers. Experience should teach us caution. Many, perhaps an increasing number, feel quite satisfied and content with what this world with its achievements has to offer.[11]

The unbeliever seemed more often satisfied than searching, and was concerned, in numerous cases, about life's problems.

He was engaged in poverty programs, housing projects, areas

of racial tension, programs of mental health, and in every form of civic and fraternal service. He believed in many things, and yet he did not believe in a supernatural revelation from God to men. He was an unbeliever in the classical sense, an unbeliever difficult to approach with the reality of a revelation. Frequently he was open to discussion. It was not easy, however, to bombard him with the traditional arguments about God's existence or the Church's claims. He did not think in terms of metaphysical arguments from causality and order, nor did he see the Christ-experience as the unique source of value in society.

His values came from other sources. Life in a complex society demanded them. His love for his family required a kind of purity and sacrifice. His concern for economic stability taught him sobriety and restraint. The tensions of modern existence forced him to consider his health and the self-denial necessary to maintain it. A growing impersonalism in society taught him the value of a few close and trusted friends. He was opposed to dishonesty because it was both unrewarding and dangerous. Even adultery was risky, expensive, and unsatisfying. Most moral failures of the traditional kind did not make sense. Domestic and economic concerns seemed to give him goal enough. Sophisticated and passive forms of recreation gave him relief. There were opportunities never dreamed of by his parents: vacations to sunny isolation or foreign lands; communication techniques which permitted new horizons, new ideas, new sources of concern and curiosity; educational opportunities which challenged him and his family.[12]

These and a hundred other changes marked the man in the new society. The fathers of Vatican II recognized that the modern unbeliever is no longer the strange exception:

Unlike former days, the denial of God or of religion, or the abandonment of them, are no longer of unusual and individual occurrence. For today it is not rare for such things to be presented as requirements of scientific progress or of a certain new humanism. In numerous places these views are voiced not only in the teachings of philosophers, but on every side they influence literature, the arts, the interpretation of the humanities and of history and civil laws themselves. As a consequence, many people are shaken.[13]

Nor do the council fathers see this as a temporary unrest. Rather they consider it "a new stage in history," a condition whereby "the human race has passed from a rather static concept of reality to a more dynamic, evolutionary one."[14] They reecho the words of Scheler when they insist that the changes of modern life are "part of a broader and deeper revolution," wherein "intellectual formation is ever increasingly based on the mathematical and natural sciences and on those dealing with man himself, while in the practical order the technology which stems from these sciences takes on mounting importance.[15]

Vatican II, however, does not sit in proud judgment on the unbeliever. Again voicing the sentiments of Blondel and Scheler,[16] it reminds the man of faith of his own responsibility for irreligion in the world:

Yet believers themselves frequently bear some responsibility for this situation. For, taken as a whole, atheism is not a spontaneous development but stems from a variety of Causes, including a critical reaction against religious beliefs, and in some places against the Christian religion in particular. . . . To the extent that they (believers) neglect their own training in the faith, or teach erroneous doctrine, or are deficient in their religious, moral or social life, they must be said to conceal rather than reveal the authentic face of God and religion.[17]

Scheler had pointed to the First World War in Europe and reminded Christians that a lack of love in the world is but a reflection of the lack of love in one's personal life.[18] Blondel had based the validity of his whole apologetic of *L'Action* on a Christian's own awareness of the need for conversion.[19] It was also Blondel who came out into the market place when he saw the scandal involved in the Church's alliance with the Action Française movement. In a world which was crying out for human freedom, the Church had allied itself with a dying monarchy. This was to abandon the mainstream of man's evolution.[20] Again, Vatican II admits failure in this regard and echoes the words of Blondel:

The Church, by reason of her role and competence, is not identified in any way with the political community nor bound to any political system. She is at once a sign and a safeguard of the transcendent character of the human person.[21]

Vatican II has admitted the birth of a new man, a man without God and religion, and has publicly acknowledged Christianity's guilt in his creation. The Church has become "conscious of how weighty are the questions which atheism raises, and motivated by a love for all men, she believes these questions ought to be examined seriously and more profoundly."[22]

This is what we believe is the modern apologetic problem: to examine the questions raised by modern unbelief and to attempt to answer them. Although Vatican II tells us that "the remedy which must be applied to atheism . . . is to be sought in a proper presentation of the Church's teaching, as well as in the integral life of the Church and her members,"[23] the entire spirit of the *Constitution of the Church in the Modern World* encourages the believer to seek out the unbeliever in open dialogue. The modern apologete must recognize, as Vatican II does, that he will not come to us. Very often, as a modern author says, "the modern post-Christian man has abandoned the 'age-old classical theories of commitment' —such as religion, supernaturalistic or secular, that meagrely and apologetically still manage to survive in Western society—for the gospel of self-fulfillment, the 'amplitude of living itself.' "[24]

Vatican II has faced this objection and sees that the "faith needs to prove its fruitfulness by penetrating the believer's entire life, including its worldly dimensions." We hope to describe the principles that would make such contact possible.

We have tried, in a few pages, to describe the modern problem of unbelief. Yet, we know that unbelief is varied both in its cause and in its expression. As Vatican II says:

The word atheism is applied to phenomena which are quite distinct from one another. For while God is expressly denied by some, others believe that man can assert absolutely nothing about Him. Still others use such a method to scrutinize the question of God as to make it seem devoid of meaning. Many . . . contend that everything can be explained by some kind of scientific reasoning alone or, by contrast, they altogether disallow the fact that there is any absolute truth. Some laud man so extravagantly that their faith in God lapses into a kind of anemia. . . . Again some form for themselves such a fallacious idea of God that . . . they are by no means rejecting the God of the Gospel. Some never get to the point of raising questions about God, since they seem to experience no religious stirrings. . . . Moreover, atheism results not rarely from a violent protest against the evil in the world, or from the absolute character with which certain human values are unduly invested.[25]

Such a manifold problem can have no simple solution. This is why we have proposed to offer "some beginning reflections" on a solution to the modern apologetic problem. Scheler, Blondel, and Newman have offered us valuable principles; Vatican II has accepted and developed these principles and has offered a challenge to speak "in language intelligible to each generation" in order to "respond to the perennial questions which men ask about this present life and the life to come, and about the relationship of the one to the other."[26] We accept the challenge humbly and hopefully.

Key Apologetic Principles in an Apologetic Program for the Unbeliever

A. *Preliminary Considerations*

1. THE PROBLEM OF ECCLESIOLOGY.   When we speak of an apologetic program for the unbeliever, we immediately face the problem of ecclesiology: What is the Church? What is its relationship to the unbeliever? Do we seek to convert him? Do we seek to lead him closer to the fullness of Christ? What must be our intentions?

We cannot resolve these problems since the theological discussions were directed but not closed by the *Constitution on the Church* of Vatican II. The theologians still have their serious differences.[27] Yet, we cannot deny that the Church struggles courageously to lead men to the faith. The *Constitution on the Church* tells us that "by the proclamation of the Gospel she [the Church] prepares her hearers to receive and profess the faith."[28] It says that "all men are called to be part of this catholic unity of the people of God" and that "the Church both prays and labors in order that the entire world may become the people of God."[29] From such indications it would seem wrong for us to discourage programs of conversion.

Yet, we know that all men will not come to the fullness of the faith within our lifetime, perhaps not within any lifetime. Vatican II recognizes this and gives a positive value to the people who "are related to [the Church] in various ways."[30] Among these are "those who have not yet arrived at an explicit knowledge of God and with His grace strive to live a good life."[31] The council fathers recognized that "whatever good or truth is found among them is looked upon by the Church as a preparation for the Gospel."[32] In the *Declaration on the Relation of the Church to Non-Christian Religions,* we read that fathers of the council were concerned above all with "what men have in common and what draws them to fellowship."[33] In an important passage, this same *Declaration* states:

One is the community of all peoples, one their origin, for God made the whole human race to live over the face of the earth. One also is their final goal, God. His providence, His manifestations of goodness, His saving design extend to all men, until the time when the elect will be united in the Holy City.[34]

The *Declaration* points out that the basis of any dialogue is "the good things, spiritual and moral, as well as the socio-cultural values found among these men."[35] This same point is developed at length in part two, chapter two of the *Constitution on the Church in the Modern World: The Proper Development of Culture.* The *Constitution* reminds us not only of the necessary contribution we have to make in our society as Christians, but also of the benefit we receive from the important insights of men who do not share our faith.[36]

It becomes clear that all men who are struggling to follow their personal light are in some way related to us. Our obligation becomes not so much that of bringing about their conversion as that of an open, honest, and loving dialogue in a search for the full dignity and freedom of man. We may well hope that this search will lead to the fullness of dignity offered by a complete sacramental communion with the Church. But we do not know the clear outlines of God's plan for men. We can only struggle to "live in very close union with the other men of [our] time and . . . strive to understand perfectly their way of thinking and judging, as expressed in their culture."[37] The Church is concerned with numerous values short of conversion, and there could be a question about the sincerity of a love that would not be interested in less. Vatican II says:

Therefore, the duty most consonant with our times, especially for Christians, is that of working diligently for fundamental decisions to be taken in economic and political affairs, both on the national and international level, which will everywhere recognize and satisfy the right of all to a human and social culture in conformity with the dignity of the human person without any discrimination based on race, sex, nation, religion or social condition.[38]

This was the kind of ecclesiology which characterized Scheler's discussion on the hierarchy of values. He taught that values at every level were positive and real. Yet he did not hesitate, in loving dialogue, to encourage men to push on to the highest value, the *Summum Bonum*.[39] Blondel, even more emphatically, asked the Christian to recognize the germ of truth everywhere and to join in man's struggle for freedom and truth.[40] This is the spirit of the ecclesiology of Vatican II, a spirit which constantly reminds us of our communion with all men. It is the ecclesiology with which modern theologians are struggling. Jerome Hamer discusses the various usages of the word *Church*:

It is doubtless, not necessary to understand the word Church every time it is used in its proper sense, with the full weight of its meaning and all the characteristics which constitute the definition of the Church. But if not, then the theologian must be aware of what he is doing. "Church" can and does designate not only the visible society of Christians, but also the clergy, or the episcopate, . . . or the Supreme Pontiff himself. *Each of these usages is legitimate and accurate,* but none of them exhausts the connotation of the concept. . . . In fact, the Church is at once a visible society and an inner community. Where nothing remains of the inner communion (unformed supernatural faith being the absolute minimum), then the Church as such has lost its roots.[41]

When we enter into communion with the unbeliever in the search for values short of conversion, we do the work of the Church. This is not to deny the hope for conversion, rather it is to admit the presence of Christ in the world. The Incarnational context from which Newman, Blondel, and Scheler spoke of the world is reflected also in the words of Vatican II:

Since human nature as He assumed it was not annulled, by that very fact it has been raised up to a divine dignity in our respect, too. For by His incarnation the Son of God has united Himself in some fashion with every man.[42]

Scheler recognized this in the very title of his most famous religious work, *On the Eternal in Man*. It was expressed in his insistence that man would contact the divine in "things" and would look for revelation to answer the need for the transcendent.[43] Blondel could see in the unbelievers "a true generosity in their rejection of the truths in which I believe, and in their very appearance of misrepresenting these truths, they do not cease to share in them invisibly."[44] Christ is in the world and the true worldly values are of Christian concern. Perhaps we can sum up our approach to ecclesiology in this dissertation with the words of Vatican II:

Christ, to be sure, gave His Church no proper mission in the political, economic, or social order. The purpose which He set before her is a religious one. But out of this religious mission itself comes a function, a light and an energy which can serve to structure and consolidate the human community according to the divine law. As a matter of fact, when circumstances of time and place produce the need, she can and indeed should initiate activities on behalf of all men, especially those designed for the needy, such as the works of mercy and similar undertakings.[45]

The "circumstances of time and place" have produced the need. The unbeliever has found the Church irrelevant. Our ecclesiology seeks to meet him where he is and to join with him in the search for greater light.

2. THE ECUMENICAL ADVANTAGE IN AN APOLOGETIC FOR THE UNBELIEVER. Since we are concerned with the unbeliever, the man who does not accept a revelation from a personal God, our apologetic should be of advantage to Protestants and Jews as well. They too are concerned with the problem of irreligion in our society.[46] Consequently, our apologetic will have ecumenical overtones. This does not mean that we are indifferent to the very real differences which exist between Catholicism and other formal religions. It only means that we recognize with Vatican II the necessary communion that should exist between men of all faiths. With regard to other Christian religions, the Council states:

Since co-operation in social matters is so widespread today, all men without exception are called to work together; with much greater reason are all those who believe in God, but most of all, all Christians in that they bear the seal of Christ's name. Co-operation among Christians vividly expresses that bond which already unites them, and it sets in clearer relief the features of Christ the Servant. Such co-operation, which has already begun in many countries, should be developed more and more.[47]

With regard to Jews, the Council says: "Since the spiritual patrimony common to Christians and Jews is thus so great, this Sacred Synod wants to foster and recommend that mutual understanding and respect which is the fruit, above all, of biblical and theological studies as well as of fraternal dialogues."[48]

Any religious person who is aware of the signs of his own times recognizes the problem of unbelief.[49] Protestant theologians have made sincere and intelligent efforts to reach the unbeliever.[50] Many Catholics are familiar, at least in a general way, with the efforts of Bonhoeffer, Bishop Robinson, Harvey Cox, Paul Tillich, and the various spokesmen for the "God-is-dead" school. All of these men have recognized the problem of unbelief, and are concerned with making religion speak to the men of our times.[51] Perhaps Karl Rahner has spoken as clearly as anyone on the need for joint efforts by all men of faith in reaching the unbeliever:

Today all religions, Christianity included, possess a common enemy—a complete lack of religion, a total denial of religion, a denial which displays the religious fervor of an absolute and holy system paradoxically presenting itself with its official organization as *the* religion of the future, the crystallized, absolute secularization and final formula of human existence. Yet it remains true that precisely this denial, which threatens religion as a whole, possesses one of its most potent weapons in the lack of union within the religious world today.[52]

Consequently, the program we offer should have meaning for all religions in the important work of making religion mean something to the modern unbeliever. We hope that the program will not be too "American" in its flavor. It is difficult, however, to avoid that charge since our own experience has been largely with the American unbeliever.[53]

B. *Key Principles of an Apologetic for the Unbeliever*

1. THE MODERN APOLOGETIC SHOULD BEGIN WITH MAN. Any effort, whether personal or programmed, to reach the unbeliever should begin with man. In the past apologetic, [54] the method of argument centered around the rights of God and the obligation of man to recognize these rights. Thus, metaphysical arguments were used to establish God's existence and nature, and historical arguments were used to show that God had truly spoken to man in Christ. We have shown that Scheler, Blondel, and Newman re-

jected such an approach.[55] Scheler spoke of a metanthropology replacing the metaphysics of the past. Man must find God in his search for true values,[56] and such a search should lead to the performance of the religious act. God stood at the end of man's search as the peak of a hierarchy of values. Blondel, too, centered his apologetic in man's effort to resolve the tension between the *volonté voulante* and the *volonté voulue*. Man would discover his need for the transcendent in the midst of this tension.[57] For Newman, the personal conscience was the road that led to God. Man must recognize and interpret his own religious feelings and the personal God Who is at the root of such feelings.[58]

Vatican II follows the same direction, indicating that our common humanity is the true source of dialogue: "According to the almost unanimous opinion of believers and unbelievers alike, all things on earth should be related to man as their center and crown."[59] In another place the Council says:

The truth is that the imbalances under which the modern world labors are linked with that more basic imbalance which is rooted in the heart of man. For in man himself many elements wrestle with one another. Thus, on the one hand, as a creature he experiences his limitations in a multitude of ways; on the other, he feels himself to be boundless in his desires and summoned to a higher life.[60]

The unbeliever is generally not concerned with what nature has to say of God. Nor, as Blondel pointed out, is he much moved by a fact of history which claims to stand apart from all other contingent events.[61] He is concerned about himself, his own struggles, his own search for wholeness. An apologetic for the unbeliever must begin here.

2. THE MODERN APOLOGETIC CENTERS IN A SEARCH FOR MEANING IN LIFE. This was the very starting point of Blondel's original *L'Action*.[62] Man was struggling to make sense out of existence, and Blondel proposed that he not give up the quest by accepting partial answers. Scheler approached the same problem with a different terminology. He spoke of man's search for values and the need of a community of love to support the unbeliever in his efforts.[63] Both Blondel and Scheler recognized that the believer himself had not yet arrived at the fullness of life's meaning, and he must honestly, humbly, and in a disciplined way join in the

search.[64] Together with Newman, they saw God calling out to man in the midst of his own labors, and asked only that man would not silence the voice that spoke to him.[65] Paul Tillich describes the same problem:

Since the middle of the nineteenth century, a movement has arisen in the Western world which expresses the anxiety about the meaning of our existence, including the problems of death, faith, and guilt. In our present day literature, many names are given to this phenomenon . . . Wasteland . . . No Exit . . . Age of Anxiety . . . Neurotic Character of Our Times . . . Man Against Himself . . . Encounter with Nothingness . . .[66]

Tillich insists (in the same chapter) that this phenomenon of unrest is not restricted to the Western world, but is universal. It is the kind of "existential anguish" that Camus, Sartre, Bergman, Albee, and others have isolated and described. It would be pedantic to insist that the simple would experience this anguish as a Camus would describe it, but it exists nonetheless. As Gerard Philips says:

The world, said to be a-religious, whether it admits it or not, suffers a deep anguish, at least when confronted with death. It is not only the atomic bomb that is frightening; we are waging war with an enigma we cannot solve: what is the meaning of life? . . . Would the only answer be: all is absurd, a source of eternal disillusionment?[67]

Alfred Dondeyne, in a remarkable essay, speaks of much the same thing. He senses the finality of the fight with what he calls "materialism." He quotes Camus' *Mythe de Sisyphe*: "To decide whether life is worth living or not is to answer the fundamental problem in philosophy." Dondeyne comments on this thought:

In the eyes of the believer the answer to this problem is faith. It goes without saying that this answer has no sense, and no value as an answer, for any but the person who asks the question. It is one that anyone can ask himself. It is one that he must ask. Or to be more precise, it is one which, by an act of faith in the mystery of being that is ourself, we must allow to rise in us, to develop without hindrance, to become urgent.[68]

Vatican II has recognized this spirit of unrest in the world, and encourages the believing Christian to join his brother everywhere in the search for an answer to the problem. The spirit of the Council decrees is not one of arrogance or complacency. It recognizes the sincerity of the unbeliever and the validity of the questions that confront him. The Council lists the questions that puzzle men:

What is man? What is this sense of sorrow, of evil, of death, which continues to exist despite so much progress? What purpose have these victories secured at so high a cost? What can man offer to society, what can he expect from it? What follows this earthly life? . . . What does the Church think of man? What needs to be recommended for the upbuilding of contemporary society? What is the ultimate significance of human activity throughout the world?[69]

When dealing with such relevant questions as these, directed at the believer and the unbeliever alike, the Church has captured the spirit of our times. The faithful are asked that "by unremitting study they should fit themselves to do their part in establishing dialogue with the world and with men of all shades of opinion."[70] It is not a request for conversion but for honest dialogue. We are asked to enable man to become more fully human and to recognize what this responsibility entails. In an important passage the Council states:

Thus, far from thinking that works produced by man's own talent and energy are in opposition to God's power, and that the rational creature exists as a kind of rival to the Creator, Christians are convinced that the triumphs of the human race are a sign of God's grace and the flowering of His own mysterious design.[71]

The mission of the Church becomes one of service to man. We learn to recognize the needs of our own times: "Motivated by this faith, [the People of God] labor to decipher authentic signs of God's presence and purpose in the happenings, needs and desires in which this People [have] a part along with other men of our age."[72] This sentiment is in harmony with Scheler's admonition that we must recognize that we too are "swayed by the rhythm" of our times,[73] and Blondel's suggestion that the obstacles to conversion must be seen within our own soul.[74] With an awareness of our common humanity, we can join the unbeliever in a search for meaning in the face of death. As Vatican II says:

It is in the face of death that the riddle of human existence grows most acute. Not only is man tormented by pain and by the advancing deterioration of his body, but even more so by a dread of perpetual extinction. He rightly follows the intuition of his own heart when he abhors and repudiates the utter ruin and total disappearance of his own person. He rebels against death because he bears in himself an eternal seed which cannot be reduced to sheer matter.[75]

Here is the framework for dialogue. Here is a problem that concerns every man and influences his view of life. This is where an apologetic for the unbeliever should begin: What does life mean? Or, in the words of Blondel, *"Oui ou non, la vie humaine a-t-elle un sens, et L'homme a-t-il une destinée?"*[76]

3. THE MODERN APOLOGETIC CENTERS IN VALUES WHICH ARE COMMON. It is difficult to prevent overlapping in our principles. There is a close connection between this principle and the previous one. Here, however, we are writing from a more general view of the values shared by believer and unbeliever alike. Blondel was insistent on this point, urging that we approach every man openly, and recognizing that there was some validity in the solutions the unbeliever offered to real problems.[77] This was a central consideration in Blondel's evaluation of the Modernists. He insisted that they had valid insights, and he despised the man who could see only one side of a question. There was good to be found everywhere, and the believer had much to learn from his unbelieving brother. Blondel's correspondence with Chardin showed clearly his recognition of human values and the esteem in which he held human progress.[78] Scheler's discussion of the hierarchy of values displayed the same kind of awareness.[79] We also noted that Newman did not hesitate to discover grains of truth everywhere.[80]

Vatican II continues and develops this spirit. In the *Declaration on Non-Christian Religions,* we read: "She [the Church] regards with sincere reverence those ways of conduct and life, those precepts and teachings which, though differing in many aspects from the ones she holds and sets forth, nonetheless often reflect a ray of that Truth which enlightens all men."[81] Even more clearly it is stated in the *Constitution on the Modern World:* "In our times a special obligation binds us to make ourselves the neighbor of every person without exception, and of actively helping him when he comes across our path, whether he be an old person abandoned by all, a foreign laborer unjustly looked down upon, a refugee, a child born of an unlawful union, . . . or a hungry person."[82]

It becomes clear in the Council's discussion of the modern

world that we are concerned with values short of the ultimate. We are concerned with man's body, man's culture, man's dignity. Often enough we entered into social programs with a spirit of conquest and conversion. The Council indicates that we should rather join with our brothers in any honest search for real values. Thus it says:

Individual men, in order to discharge with greater exactness the obliga-tions of their conscience towards themselves and the various groups to which they belong, must be carefully educated to a higher degree of culture through the use of the immense resources available today to the human race. . . . The education of youth from every background has to be undertaken. . . . Man can scarcely arrive at the needed sense of responsibility, unless his living conditions allow him to be conscious of his dignity. . . . Hence, the will to play one's part in common en-deavors should be everywhere encouraged.[83]

How often in the past have we been interested in social values only when some "Catholic" cause seemed to be served. Vatican II, in the spirit of Blondel and Scheler, is asking us to share in the pursuit of any value that serves man. Nor do we join in some dialogue as if we have nothing to learn. It is a common search for truth and justice, and all men have something to give and receive. As the Council says: "In fidelity to conscience, Christians are joined with the rest of men in the search for truth, and for the genuine solution to the numerous problems which arise in the life of individuals and from social relationships."[84] Such statements are a declared end to the ghetto mentality, and reflect the spirit of Scheler, Blondel, and Newman.

4. THE MODERN APOLOGETIC TAKES PLACE IN A COMMUNITY FRAMEWORK. We have recognized for centuries the place of the community in man's development. Not only do we recognize that he is a social animal, but of latter years we have emphasized the importance of community acceptance in the learning process.[85] It is almost a truism to insist on the place of community in any program of apologetics for the unbeliever. Newman stressed the importance of each man's presuppositions in the search for truth, and was well aware of the social framework in which such pre-suppositions were formed.[86] When Scheler pointed out that the love of God actually precedes in human consciousness the positing

of God's existence, this idea flowed from his general awareness that a person does not truly exist in the eyes of another until he exists *for* the other in love. Such love is found only in the community of love, where love itself becomes the source of knowledge.[87] Blondel's persistent emphasis on the need for the unbeliever to be given an open hearing and a chance to join the believer in some form of "liturgical" expression presumes the presence of some form of community.[88]

Blondel and Scheler, following the spirit of Pascal, insisted that there must be some place for the unbeliever in the community of the faithful.[89] Each realized that he would find faith only when joined in a common family of love. Vatican II, by its strong insistence on the community of men and the positive values which we share, continues this spirit. The Council does not seem to recognize, as Newman did,[90] that there are many unbelievers within the framework of the Church who are still seeking to discover God in Christ Jesus. At any rate, there seems to be no special treatment of this important area. Perhaps it is taken for granted, since there is such broad sympathy and understanding offered to the unbeliever outside the community. The dialogue recommended by Vatican II seems to presuppose some kind of place within the community for the man in search of truth and life. We are reminded by the Council that:

from the beginning of salvation history He [God] has chosen men not just as individuals but as members of a certain community. . . . This communitarian character is developed and consummated in the work of Jesus Christ. . . . Willingly obeying the laws of His country, He sanctified those human ties, especially the family ones, which are the foundation of social structures. He chose to lead the life proper to an artisan of His time and place.[91]

The unbeliever certainly makes contact with believers who are open to him in loving dialogue. Unquestionably there have always been those individuals who are marked with an all-embracing love. Furthermore, the spirit created by the person of Pope John and the work of the Council made such encounters more frequent and more meaningful. The "communitarian character" of man, however, demands more than this. There is need for a community approach. The establishment of the Vatican Secretariat for Non-

Believers is a step in the right direction. It is engaging in worthwhile dialogue as recommended by Vatican II. We will attempt, in
an epilogue, to describe the spirit and outlines of a possible
communal program for the unbelievers, whereby we seek to meet
them "in the integral life of the Church and her members."[92]

5. A MODERN APOLOGETIC MUST RECOGNIZE MAN'S RELIGIOUS
NEED.   Blondel and Scheler were both convinced that man would
discover his need for the transcendent in his active pursuit of
value.[93] This need was the tension of which Blondel spoke. It was
the demand for an answer from a personal God which preoccupied
Scheler. Newman saw the need in man's awareness of his own
sinfulness and the redemption for which he longed.[94] Each recognized, optimistically, that God had left His mark on men, and was
calling to them amid the distractions of the world. The believers
should be concerned about letting this need cry out.[95] Once this is
recognized, that man has this need for God, the apologetic approach which stresses man's moral obligation and religious duties
appears ineffective. Thus, Ignace Lepp, speaking of his own
atheism, says: "It is important for religious people never to forget
the ancient truth that acceptance of divine revelation presupposes
in the subject a natural awareness of insufficiency or dissatisfaction. . . ." He then goes on to describe his own rejection of
Communism and the existential need that brought him to Christianity.

After several months of "negative atheism," I was to experience for
want of a better name, what might be called a metaphysical anxiety. In
truth, my anxiety was not very "metaphysical" in any sense of the term.
Neither the beyond nor my own immortality concerned me. . . . More
and more frequently, however, I questioned myself about the meaning
of this life. . . . With these psychological dispositions I entered the
Christian religion.[96]

This need of man for God will, of course, express itself variously in
different men. Perhaps this religious need will not appear even long
after we have engaged in honest activity with the unbeliever. We
agree with Harvey Cox that "it is pointless and unfair to try to
force secular man into asking religious questions, consciously or
otherwise, before we can converse."[97]

     Nor do we intend to offer an apologetic which tries to tell a happy man how miserable he is. We do not have in mind some artificial form of bullying. Bonhoeffer describes the futility of such an approach to arouse the religious need: "If, however, it [our apologetic] does not come off, if a man won't see that his happiness is really damnation, his health sickness, his vigor and vitality despair; if he won't call them what they really are, the theologian is at his wits' end."[98] Bonhoeffer was not opposed to an apologetic which asked man to face the true meaning of life. He opposed a Christianity that called true human values a barrier to God. Like Scheler,[99] Bonhoeffer resisted an apologetic which made man crawl to God in weakness, or which aroused a religious need by attacking all that man held dear:

I am so anxious that God should not be relegated to some last secret place, but that we should frankly recognize that the world and men have come of age, that we should not speak ill of man in his worldliness, but confront him with God at his strongest point, that we should give up all our clerical subterfuges, and our regarding of psychotherapy and existentialism as precursors of God. . . . The Word of God is far removed from this revolt of mistrust.[100]

Similarly, when Vatican II speaks of man's religious need, it does not expect first to reduce man to helplessness and then to pick him up. It rather recognizes that man is already asking religious questions and makes itself available to answer them:

Though mankind is stricken with wonder at its own discoveries and power, it often raises anxious questions about the current trend of the world, about the place and role of man in the universe, about the meaning of its individual and collective strivings, and about the ultimate destiny of reality and humanity. . . . The Council can provide no more eloquent proof of its solidarity with, as well as its respect and love for, the entire human family with which it is bound up, than by engaging with it in conversation about these various problems.[101]

There is a tremendous note of optimism here, a deep awareness that Christ's presence in the world has in some way touched all men. The Council knows that men v·"l continue to ask and to wonder, because the wholeness of life is possible only in Christ. This dialogue cannot be pushed or forced. But man has a deep religious need and the very changes within society "lead men to look for answers; indeed . . . force them to do so."[102] The

Church has reason to be optimistic. Vatican II puts in words the very thought of Scheler and Blondel, the thought which fifty years ago might have seemed to smack of Modernism:

Above all the Church knows that her message is in harmony with the most secret desires of the human heart when she champions the dignity of the human vocation. . . . For by His incarnation the Son of God has united Himself in some fashion with every man. . . . All this holds true not only for Christians, but for all men of good will in whose hearts grace works in an unseen way.[103]

In another place the Council tells us:

[The Church] also knows that man is constantly worked upon by God's Spirit, and hence can never be altogether indifferent to the problems of religion. . . . For by His incarnation the Father's Word assumed, and sanctified through His cross and resurrection, the whole of man, body and soul, and through that totality the whole of nature created by God for man's use.[104]

Man has this religious need to provide meaning in his life. At times it will be difficult to recognize; at times we will see only its outlines. But always we must recognize that God is calling out to man through the spirit of Jesus, and where there is truth and love, there is God.

6. THE MODERN APOLOGETIC IS CHARACTERIZED BY FREEDOM. The spirit of freedom necessary for a modern apologetic flows from the above-mentioned spirit of optimism. It means that we must believe in man. Newman was insistent on the freedom of conscience necessary to produce faith.[105] Blondel was criticized for his open-mindedness. He replied:

My goal has been to accept the differences of human consciences without discouraging good will, without questioning sincerity. And if at times I have appeared to support closed minds or weak and sluggish consciences, it is only to lead them where I think their secret will is taking them, and to give them more when they were satisfied with less.[106]

Newman had explained the need for freedom in any Catholic educational program, and his *Idea of a University* summarizes his views on the "elbow room" needed for the development of judgment and creative thought.[107] He also pointed out that religion was a system which permitted various kinds of assent, and that too often in the Church there was no distinction between opinion and certitude.[108] Such a lack of freedom within the Church would push the unbeliever away. Blondel asked the Church to be careful about sudden and peremptory condemnations of sincere thought. He asked that a man be given a chance to defend himself, and insisted on the germ of truth everywhere. Scheler was extremely conscious of the social consequences produced by an authoritarian Church. It made for a passive membership and prevented the personal religious commitment that would acknowledge guilt in the face of war.[109] In general, our historical sources emphasized the freedom necessary for faith and love. If the Church was not seen by the unbeliever as a protector of human freedom, he could not consider her as a serious answer to his religious need. Again, it should be said, our primary concern is not with conversion, but with the opportunity to render service to all men in the search for the light.

The problem of freedom within the Church is still a serious one, although Vatican II has initiated a vigorous force to resolve this problem. If the unbeliever were given one word to describe the attitude of the Catholic Church prior to Vatican II, the word selected would likely be "authoritarian," or "narrow," or possibly dogmatic. Monica Lawler describes the Catholic undergraduate in the state university in this way:

Catholic students are distinguishable as a group; the effect of having been at a Catholic school is not negligible. . . . The efforts of an authoritarian system of education have, however, aspects more destructive of intellectual endeavor. . . . These are roughly comprehended in an unwillingness to think independently.[110]

In Gerhard Lenski's study of the religious attitudes among people in the Detroit area, he speaks of the social values of the Catholic clergy:

Of all the differences between the Protestant and Catholic clergy, few are more pronounced than those involving the question of what a child must learn to prepare him for life. . . . The Catholic clergy overwhelmingly stressed the importance of obedience and ranked it well ahead of intellectual autonomy. . . . The strong concern for authority of the Catholic clergy manifested itself at numerous points in our interviews with them. In response to questions, priests often replied,

"The Catholic Church teaches . . ." or "The Catholic Church's position is . . .", even when the questions dealt with matters where Catholic teaching permits some latitude for individual differences of opinion.[111]

Scheler, Blondel, and Newman had a certain underlying trust in man, a respect for his sincerity, a consciousness that man had the mark of God upon him. This mark of God was rooted deep within man and could not easily be disregarded. The mark would only be recognized in the freedom of man's struggle. The words of Vatican II reflect this same spirit, offering us new hope and new horizons within the Church because the Council acknowledged our own sinfulness and neglect and it recognized the rights of the unbeliever. The *Declaration on Religious Freedom* says:

A sense of the dignity of the human person has been impressing itself more and more deeply on the consciousness of contemporary man, and the demand is increasingly made that men should act on their own judgment, enjoying and making use of a responsible freedom, not driven by coercion but motivated by a sense of duty. . . . The truth cannot impose itself except by virtue of its own truth, as it makes its entrance into the mind at once quietly and with power. . . . The inquiry [for truth] is to be free, carried on with the aid of teaching and instruction, communication and dialogue, in the course of which men explain to one another the truth they have discovered, or think they have discovered, in order thus to assist one another in the quest for truth. . . . [Man] is not to be forced to act in a manner contrary to his conscience.[112]

Herein is expressed the ideal for which Scheler, Blondel, and Newman fought. The Council was not afraid to admit that there had been true progress in the new understanding of man:

The declaration of this Vatican Council on the right of man to religious freedom has its foundation in the dignity of the person, whose exigencies have come to be more fully known to human reason through centuries of experience. . . . It is therefore completely in accord with the nature of faith that in matters religious every manner of coercion on the part of men should be excluded.[113]

This is the necessary freedom for any program of apologetic for the unbeliever. The Council emphasizes that "men explain to one another the truth they have discovered," and in this way permit true dialogue. The words of Robert McAfee Brown on ecumenism are relevant in any consideration of an apologetic program: "Ecumenism must be a path on which *both* partners are trying to move toward one another, [and not] a static and passive attitude on the part of Catholicism."[114] Freedom might well be the motif of Vatican II. Any apologetic program can now discover new and positive direction from its words:

Conscience is the most secret core and sanctuary of a man. There he is alone with God, Whose voice echoes in his depths. . . . Only in freedom can man direct himself towards goodness. Our contemporaries make much of this freedom and pursue it eagerly; and rightly to be sure. . . . Man's dignity demands that he act according to a knowing and free choice that is personally motivated and prompted from within, not under blind internal impulse nor by external pressure.[115]

No longer are we weighed down by such narrow shibboleths as "error has no rights." The clear words of Vatican II make a searching and honest dialogue possible:

The more deeply we come to understand their [other men's] ways of thinking through such courtesy and love, the more easily will we be able to enter into dialogue with them. . . . It is necessary to distinguish between error, which always merits repudiation, and the person in error, who never loses the dignity of being a person even when he is flawed by false or inadequate religious notions.[116]

7. THE MODERN APOLOGETIC ATTACKS THE "IDOLS" OF OUR SOCIETY IN A SEARCH FOR TRUE AND COMMON VALUES. The attack on "idols," or the false values of our society, was an important part of the work of Max Scheler: "What I have called the 'shattering of idols' is the principal (and only) way to prepare the religious development of the personality."[117] Scheler did not deny the importance of the positive values short of God himself. He stressed, rather, that Christianity must constantly reappraise its own aims and recognize how easily "scientism" and "humanism" can take the place of faith and love.[118] He saw Christianity standing above the hopes of any single nation as the one source of peace and love. Blondel recognized the danger of the Church's identification with any decadent form, such as the monarchy in France, which had aided its cause in the past.[119] The values of society require the constant and prophetic vision of Christianity.

There are numerous values in our society that require a careful scrutiny in the framework of a loving dialogue. The unbeliever is also concerned about such areas as the meaning of speed and material progress, the emotional prison of the organization man, the trauma of television, the passionless career of cybernetics, the growing depersonalization and specialization of society. These and hundreds of other concerns affect the modern unbeliever. The prophetic vision of the Church could be of great service in such areas, and the insights of the unbeliever would broaden the vision of the Church. Our prophetic role in the past seemed often enough to be related only to the values which were important to the Catholic community. Consequently, we were concerned about Communism as a threat to the faith, secular education as a challenge to Catholic students, divorce and birth control laws as hostile to the Catholic position. There are numerous spheres of concern which we share with the unbeliever. Herein we can jointly attack the idols of our society which threaten the freedom and dignity of man. This was the spirit of Blondel and Scheler, and it has been carried through by the directions of Vatican II:

The Church, sent to all peoples of every time and place, is not bound exclusively and indissolubly to any race or nation, any particular way of life or any customary pattern of life recent or ancient. . . . She can enter into communion with the various civilizations, to their enrichment and the enrichment of the Church herself.

The Gospel of Christ constantly renews the life and culture of fallen man; it combats and removes the errors and evils resulting from the constant allurement of sin. It never ceases to purify and elevate the morality of peoples.[120]

The Council reminds us that the prophetic mission of the Church should not lead us "into the temptation of not acknowledging [society's] positive values":

Among these values are included: scientific study, . . . the necessity of working together with others in technical groups, a sense of international solidarity, a clearer awareness of the responsibility of experts to aid and even to protect men, the desire to make the conditions of life more favorable for all, especially for those who are poor in culture or who are deprived of the opportunity to exercise responsibility.[121]

The Church is not alone in her struggle for truth and love. There are men on all sides who do not share our faith, and yet they share our concern about the permanence of marriage, the dignity of the individual, the senselessness of war, the glamorization of sex, the death of creativity, the scandal of racism, and numerous other areas of importance. Vatican II, following the spirit of Blondel and Scheler and Newman, asks us to join with all men in a frontal attack on the idols which debase man and still the cry for a personal God. Such a joint attack on society's idols is an important part of a modern program of apologetics for the unbeliever: "No foundation therefore remains for any theory or practice that leads to discrimination between man and man or people and people, so far as their human dignity and the rights flowing from it are concerned."[122]

CONCLUSION. The seven principles listed in this chapter are an attempt to synthesize the apologetic principles approved by Scheler, Blondel, and Newman and adopted by the spirit of Vatican II. Thus, it should become evident that our historical sources, although men far ahead of their times, are very much in the mainstream of present thought in the Church. The Church has moved in the direction that Scheler, Blondel, and Newman marked out. A relevant apologetic for the unbeliever now becomes a possibility. The principles we have listed should characterize such a program.

Blondel and Scheler espoused openly the need for an apologetic of action.[123] We shall attempt, in an epilogue, to describe such an apologetic of action in the light of the principles we have established. Such an apologetic would not consider Christianity to be merely an idea to be held comfortably in the mind. It must be involved in man's struggle for life and meaning. Blondel proposed that Christianity offered an answer to a man who was forced to ask questions at the level of life and action.[124] Man had first to recognize the tension that existed between the meager man that he was and the man he knew he wanted to be. Such a tension would be the experience of the believer and the unbeliever alike. The believer would have to recognize the unbelief that marked his own struggle for meaning. If he needed proof of his unbelief, *L'Action* offered it to him: the poverty of his own commitment. Faith was far more than an intellectual acceptance of certain doctrines. It was the adoption of a new way of life. The resistance to conversion in the life of every believer became the source of his dialogue with an unbelieving world.

Scheler recognized the same phenomenon. He was vigorous in his criticism of a complacent and self-righteous Christianity. If Christianity were merely the acceptance of an idea, or the admission of a body of propositions, then there was good reason for a Christian's self-congratulations. If, however, Christianity were a unique way of love, and not merely another form of humanitarianism, then its goals and actions should be recognizably different. The tragedy of World War I made Scheler aware of Christianity's failure to reach men in the real decisions of life.[125] The true believer had to recognize that he personally danced before the idols of society, and to realize that the unbeliever was often deeply committed to Christian principles.

Newman, too, was well aware that faith was very often mere superstitious allegiance. He recognized that many believers were merely conforming and had no real assent.[126] They assented to an idea, but when the idea was challenged by life, only then would it be clear whether or not faith were real assent. Thus Newman, in speaking of personal conscience, insisted that moral awareness was only one side of this God-given power. The other side was responsibility, moral responsibility, a sense of duty. Man must measure his religious commitment in terms of action and decision.

We have experienced this shallow kind of Christianity in our day. Faith could somehow avoid the real issues. Thus it was possible to share fully in every visible measure of Christian life, and yet harbor a bitter and righteous hatred in racial matters. At the same time, the most charitable persons, steeped in the deepest traditions of social justice, could be cut off from this same visible support of the Christian community, if they were living in an impossible marriage situation. As long as Christianity remains merely an institution, this ambiguity is possible. To the extent that it becomes a community of love, such cruel categorization becomes proportionately impossible. With the direction of Scheler, Blondel, and Newman and the eloquent encouragement of Vatican II, we would like to look to the future and describe, in our epilogue, the community apologetic for the unbeliever. We do not presume to exhaust the possibilities, but merely to describe the spirit and form of one such possibility.

EPILOGUE

The present framework of the Catholic parish has little to offer the modern unbeliever. The liturgy is strange to him even in the vernacular. The prayers seem to take no cognizance of him. This is the service of the believer. More often than not, the sermon is mediocre,[127] and even when well prepared it often deals with questions or answers that are unacceptable to him. He is not permitted to share in the common table. There is generally nothing to attract him, other than the sense of prayer and sacredness which often accompanies the Catholic liturgy.

In addition to the liturgy, the ordinary parish offers a course of instructions or, if it is a particularly progressive parish, a few courses in "theology" or training courses for religion teachers. Such courses, however, generally begin with the presumption that he is committed to a personal God. They do not reach him. The questions he would like to ask, when he attends, would only delay the progress of the others, who are planning to marry a Catholic, or who hope to embrace the Catholic faith.

There are broadminded individuals within the community who make some attempt at dialogue with the unbeliever. But there is nothing offered in a communal way, nothing which helps him discover himself, nothing which makes him feel comfortable short of conversion. The instruction class is usually geared to convince; the liturgy presumes conviction. We propose a kind of church, or community, for the unbeliever, promoted by the Catholic parish. Undoubtedly, it would have to prove itself to the unbeliever, that is, it would have to make clear that it did not seek to convert him, but would assist him in his search for value and meaning and listen to him in his revelation of valid insights. Such a community might at first appear as a kind of artifice to entice the unbeliever directly into the Catholic fold, but time and honest communication could dissipate such suspicions. Permit us to hypothesize about such a community.

The Community of the Unbeliever

1. FORMATION OF THE COMMUNITY. Once the program for the community (see step 2, which follows) was initially outlined, a brochure could be prepared for distribution. Newspaper publicity would also help to provide a community airing of the proposed program. Protestant ministers should be assured that we are not attempting to invade their parishes, but rather to offer some structure to form, challenge, and discover the value-orientation of the unbeliever. Our Protestant and Jewish brothers might well want to join us in such an important work. Members of any religion would be welcome, but the primary concern of the community would be the unbeliever, who is not formally attached to any faith. The greatest care would have to be exercised to make clear that the community is not intended to be a clever way of luring the unbeliever into the Church, but that it has positive value in itself.

2. THE NATURE OF THE SERVICE. The service would vary according to the community with which we were dealing. In a suburban area, it might well match the Unitarian motif. There would be a sermon, sophisticated and well delivered, that would challenge the values of the community. For example, it would recognize the idols in daily life that are mere substitutes for real meaning and light. The modern unbeliever would appreciate a consideration of the effects of speed and fast living on our lives. He knows that he lives too fast; he knows that he is working too hard and is concerned with social trifles. He also knows that the pressure of success is a one-way street, moving a father away from his wife and children, moving a man away from himself.

Discussions would not require the direction of a priest. A layman could direct the program. The service could be held in a church or in private homes. It could be held on Sundays or other days, but it would fulfill the need that the modern unbeliever has to come to grips with meaning. It might well satisfy the religious sense that lurks in the heart of man, the appetite for the holy.

A psychologist could talk about the fear that underlies the drive of the businessman or his overextended spouse. He could discuss the pressures on children when parents live out their frustrations in the success of their offspring. He could describe the difference between recreation and diversion, or discuss the loss of man's reflective sense. A sociologist could talk about the changes that have taken place in family life. A discussion of the loss of creativity and individuality in American life would be appreciated. So would a dialogue on the significance of an educationally oriented society. There could be programs outlined to awaken a sense of responsibility for the poor, the retarded, the emotionally disturbed.

There would be opportunity for discussing the significance of modern literature and drama. Many would like to hear what a diet of television has done to the esthetic sense. Efforts could be made to secure better entertainment in the theaters, to promote dramatic societies, to host programs for the development of the arts. There is no end to what could be done in such a program.

If the priest were to be a part of such a program, he would have to be aware and open, an exceptional speaker, a man concerned about society and community, a man who did not believe that conversion to Catholicism was the only worthwhile goal in the unbeliever's search.

Some form of prayer could be offered in keeping with the goals of the community. Perhaps suitable hymns could be selected; a fellowship service could be offered, in which the symbols agreed upon might speak meaningfully to the community. Selections from Scripture would be in order; perhaps each member of the community could be invited to read, on occasions, his favorite text or story. Whatever was done would be done in a spirit of openness and dialogue.

For the poor, for the Negro in the ghetto, the nature of the service would be different. It might mean a program of self-help. Economists could speak about job opportunities; members of the community could speak about the dangers of indifference or irresponsibility, or about school dropouts. With the present poverty programs and civil rights activities, there would be numerous outlets for the community. Hymns and scriptural readings would have an important place. Recreation and education would be of primary concern. Courses in preparation for marriage could be offered; programs to prevent divorce could be formed.

There is no reason not to have several communities within the same parish. Nominal Catholics who cannot reconcile themselves to the formalism of their faith, or who have made no personal commitment to their traditional creed, might search for God in such a community. It has been our impression that many Catholics, especially among the post-adolescent group, who presently are abandoning formal religion, would find an important help in such a program, a help in finding their own identity and in discovering God.

3. OTHER ACTIVITIES WITHIN THE COMMUNITY OF UNBELIEVERS. Community programs could be encouraged outside the Sunday service. Groups could take an interest in the civic library, the city government, housing developments, urban planning, mental health, scholarships for the underprivileged, art centers, schools for beginning writers, neighborhood welcoming activities. There would be countless opportunities in a community which recognized that values short of the ultimate are values still.

4. VALUE TO THE CATHOLIC COMMUNITY. The community of the unbeliever, supported and encouraged by the Catholic Church, would offer an important "witness" to the sacramental Catholic. At first he might look upon this community of the unbeliever with amusement or disdain. Gradually, if the proper clerical support and public relations were maintained, he would be impressed by the sincere "witness" of the man struggling for some kind of commitment. Too often in the past the Catholic in society has represented a defensive protection of minority views. He was interested in the birth control issue to protect the Catholic position. The larger issue of overpopulation was seldom his concern. He simply insisted that the world could feed ten times its present population, and he accused the proponents of the pill and contraceptive literature of selfishness and immorality. He sometimes impugned the motives of the doctor who performed therapeutic abortions, calling his dedication self-centered and egotistical. The Catholic

did not always face honestly the human suffering and mental breakdowns that such a doctor experienced in his practice. Or if he faced such problems, too often he met them with pious clichés whose meanings he had never known firsthand. It was much the same with divorce. Rather than face the fact that divorce will take place within our society, and instead of helping to improve the existing laws and mitigate the social consequences, the Catholic could sit comfortably back and disapprove. The presence of the unbeliever in our midst could open up to the Catholic a new interest in the values and concerns of our society, and not merely in a negative and judgmental way. Vatican II has reminded us that Catholics are in the world, and such a program would give meaning to its hopes.

5. JOINT ACTIVITIES OF BELIEVER AND UNBELIEVER IN A COM-MUNITY FRAMEWORK. The *Constitution on the Church in the Modern World* has declared an end to the Catholic ghetto. It has called a halt to pharisaism, or self-righteousness. The opportunity for the believer and unbeliever to recognize how much they have in common has never been better. Even apart from such a program as we recommend, the Catholic must enter into the concerns and hopes of the world with a spirit of love and with a willingness to help. The unbelieving community in our midst, however, would make firm the conviction that the Catholic in society must witness and serve, must recognize the genuine sincerity and concern of his unbelieving brothers. Intercommunal activities would not be difficult to develop. The results could be as thrilling as Vatican II suggests they should be.

There is need in our society for vast programs to help the young prepare for marriage. In the past, the Catholic community has been largely concerned with preparing its own. Yet, we know that the stability of our society depends upon the strength of its families. We know this, but have done little or nothing to help develop such strength outside the Catholic community. Civil law demands blood tests and other physical requirements. It does not require emotional preparedness, nor any specific knowledge of the nature of the marriage union. The Catholic community, although laden with pre-Cana programs of one kind or another, has done little or nothing to secure better legislation for marital prerequisites. Nor have we done anything practicable to remedy the frightening divorce rate throughout the world. It is feasible that some marriage counseling could be required of the parties to a divorce if experimental programs were begun and serious legislation were introduced. The Catholic concern, however, has been with the Catholic community. The presence of the unbeliever in our midst would arouse new visions of our responsibility to the total community. Such responsibility is the heart of Vatican II's plea to the Church in the modern world.

6. CONCLUSION. It would not be difficult to multiply examples of areas of value common to all men. The Catholic concern has largely ended with the Catholic community. Consequently, the presence of the Catholic Church has scarcely been felt in large and important areas of our society, such as the secular campus, the public schools, the courts of law, the programs for world peace and the development of young nations. The presence of the Church has scarcely been felt because the Catholic Church was seen as a powerful religious body concerned with the protection of its vested interests. It is hard for the world to trust the words of a community which could accept no goals short of its own absolutes. Fortunately, there are signs in the world that all of this is beginning to change. Vatican II has given us a start.

Our primary concern is not to impose the Catholic way of life on the world. Nor can it be with new and clever methods of convert making. It must be the "witness" of service, of openness, of concern for all that is good. Then will the Church's voice be heard and pondered in an unbelieving world. Pope John was a breath of fresh air, or even more, a veritable change in climate. The world seemed to embrace him because he brought to the Church a new respect for the individual, a trust in mankind, a new vision of freedom. Vatican II, the reflection of his spirit, could offer us new hope and new horizons, because it recognized our own sinfulness and neglect, and acknowledged the rights of all men.

While we begin to go out to the unbeliever and to welcome him into our midst, we must recognize the need to improve the image of the Church in the world. Within the Church itself there must be a new respect for the individual if the apologetic programs for the unbeliever are to have any meaning. There is a place for pacifists in the Church; there is also a place for traditionalists, even vocal and imprudent ones. If a community cannot tolerate outbursts and opposition, even of a dramatic kind, then it is not a community, only a closed society. As long as the Church reaches out and silences its members, even its officers, without a hearing, then the world cannot be much impressed by our eloquent constitutions. The unbeliever cannot find a home in the Church, cannot even regard the Church worthy of serious concern, until he knows that his views will be given a hearing. If the Church policy on the intricate problems of modern existence is already decided, if only the hierarchy can speak, cautiously and prudently, requiring other members to follow the party line with scrupulous care, then we ask a man to abandon his essential personality before he joins us in community. Modern man has no such intentions. The apologetic for the unbeliever can be severely incapacitated or mortally wounded by the image of an intolerant Church. No matter what the efforts of the individual to improve that image, he will be seen largely as an exception who, at any moment, may be silenced or sent away.

This, then, is the modern apologetic problem: to say something to the modern unbeliever. The principles we have offered will serve as a guide in our beginning reflections on the most effective ways in which to resolve this problem. Unquestionably, we shall make mistakes. This is the freedom, however, that Scheler, Blondel, and Newman realized was the key to an honest search, the key to a sincere discovery. Vatican II, adopting their spirit, has once again sent us forth into the world humbly and hopefully to offer the service of our "witness," to attempt a resolution of the modern apologetic problem:

The joys and the hopes, the griefs and the anxieties of the men of this age, especially those who are poor or in any way afflicted, these are the joys and the hopes, the griefs and anxieties of the followers of Christ. Indeed, nothing genuinely human fails to raise an echo in their hearts. For theirs is a community composed of men. United in Christ they are led by the Holy Spirit in their journey to the Kingdom of their Father and they have welcomed the news of salvation which is meant for every man. That is why this community realizes that it is truly linked with mankind and its history by the deepest of bonds.[2]

NOTES

PREFACE

1. Johann Peter Steffes, *Glaubensbegrundung: Christlicher Gottes-glaube in Grundlegung und Abwehr,* I Band: *Methodische und Geschichtliche Einführung Anthropologische Grundlegung Religionsphilosophie* (Mainz: Matthias Gruneward Verlag, 1958), p. xiv, wherein Steffes describes what happens when we fail to recognize cultural changes: ". . . *die Apologetik befolge eine falsche Methode, indem sie entweder Argumente vorlege, denen seitens kritischer Denker die Zustimmung versagt bliebe, oder aber sie entwickele ihre Gedanken in einter Form, die Keine Notiz von der Seelenlage des modernen Menschen nähme.*"

2. Emil Brunner, *Man in Revolt, A Christian Anthropology,* trans. Olive Wyon (Philadelphia: The Westminster Press, 1957), especially Chapters 1 and 2. Brunner shows in Chapter 2 that Darwin, Marx, Nietzsche, and Freud each offered a particular view of man, and from this flowed the social consequences of the theory. No real apologete can ignore man's changing image of himself. *Cf.* Gustave Weigel's "The Historical Background of the Encyclical *Humani Generis*" in *Theological Studies,* XII (1951), 208–230.

3. We have carefully examined such works as: F. J. Sheed, *A Map of Life* (New York: Sheed & Ward, 1933); A. Tanquerey, *Synopsis theologiae dogmaticae fundamentalis ad mentem S. Thomae Aquinatis, hodiernis moribus accommodata,* Vols. I and II (24th ed.; (New York: Benziger Bros., 1943); Anthony Alexander, *College Apologetics* (Chicago: Henry Regnery Company, 1954); Gabriel Brunhes, *La Foi et sa justification rationelle* (Paris: Bloud and Gay, 1928); Martin D'Arcy, *Mirage and Truth* (New York: The Macmillan Company, 1933); Joseph Fichter, *Textbook in Apologetics* (Milwaukee: The Bruce Publishing Company, 1947); John Cardinal Heenan, *The Faith Makes Sense* (New York: Sheed & Ward, 1948); Arthur Patrick Madgett, *Christian Origins* (Cincinnati: Xavier University Press, 1943); Walter Devivier, *Christian Apologetics,* trans. from the French (New York: Wagner, 1924); Wilhelm Wilmers, *Handbook of the Christian Religion,* trans. from the German (New York: Benziger Bros., 1905).

4. Alec Vidler, *Prophecy and Papacy: A Study of Lammenais, the Church and Revolution* (New York: Charles Scribner's Sons, 1954), pp. 68 ff.

5. Alec Vidler, *The Church in an Age of Revolution* ("The Pelican History of the Church," Vol. 5; Baltimore: Penguin Books, Inc., 1965), pp. 31–32.

6. *Ibidem*, pp. 146 ff., 180–81.

7. When we speak here of the traditional apologetic, we have in mind the standard treatment offered in the textbooks on fundamental theology. This would include the proofs for the existence of God, the nature of religion, the proof of the Christian revelation through miracles and prophecies, and the living wonder of the Church. There would be refinements offered to include the inexplicable wonder of Christ's person, the unparalleled beauty of Christian doctrine, and a variety of popular approaches. We are not concerned with the variety of attempts, but rather with their underlying assumption that these discussions were the demonstrative proof drawn from "history" and "reason." We will bring this out more clearly as we go along, but a classical summary of the traditional apologetic would be L. Maisonneuve's "Apologétique" in *Dictionnaire Théologie Catholique* (Paris: Librairie Letouzey et Ané, 1931), pp. 1511–80, and Jean Levie's *Sous les yeux de l'incroyant* (Paris: Desclée, 1946), p. 18.

8. Roger Aubert, *Le Problème de l'act de la foi, donnés traditionelles et resultats des controverses récents* (Louvain: E. Warny, 1950).

9. It is extremely tempting in a work such as this to show precisely what intellectual opponents were the source of our inherited apologetic approach. This would mean showing the effect of Kant and the neo-Kantians in Germany and also in France, the survival of the Hegelian strain, the persistence of Cartesian dichotomies in French thought, the reaction to Locke and Hume, the effects of Sabatier, the positivism of Comte, the sentiment of Schleiermacher, the vitalism of Bergson, the growth of pragmatism and numerous other elements. Such an investigation would be well beyond our capacity and the scope of this dissertation. From time to time it will become clear that one or the other of the above, most especially the positivists, the neo-Kantians, and Schleiermacher were the contemporary targets in apologetics. However, we will occasionally point out such matters when they bear directly on the principal subjects of our historical research. For good background material on the philosophical influences on religious thought in the late nineteenth and early twentieth centuries, we have found helpful: John Macquarrie, *Twentieth Century Religious Thought* (New York: Harper & Row, Publishers, 1963); I. M. Bochenski, *Contemporary European Philosophy*, trans. Donald Nicholl and Karl Aschenbrenner (Berkeley: University of California Press, 1965); G. R. Cragg, *The Church and the Age of Reason* ("The Pelican History of the Church," Vol. 4; Baltimore: Penguin Books, Inc., 1961); Vidler, *The Church in an Age of Revolution*; A. Gardeil, "Crédibilité," *DTC*, III, 2e part, especially pp. 2300–2308. Gardeil offers a fine presentation of the apologete in Germany, France, and England and his opposition. *Cf.* also, Gustave Weigel, *op. cit.*, and Jean Levie, *op. cit.*, pp. 17–18 and the following two chapters. See also the work of Johann Steffes already cited, especially the Introduction, pp. xiii ff.

10. On the distortions of Newman by the French immanentists, *cf.* Aubert, *op. cit.*, p. 343. The work of the Germans was more faithful to

Newman, especially the efforts of Erich Przywara, S.J., but this revival was only around 1920. *Cf.* Aubert, *op. cit.*, p. 565. It is interesting to note that Maisonneuve, *DTC*, I, 1565–66, mentions Newman only briefly among the new apologetes, but does not even list his *Grammar of Assent*, which we consider his foremost apologetical work. Maisonneuve, however, appears to have written this article only shortly after 1900, judging by his citations, although the revised publishing date of the volume of *DTC* in question is 1931. If we study the reflections of Gardeil on Newman in Vol. III of the *DTC* we can see how well received were the offerings of Newman—at least at the scholarly level—in 1938, especially pp. 2303–2304. However, the conclusions of Gardeil indicate that he had not absorbed the essential insight of Newman. More of this later in the pages which follow.

11. It is interesting to note that after a painstaking selection of our key historical sources—which meant excluding from predominant consideration such men as Möhler, Scheeben, Lammenais, Cardinal Dechamps, Gardeil, and Rousselot—in the apologetical problem, we discovered that Kevin McNamara, "Nature and Recognition of Miracles," *Irish Theological Quarterly*, V (1960), 295, singles out Newman, Blondel, and Scheler as the men "capable of making an important and indeed vital contribution to Christian Apologetics." He sees them continuing in the spirit of Pascal.

12. Yves Congar, "Théologie" in *DTC*, XIV (1946), 440–46, brings out the nature of the Modernist crisis, namely, that in trying to "remove the conceptual and philosophical image" of scholastic thought they [Modernists] tend to remove the intellectual content from the dogma itself. It was relevance at the expense of dogma, when it should have been dogma at the expense of fruitless speculation. When the Church refused to engage in dialogue with the Modernists (p. 446), it was easy to lump Blondel and Newman with Tyrell and Loisy. Gustave Weigel also brings this out clearly in his article in *Theological Studies*, XII (1951), 212–14. "The discontent that many theologians felt with the state of their discipline could not be voiced because it exposed them to the danger of being considered modernists." (p. 214) The distinction that Weigel makes between the negative and positive sides of the Modernist movement, wherein he recognizes their dissatisfaction with a conceptualist theology as valid and rejects their dismissal of dogma, is a better critique than that of John Macquarrie, *Twentieth Century Religious Thought*, pp. 181–86, wherein he attempts to show that the views of Tyrell, LeRoy, and others were not of the positivistic and heretical variety. A good treatment of Loisy's loss of faith and the setting of the Modernist problem is contained in Jean Levie's *Sous les yeux*, pp. 191–214. There is also a good treatment of the influence of Tyrell and Loisy on the American scene and the silence that followed the *Syllabus* in John L. Murphy's "Seventy-Five Years of Fundamental Theology in America," *American Ecclesiastical Review*, X (1964), 392–93. For a further development of the fear bred of the modernist crisis and its consequent condemnation, see the critics of Gardeil's extremely orthodox views, Aubert, *op. cit.*, pp. 407 ff. Also, the critics of Rousselot and his "Les Yeux de la foi" in Aubert, *op. cit.*, pp. 470 ff. *Cf.* also, Vidler, *Prophecy and Papacy*.

Certainly, the replies of the Biblical Commission between 1906 and 1914 reflect this same attitude of fear. We do not mean to imply that their fear of Modernism was not warranted, but this reaction has a profound effect on the slowing down of an apologetic which saw in Sacred Scripture a special kind of "history," and saw "miracle" as a special kind of "sign." The replies of the Biblical Commission assuredly made the work of the "new apologist" more difficult. *Cf.* Jean Levie, *The Bible, Word of God in Words of Men*, trans. Geoffrey Chapman (New York: P. J. Kenedy & Sons, 1961), pp. 70–76, 122–28, 186–90. There is an abundance of literature on this entire question.

It would be wrong to blame the entire hesitancy to move ahead in apologetics on the modernist controversy. In Gardeil's article on "Crédibilité," he shows the shaping influence on apologetics of the continuing reaction to Kant and Schleiermacher (p. 2301) and reassertion of the "objective apologetic" of proof and logic. He shows similar developments in France, even in the work of Lammenais with the "four marks of the Church" and the traditional use of miracle and prophecy in reaction to the Deists and the introduction of Kant. Modernism was not born without ancestors, nor was the traditional apologetic which hoped to temper the Modernists. Vidler, *Prophecy and Papacy*, pp. 88 ff. also offers a similar critique of Lammenais. In any discussion of Modernism we should mention Émile Poulat's *Histoire dogme et critique dans la crise moderniste* (Paris: Easterman, 1962).

13. *Cf.* Congar, *DTC*, pp. 392–97, wherein the author shows the recurrence of this theme in theology and its ever-important dimension. He shows in pp. 434 ff. how it was temporarily lost. *Cf.* also, McNamara, *op. cit.*, pp. 294–95, for a development of this theme.

14. McNamara, *op. cit.*, p. 296. These "insights" are called by the author "a powerful current of thought of a strongly subjectivist character which, despite serious dangers that have become only too obvious in the past, has increasingly come to be recognized as making an important, and indeed, vital contribution to Christian apologetics." (p. 295) *Cf.* Aubert, *op. cit.*, pp. 658, 665–66, wherein he asks for more "scientific" conversion stories. Also, on p. 407, where he challenges Gardeil from his own experience in the work of conversion.

CHAPTER I

1. Congar, *DTC*, pp. 445–46; Aubert, *op. cit.*, p. 649; Gardeil, "Crédibilité," pp. 2300–08.

2. St. Thomas' discussion of "unbelief" and "heresy" in the *Summa Theologica*, IIa, IIae, q. 10, 11, shows that even the balanced mind in the "Age of Faith" lived totally in the climate of a believing world. *Cf.* also, Aubert, *op. cit.*, pp. 650–51.

3. Aubert, *op. cit.*, p. 653.

4. *Ibidem*, pp. 654–55.

5. *Ibidem*, p. 256, where Aubert points out that even the Thomists in the early twentieth century did not recognize the seventeenth century Jesuit influence on the thought of St. Thomas. When they would say that signs gave rational certitude of revelation, or that revelation *quo ad modum* could be grasped by reason, this was not true Thomism. *Cf.* also, Congar, "Théologie," pp. 382–83, wherein he shows Rousselot's rejection (*L'Intellec-*

tualisme de Saint Thomas) of a philosophic demonstration of the *prae-ambula fidei* as the true mind of Thomas. Rousselot asserts that Thomas' use of *Patet, necesse est*, or *oportet* has to be established contextually as to its rigor.

It might be well here to cite the opinion of Carlos Cirne-Lima, *Personal Faith*, trans. G. Richard Dimler, S.J. (New York: Herder and Herder, Inc., 1965), wherein he shows the clear distinction that Thomas makes between *"ratio"* and *"intellectus"* (p. 103), where he puts in contemporary language: "Intuition (*intellectus*) is the starting-point as well as the goal of discursive, conceptual (*ratio*) thought. Intuition is that undivided simple kernel, that oneness in which many things are made manifest. Out of this intuition then arise by analysis . . . concepts, judgments, and syllogisms." Cirne-Lima makes it clear that, in his opinion, not only has Thomas' theology of faith been distorted, but his epistemology as well. We shall speak more of this later, when we have occasion to develop Scheler's thought. *Cf.* Gerard McCool, "Primacy of Intuition," *Thought*, XXVII (1962), 68.

6. Cragg, *op. cit.*, pp. 11–13, 234 ff., 246, 250–51.

7. *Ibidem*, p. 13.

8. *Ibidem*, p. 235.

9. *Ibidem*, pp. 236–50.

10. *Ibidem*, p. 246.

11. Vidler, *Prophecy and Papacy*, pp. 70 ff.

12. *Ibidem*, pp. 109 ff.

13. Vidler, *Prophecy and Papacy*, pp. 79–101. F. Lammenais, *Essai sur l'indifférence en matière de religion*, 4 vols. (Paris: Garnier, 1895), especially the latter part of II, 365 ff., 384 ff.

14. Vidler, *The Church in an Age of Revolution*, p. 156.

15. Such questioning was the result of Rousseau's work, and especially that of Schleiermacher and Kant.

16. The defensive nature of apologetics naturally grew in an effort to meet the mounting threat of Protestantism, Deism, Rationalism, Scientism, and other varieties of -isms. (*Cf.* Levie, *op. cit.*, p. 18.) An examination of dozens of apologetic manuals of the nineteenth and twentieth centuries (which we cursorily made, *cf.* Introduction, note 3 above), many of them popular editions, shows that innumerable "logical reasons" and scriptural texts used as "history" were heaped up against the Protestants and unbelievers. It is not our intention here to discuss these clever and well-intentioned (and often successful) efforts. We intend, rather, to point out that these zealous attempts were marked by a medieval framework which took for granted that the world was largely believing, clearly "rational" (in the apologete's own sense of that word) and rejecting the Church by a kind of stubborn pride which prevented it from "reasoning." Even though it became clear that the "unbeliever" was a unique problem at the turn of the twentieth century (*cf.* Aubert, *op. cit.*, pp. 265, 512) and the Protestant-Catholic argument was somewhat expanded to include the unbeliever, we still continued to speak of "reason," "nature," and "history" as if nothing had changed. Man was still the neat division of "faith" and "reason" that the Middle Ages saw. (*Cf.* Johann Steffes, *Religionsphilosophie* [Munich:

Kösel and Pustet, 1925], p. 1: "The protective covering, upon which the world had relied in philosophy, appeared undermined with the onset of the New Age." Steffes then brings out clearly the slowness in realizing that "nature" and "history" had lost their univocal and probatory meaning. [Cf. pp. 2–3.])

In a work reissued hardly ten years ago, Canon George Smith, in his book, *The Teaching of the Catholic Church*, Vol. I (New York: The Macmillan Company, 1953), assures us that to *prove* that "the Catholic Church is the divinely appointed Teacher of Revelation" (p. 13) is only a matter of using the "human mind" and examining the report of "history." Here is a rather sophisticated apologetics that could ignore the epistemological atmosphere of its own world and speak from the Middle Ages. *Cf.* also, "The Case for Traditional Apologetics," by J. C. Fenton, as late as 1959, in *American Ecclesiastical Review*, CXLI (December, 1959), 406–416.

It is also informative to glance through Adolph Tanquerey's *Synopsis Theologiae Dogmaticae*, Vols. I and II, a book which is still being sold. He asks us to confront the "empiricists" and "positivists," "moderns," and others with the clear, coldly logical tool called "reason." Man must only have the right dispositions. (II, 228–47) When discussing the Trinity, he says that it is "proved by revelation," rather than saying simply, "It is revealed," indicating the "Middle-Aged" epistemology that our age would not recognize (p. 347).

17. Aubert, *op. cit.*, p. 283.

18. Macquarrie, *Twentieth Century Religious Thought*, pp. 75–94; Bochenski, *op. cit.*, p. 95.

19. Aubert, *op. cit.*, pp. 655–56; Levie has a long treatment of this fact in Chapter II, *op. cit.*, pp. 67–106. In speaking of the apologetics of the past, he says (p. 20): "It fails to consider the essential role of the subject in the apologetic study. And it limits the object of apologetics to the narrow limits of controversy with the unbelievers, rather than selecting as its foundation *the entirety of the Christian event*." *Cf.* also, the remarks of René Latourelle, S.J., *Théologie de la révélation* (Paris: Desclée, 1963), pp. 472–74, wherein he shows the four aspects of revelation, namely, mystery and divine action, an event of history, knowledge, and encounter. He points out that man is apt to exaggerate or underestimate any of these aspects, or oppose them. This is precisely what Aubert concludes (p. 784), and in his treatise one can see faith—through history—pass from a belief in a body of propositions in the nineteenth century to a personal act of encounter in the twentieth. When faith is seen somewhat apart from the subject, it is easy to support it with the *praeambula fidei* whether it moves people or not. The job of the conceptualist is done. As the personal side of faith was emphasized, such an apologetic became obviously ineffective. (Pp. 655–66, 658–59, 754) He brings out clearly (p. 659) that a medieval epistemology will fail. *Cf.* the excellent article by G. Philips, "Deux tendances dans la théologie contemporaire," *Nouvelle Revue Théologique*, LXXXV (1963), 227–29, wherein he speaks of these two aspects of the mystery of faith and the two approaches in theology. It would be another exaggeration, he points out, to go too far in the other direction and lose the "content" side of the mystery. Aubert brings out this same point on p. 695. Several authors quote St. Thomas on this point (*e.g.*, Aubert, *op. cit.*, p. 701), to show the balance he had. Faith in Thomas is not concerned with content for its own sake, but

to lead us into personal encounter with God: "*Solum cognitio finis super-naturalis, et eorum quibus in finem illum supernaturaliter ordinamus.*" Or, as Thomas says in IIa, IIae, q.1, a.2, ad.2: "*Actus credentis terminatur non ad enuntiabile sed ad rem.*" In this light, faith becomes a personal act, and its defense could not ignore its own culture. *Cf.* McCool, *op. cit.*, p. 68 and Cirne-Lima, *op. cit.*

20. R. Rousselot (died 1915), author of the famous *Les yeux de la foi,* was certainly one such exception, as were Gardeil, Dechamps, and the men we have selected for special historic research. Aubert has an extensive treatment of Rousselot's thought, pp. 451–511. *Cf.* also, Congar, "Théologie," p. 383 and Weigel, "The Historical Background . . .," pp. 215–17. Our reason for not selecting Rousselot as a major source of our research was the fact that, by his own admission, he is heavily indebted to Newman (Aubert, *op. cit.*, p. 468). He attempted to meet the mind of the modern man who was preoccupied with inductive reasoning. (Aubert, *op. cit.*, p. 458) He resisted the tendency to exclude grace from the motives of credibility, and said that "reasonable" did not mean accessible to reason alone. Love would give "new eyes," and truth has a certain fascination. He is truly a modern apologist, but we judge that he follows in the train of Newman, Scheler, and Blondel. Rousselot was also strongly influenced by Blondel, both directly and through Laberthonnière. *Cf.* Introduction to Maurice Blondel's *Letter on Apologetics,* trans. Alexander Dru and Illtyd Trethowan (New York: Holt, Rinehart and Winston, Inc., 1964), p. 14, note 1.

21. Aubert, *op. cit.*, p. 654. Our remarks on modernism (*supra*) should be read within this context.

22. *Cf.* Vidler, *The Church in an Age of Revolution,* pp. 150 ff. and p. 189.

23. *Ibidem,* pp. 655–66. *Cf.* also *supra,* p. 14, note 19. *Cf.* also, the article "Dechamps" in *DTC* (1939), 178–82. This great Cardinal of Vatican I was well aware of the failure of the rational proofs. He emphasized the place of the subject with his famous: "*Le témoin c'est vous-même.*" (p. 180) Theological development had not gone far enough along the lines of the personalist view of faith to give Cardinal Dechamps the freedom he needed. He was subjected to serious criticism until his critics were "satisfied that the only truly Christian, rigorous and absolute demonstration" (p. 181) is Jesus Christ with His character, miracles, doctrine and the wonder of His Church. Mallet, who sees Dechamps as the first of the immanentists, asserts that his proof would have no value independently of the "objective" proofs. (p. 181) Dechamps, like Möhler of Germany, was so far ahead of his time, in such a position of prominence, and so devoid of the needed theological support that he was not able to develop his thought as did Newman, Scheler, and Blondel.

24. Steffes, *Religionsphilosophie,* p. 1.

25. *Ibidem,* pp. 2–3.

26. *Ibidem,* pp. 3 ff. A good discussion of Kant's effort to bridge the gap between reason and religion and to react to the rationalism of Locke is to be found in Cragg, pp. 250–51.

27. Steffes, *Glaubensbegründung,* p. xxi. In this posthumous work (1958), Steffes distinguishes between "*Beweis*" and "*Aufweis,*" between "proof" and "exposition." "*Beweis*" had become a tendentious word, re-

sounding with Kantian overtones and the inductive approach of positive science. It established a cultural barrier between the apologete and the word, especially when the apologete did not acknowledge (as Rousselot saw so clearly) the place of grace and faith influencing his reason. In an earlier passage (p. xiv) Steffes likens the apologete to a lawyer who wants to win at any cost, and brings up anything, true or untrue, objective or not, to rescue his client. Most of us need no examples of what he means.

28. *Cf.* "Crédibilité" (Gardeil), *DTC*, pp. 2298–99, 2302, 2308. *Cf.* also, "Apologétique" (Maisonneuve), *DTC*, pp. 1511, 1529, 1579.

29. Aubert, *op. cit.*, p. 228; Gardeil, "Crédibilité," pp. 2299–2301; Weigel stresses the influence of Hegel and scientism, and Maisonneuve sees other sources, but we are more concerned with the type of apologetics used than with a specification of its opponents. (*Cf.* Introduction, note 9.)

30. *Ibidem*, p. 229.

31. Maisonneuve, *op. cit.*, p. 1579. Here Maisonneuve cites with approval the letter of Monsignor Mignot on contemporary apologetics, the letter appearing in *Revue du Clergé Française*, XXIV, 561–85. *Cf.* also, Levie, *op. cit.*, pp. 19–21.

32. J. St. Harent, "Foi," *DTC*, VI, 391.

33. Aubert, *op. cit.*, p. 230.

34. *Ibidem*, p. 230.

35. Maisonneuve, *op. cit.*, p. 1511.

36. *Cf.* Aubert, *op. cit.*, p. 269 for important selections from the work of Ollé-Laprune.

37. Maisonneuve, *op cit.*, pp. 1573–78.

38. *Ibidem*, p. 1579. Here is another example where theology had not developed adequately to permit the theologian to take an honest look at the problem. As long as the "gratuity of grace" was threatened, he was paralyzed. *Cf.* p. 16, note 24.

39. Aubert, *op. cit.*, pp. 395, 403–404.

40. *Ibidem*, pp. 393–96. Our treatment of Gardeil is based largely on his article in the *DTC* and the commentary of Aubert.

41. J. St. Harent, "Foi," *DTC*, VI, p. 2203.

42. *Ibidem*, pp. 2211–12, 2221–23.

43. *Ibidem*, pp. 2223 ff. *Cf.* also, Aubert, *op. cit.*, pp. 397 ff. Aubert shows that Gardeil was trying to avoid the "extrinsèque" label which the Blondelians hurled at him. Gardeil attempts, in a painfully elaborate way, to analyze the act of faith as St. Thomas had done with the *actus humanus*. This appears in pp. 2205–2206, and was upsetting and pedantic to the Blondelians. Gardeil, however, was attempting to compromise, and thought the Blondelians were sacrificing the "gratuity of grace and the supernatural order."

44. Aubert, *op. cit.*, p. 401; Gardeil, "Crédibilité," pp. 2221 ff. This second step has been traditionally referred to as *actus credentitatis.*

45. *Ibidem*, pp. 404–405.

46. Gardeil, "Crédibilité," p. 2226.

47. Aubert, p. 407; Gardeil, "Crédibilité," pp. 2221–22.

48. *Ibidem.*

49. *Ibidem.*

50. *Ibidem*, p. 418.

51. *Ibidem*, pp. 122–24.

52. *Ibidem*, p. 434. B. de Sailly, *Comment réaliser l'apologétique intégral?* (Paris, 1913). This is a pseudonym of Blondel, a fact which Aubert apparently did not realize.

53. Weigel, "The Historical Background . . .," *Theological Studies*, XII (1951), 216.

54. Gardeil, "Crédibilité," p. 2308. Gardeil, it should be noted, was opposed to the separation of apologetics from the tract *De Fide*, which took place in the nineteenth century. *Cf.* p. 2298.

55. *Cf.* Aubert, *op. cit.*, p. 234.

56. J. Coppens, "Un Essai de synthèse apologétique," *Ephemerides Theologicae Louvanienses*, IV (1937), 447–66. Here 453.

57. *Ibidem*, p. 453.

58. *Ibidem*, p. 457.

59. *Ibidem*, pp. 448–49.

60. *Ibidem*, pp. 457, 464.

61. This partially explains the popularity of the vast number of the lives of Christ offered by Ricciotti, Lagrange, Lebreton, Fouard, Grandmaison, and numerous others. I do not question their value in counteracting the attacks on the historical Christ and their capacity to inspire, but they were not an apologetic for the unbeliever. *Cf.* the apologetic of Eugene Joly, *What Is Faith?* trans. Illtyd Trethowan (New York: Deus Books, 1963), pp. 19–31; Karl Adam, *The Christ of Faith*, trans. Joyce Crick (New York: Mentor-Omega, 1962), pp. xviii and 31–32. Adam does not offer this as an apologetic for the unbeliever, but we cite this work for its description of the ethical character of Christ, most useful in the type of apologetics herein discussed. Adam has made use of modern theological insights in his apologetic, but the person of Christ would not be a primary place of encounter for the modern unbeliever.

62. *Cf.* Avery Dulles, *Apologetics and the Biblical Christ* (Westminster, Md.: The Newman Press, 1964), especially chapters I–III. *Cf.* McNamara, *op. cit.*, pp. 297 ff. *Cf.* Latourelle, *op. cit.*, p. 434 and F. Taymans d'Epeymon, "Le Miracle, signe du sûrnaturel," *Revue Théologique*, LXXVII (1955), 225–45.

63. *Cf.* Joseph C. Fenton, "The Case for Traditional Apologetics," *American Ecclesiastical Review*, CXLI (1959), 406–416. *Cf.* Thomas Pater, book review of *Apologetics and the Biblical Christ*, in *American Ecclesiastical Review*, CL (1964), 453.

64. Max Scheler, *On the Eternal in Man*, trans. Bernard Noble (London: SCM Press, 1960), p. 276.

65. Maurice Blondel, *The Letter on Apologetics and History and Dogma*, trans. Alexander Dru and Illtyd Trethowan (New York: Harper & Row, Publishers, 1964), pp. 129–30.

66. John Henry Newman, *The Grammar of Assent* (New York: Image Books, 1955), p. 319.

CHAPTER II

1. Aubert, *op. cit.*, pp. 518 ff. The efforts of Drey and Möhler had been largely neutralized during the reign of Pius IX. *Cf.* Vidler, *The Church in an Age of Revolution*, pp. 31–32. We will see under Blondel in a later chapter that he learned only after he had finished school of the efforts of the Möhler and Tübingen School. *Cf.* Bochenski, *op. cit.*, pp. 140–53. Bochenski gives a good treatment of the phenomenological method on pp. 135–39. *Cf.* also, Macquarrie, *Twentieth Century Religious Thought*, pp. 218–23. For an extensive treatment of both the method and its application to faith, *cf.* Raymond Vancourt, *La Phénoménologie de la foi* (Paris, n.p., 1953). An elaborate treatment of the precise breakthrough of phenomenology in the area of theology (without an historical elaboration) is contained in E. Masure, *Le Signe* (Paris: Bloud and Gay, 1953).

2. Numerous authors list Max Scheler as a disciple of Edmund Husserl. Quentin Lauer, S.J., is perhaps more accurate in calling him a "younger contemporary," since Scheler was too old to be classified as a disciple of Husserl. *Cf.* Lauer, "Four Phenomenologists," *Thought*, XXXIII (1958–1959), 184.

3. The complete explanation of Scheler's method is contained in his classic *Der Formalismus in der Ethik und die materiale Wertethik* (Bern: Francke Verlag, 1954). The work was first published in 1916. The application of Scheler's ideas to the religion-value area is contained in *Vom Ewigen im Menschen* (Bern: Francke Verlag, 1954). This work has been translated by Bernard Noble and is called *On the Eternal in Man* (London: SCM Press, 1960). It was first published in 1921, and the Francke Verlag text is a fourth edition. The position outlined here is based largely on Scheler's *Vom Ewigen*, and pp. 66–178 in *Der Formalismus*. In applications of the theory, we make use of other works of Scheler as well.

4. Bochenski, *op. cit.*, p. 153. For significance of phenomenology, *cf.* Alfred Schutz, "Max Scheler's Epistemology and Ethics," *The Review of Metaphysics*, IX (1957–1958), 306 ff.: "Neither a new science nor a substitute for philosophy, but . . . a particular attitude of spiritual vision. . . ." *Cf.* McCool, "Primacy of Intuition," pp. 57–73, for the modern development of phenomenology in theological circles. Also, a book review by the same author, *On the Eternal in Man*, in *The New Scholasticism*, XXXVII (1963), 91. *Cf.* John M. Oesterreicher, "Max Scheler and the Faith," *Thomist*, XIII (1950), 175–76. Footnote 102, p. 175, has additional important bibliography, especially Paul Ortegat, S.J., *Intuition et religion: le problème existentiale* (Louvain: Editions de L'Institut Supérieur, 1947), who calls Scheler's work "the most remarkable contribution to the religious problem by the phenomenological school." (p. 11) *Cf.* Lauer, *op. cit.*, p. 183 and Macquarrie, *Twentieth Century Religious Thought*, pp. 223–25.

5. Aubert, *op. cit.*, p. 519.

6. Louis A. Coser, *Introduction to Max Scheler's "Ressentiment,"* trans. William Holdheim (New York: Crowell-Collier Press, 1961), p. 7. This book was first published in 1912. Other sources for the details on Scheler's life are: "Max Scheler," *Lexikon für Theologie und Kirche*, IX (Freiburg: Herder, 1964), 383 ff.; John M. Oesterreicher, *op cit.*, pp.

135–203. This article later appeared in the book, *Walls Are Crumbling* (New York: The Devin-Adair Co., 1952), pp. 135–98; Marius Schneider, *Max Scheler's Phenomenological Philosophy of Values* (unpublished doctoral dissertation, Catholic University of America, Washington, D.C., 1951), pp. 9 ff. The classic and personal study of Scheler's life and its relationship to his thought is in Dietrich von Hildebrand, "Max Scheler als Persönlichkeit," *Zeitliches im Lichte des Ewigen* (Regensburg: Habbel, 1932), pp. 368 ff. Also a recent work, Manfred Frings, *Max Scheler: A Concise Introduction into the World of a Great Thinker* (Pittsburgh: Duquesne University Press, 1965), pp. 11 ff.

7. Schneider, *op. cit.*, p. 13. For reflections on his personality and his capacity to discuss and impress, *cf.* von Hildebrand, *op. cit.*, pp. 368–69; Oesterreicher, *op. cit.*, p. 139; Erich Przywara, *Religionsbegrundung: Max Scheler—J. H. Newman* (Freiburg: Herder, 1932), p. xiii.

8. Coser, *op. cit.*, p. 7.

9. A good description of Scheler's break with the Church is given in Oesterreicher's article, *op. cit.*, pp. 197–203. Here the treatment is both plausible and sympathetic. Oesterreicher points out the growth of a kind of *ressentiment* in Scheler that led him to build a system around his marital disappointment. Ironically, this was the very quality which Scheler had attacked in its extreme form in the thought of Nietzsche (developed in *Ressentiment.*) Oesterreicher traces the loss of faith in some measure to temperamental weaknesses. For a less sympathetic treatment, *cf.* Schneider, *op. cit.*, pp. 13–14. Both Schneider and Oesterreicher seem to borrow from von Hildebrand, pp. 353 ff. Some authors emphasize rather certain lacunae in Scheler's early thought as permitting the turning away from a personal God and his defection from the Church. This would seem to be the logical conclusion of the efforts of Marius Schneider. *Cf.* also, Richard Acworth, book review *On the Eternal in Man*, in *Heythrop Journal*, II (1961), pp. 367–69. Currently, a doctoral candidate in philosophy at Columbia University, Peter Spader, to whom I am indebted for help with Max Scheler, is attempting to show that there was an actual progression in Scheler's thought, and a definite connection between the thought in his early and late periods. This is the view of Frings, *op. cit.*, pp. 166 ff. My own judgment is that somewhere in the middle lies the balance. There is evidence in *Ressentiment*, especially pp. 156–57 and 159 ff., that Scheler was overwhelmed with the vital forces that interfered with the life of the spirit, and the need for the preservation of a kind of "estate" system to tone down man's personal search for mastery and conquest. Hence, when we read in *The Nature of Man*, e.g., pp. 9, 55, 71, that the highest spiritual powers derive their energy by a repression of the lower drives, it is not a completely new thought. *Cf.* Frings, *op. cit.*, pp. 28, 196 ff., 166 ff.

10. Max Scheler, *The Nature of Man*, trans. H. Meyerhof (Boston: Beacon Press, 1961), pp. 91–92.

11. Oesterreicher, *op. cit.*, p. 202.

12. Aubert, *op. cit.*, pp. 569–70, discusses Erich Przywara's insistence that Newman was a better vehicle for a "theory of religious knowledge and faith" than was Max Scheler. It is hard to dispute Przywara's assertion when it comes to any complete theory given in an orderly fashion: "So ist das . . . *System Newmans die Erfüllung dessen worauf Schelers Person-Liebe*

System eigentlich zielt, ohne es infolge seiner systematischen Vereinseitigung und Verschalung in seinen klaren Linien zu fassen." Religionsbegrundung, p. 160.

Probably a more accurate reason for the neglect of Scheler is offered by Frings, *op. cit.,* pp. 11 ff. The works of Scheler were suppressed by the Nazis in 1933, and it was only in 1945 that his works became available. Frings also insists that the untimely death of Scheler and the unfinished quality of his works delayed his reception. Actually, even in German the works have been slow to appear. Only six volumes of the German Collected Edition have been published by Francke Verlag in Bern and Munich. Thirteen volumes is the proposed goal. In the English-speaking world, the most important works of Scheler—for an understanding of his complete philosophical thought—are not available. (Frings, *op. cit.,* p. 14) Finally, Scheler was such a versatile man that the student of his works finds himself rushing from sociology to philosophy, from theology to psychology and politics. At first blush, the work of Scheler appears hopelessly disordered. It is only later that a system begins to be discernible, and we discover that his dimension is never merely that of one discipline, but that of the whole man. Thus the work of Scheler has just begun, and Frings can call him "the most versatile and comprehensive thinker of contemporary philosophy." (Frings, *op. cit.,* p. 21)

13. Bochenski, *Contemporary European Philosophy,* p. 151. Frings, *op. cit.,* pp. 166 ff., would disagree, maintaining that this is the thinking of one who reads Scheler with a "fixed perspective." I find it hard to agree with him.

14. Lauer, *op. cit.,* p. 188, wherein he states that *On the Eternal in Man* contains the substance of Scheler's religious philosophy. *Cf.* also, Stark, Introduction to Scheler's *The Nature of Sympathy,* trans. Peter Heath (New Haven: Yale University Press, 1954), p. xiv.

15. Frings, *op. cit.,* pp. 26 ff. It does not appear to us that Frings gives enough importance to the effect that Scheler's private life had on this thought.

16. Scheler's efforts during the third period are largely metaphysical, and it does not seem that they will be of lasting concern. His phenomenology and theory of values are the areas which attract the modern student. Hence, we feel justified in stressing Scheler's middle period. It is our contention that his third period will continue to be of mere historical interest.

17. August Brunner, Introduction to *On the Eternal in Man,* p. 7. *Cf.* also, Eckhard Joseph Koehle, *Personality: A Study According to the Philosophy of Value and Spirit of Max Scheler and Nicolai Hartmann* (unpublished doctoral dissertation, Columbia University, New York, Arlington, Va.: Catholic Protectory Press, 1941), pp. 3 ff.

18. Oesterreicher, *op. cit.,* pp. 144, 164 ff. *Cf.* Yves de Montcheuil, *Mélanges Théologiques* (Paris: Aubier, 1946), p. 225, wherein he reveals the temperamental problems with which Scheler struggled. At the same time, Montcheuil is not unaware of the tremendous insights of Scheler, which were at times marred by his temperament. This also seems to be the thought of Przywara in *Religionsbegrundung.*

19. Brunner, *op. cit.,* p. 8: "[Neo-Kantianism] regarded knowledge as the formation by the categories of something given by the senses. According

to neo-Kantianism, a direct view of things that are spiritually given and which man meets with is not only impossible, but nonsense—contradicting the essential nature of knowledge." Kant was always Scheler's primary target. Cf. Schutz, *op. cit.*, p. 486.

20. Scheler, *On the Eternal in Man*, p. 60.

21. *Ibidem*, pp. 107–28, 130–60, 359–402. *Cf.* also, *Ressentiment*, Chap. V. In a kind of summary, on p. 59 of *On the Eternal in Man*, Scheler says: "All those numerous philosophies which modern man has cultivated and excogitated in evasion of the guilt growing within him—they will all have to be smashed in the process."

22. *Ibidem*, p. 120. "False belief in the inventive, creative or even revelatory power of need has led very many people today to the opinion that the Great War must of itself bring to birth a *new religion* or perhaps a new phase in the development of religion, as it were a miraculous . . . new Word in answer to the question of suffering humanity. . . ." Scheler insists that this could be more pride and egoism, and no ready disposition for revelation.

23. *Ibidem*, pp. 118–19. *Cf.* also, pp. 263 ff.

24. *On the Eternal in Man*, p. 263.

25. Macquarrie, *Twentieth Century Religious Thought*, pp. 75, 77.

26. *Ibidem*, p. 220. *Cf.* Brunner, *op. cit.*, p. 7.

27. *Ibidem*, p. 60.

28. Brunner, *op. cit.*, pp. 7–8. Scheler did not merely accept the methods of Husserl, but altered many of them. *Cf.* Frings, *op. cit.*, p. 24.

29. Bochenski, *op. cit.*, p. 152.

30. Schutz, *op. cit.*, p. 486; Koehle, *op. cit.*, pp. 1–4; Lauer, *op. cit.*, p. 185.

31. *Ressentiment*, p. 144; Coser, *op. cit.*, p. 12.

32. *On the Eternal in Man*, p. 117. This was the way of the pantheists, since the "[God of Pantheism] meekly complies with the veering currents of history." *Ibidem*, p. 180, wherein he discusses the common appearance of a man who has one way of thinking religiously and a totally different *Weltanschauung*. Here, as in his discussion of "need" as leading a man to faith, Scheler anticipates the thought of Dietrich Bonhoeffer (*cf. The Cost of Discipleship*, trans. R. H. Fuller [New York: Macmillan Paperback, 1963], pp. 45–60). We will discuss Bonhoeffer's views on religious need and "stopgap Christianity" in another place. *Cf.* also *Ressentiment*, pp. 12 and 144.

33. *Ressentiment*, p. 72, wherein Scheler discusses the reality of values in opposition to Nietzsche's thought. For an extended treatment, *cf. Der Formalismus*, Chap. II, pp. 63–130. *Cf.* Stark, *op. cit.*, p. xiv; H. Meyerhof, in the Introduction to *The Nature of Man*, pp. xvi, xix; Koehle, *op. cit.*, p. 17; Brunner, *op. cit.*, p. 8 (brief but excellent treatment) and Frings, *op. cit.*, pp. 617 ff.

34. *On the Eternal in Man*, pp. 74, 86, 88–89. Koehle, *op. cit.*, pp. 17–19, is very good on this point. *Cf. The Nature of Sympathy*, pp. 147 ff., for an extended treatment. Stark's Introduction to *The Nature of Sympathy* is excellent, especially p. xli. *Cf.* also, McCool, *op. cit.*, p. 89 and Lauer, *op.*

cit., p. 288. *Cf.* Meyerhof, *op. cit.*, p. xviii, wherein he singles out this point as one which "deserves special mention" as a "restatement of the Platonic-Augustinian view." *Cf.* Frings, *op. cit.*, pp. 49–50.

35. *Cf. Der Formalismus*, pp. 267–77, 341–55, and *On the Eternal in Man*, pp. 88–89. *Cf.* Aubert, *op. cit.*, pp. 518–19; Schutz, *op. cit.*, p. 306; Meyerhof, *op. cit.*, p. xvii. *Cf.* McCool, *The Primacy of Intuition*, p. 57, wherein he says: "Intuitive personal knowledge . . . is a rich, concrete awareness of the real, prior by nature to the judgment which merely explicates one or other of its aspects in the linking up of objective concepts." *"Anschauung"* (literally, "beholding" or "looking at") is the word used by Husserl and Scheler for the now commonly used word, "intuition." When he speaks of the intuition of values, Scheler uses numerous terms, such as *"Werterkenntnis," "Werteinsicht," "Werterfassung,"* and others. *Cf.* Koehle, *op. cit.*, p. 10 and Frings, *op. cit.*, pp.51 ff.

36. *On the Eternal in Man*, pp. 85–86 and Bochenski, *op. cit.*, pp. 143, 147. *Cf.* also, Schutz, *op. cit.*, pp. 306 and 486: "Values are to him a particular class of idea-objects which are objective, eternal, and immutable." *Cf.* also, Lauer, *op. cit.*, p. 185.

37. *Ibidem*, p. 173: "[In religious vision] . . . we are looking into a realm of being and value which is in basis and origin utterly different from the whole remaining empirical world. . . ." For the four classes of values, *cf. Der Formalismus*, pp. 125–30: 1) *Die Wertreihe des Angenehmen;* 2) *Die vitalen Werte;* 3) *Die geistigen Werte;* 4) *Die Werte des Heiligen. Cf.* Bochenski, *op. cit.*, pp. 140–46; Schutz, *op. cit.*, pp. 307, 313, 314, 491; Coser, *op. cit.*, p. 11. *Cf. Ressentiment*, p. 72, where Scheler upholds the hierarchy of values in opposition to Nietzsche. On p. 12, he insists that the weak, through *Ressentiment*, have rejected an objective scale of values to which they cannot submit. *Cf.* Frings, *op. cit.*, pp. 67 ff.

Since Scheler and Rudolph Otto were contemporaries it is hard to determine the degree of influence they had on one another. Otto's *Das Heilige* appeared in 1917. Scheler seems to deny any influence by Otto, on p. 15 of *On the Eternal in Man* (Preface to the second edition). His critique of Otto is a rejection of his "religious epistemology" while approving his descriptions of the "holy" as similar to Scheler's own. His strongest criticism of Otto accuses him of "falling into Schleiermacher's error" (p. 287) of denying the importance of religious dogmas and calling them "free-floating utterances and trial flights of expression of the numinous feeling." He also accuses him of laying disproportionate emphasis on emotion in the religious act." (*Ibidem*) We find Scheler's critique of Otto rather unfair, since Otto was largely concerned with the exaggerations that had led to such involved theorizing on dogmas that man lost the numinous sense in the process. Along the same lines we should call attention to development of Otto's thought in Mircea Eliade's *The Sacred and the Profane* (New York: Harper & Row, Publishers, 1961).

38. Meyerhof, *op. cit.*, p. xvi and Lauer, *op. cit.*, p. 185.

39. Schutz, *op. cit.*, p. xix and Stark, *op. cit.*, p. xvii.

40. *Cf. Ressentiment*, pp. 115–16. Bochenski, *op. cit.*, p. 146.

41. *On the Eternal in Man*, pp. 94, 125, 180–81. *Cf. Ressentiment*, pp. 152–74. *Cf.* Schutz, *op. cit.*, p. 494 and Stark, *op. cit.*, p. xiv.

42. *Cf.* Max Scheler, *Philosophic Perspectives*, trans. Oscar A. Haac (Boston: Beacon Press, 1958), p. 12. This work was published posthumously in 1929. *Cf.* also, *The Nature of Man*, pp. 40 and 62. *Cf.* Meyerhof, *op. cit.*, p. xx, wherein he describes the *"Realfaktoren"* as 1) material conditions, and 2) as biological drives, which "limit the range of idea possibilities that can be realized in any great historical situation."

43. Von Hildebrand discusses the "weakness of will" as Scheler's perennial problem (p. 350), his troubles with sex (p. 380), and the love for women which "became the deep tragedy of his life." (p. 382)

44. For the place of "humility" and "discipline" *cf. On the Eternal in Man*, p. 94. Coser points out his contributions to the sociological consideration of "functional analysis," *i.e.*, the influence of social institutions on man's personal struggle: (Quotes Robert K. Merton) "[He] conceives of the social structure as active, as producing fresh motivation which cannot be predicted on the basis of knowledge about man's drives." (pp. 24–25) *Cf.* Schutz, *op. cit.*, p. 305 and Brunner, *op. cit.*, p. 9, wherein he suggests that Scheler never resolved the problem presented in *The Nature of Man*. (*Cf. supra*, note 42.)

45. Schneider seems to think that Scheler's intellectual problems were never resolved. Oesterreicher would be inclined to class Scheler's struggle as the battle of the man influencing his thought. Oesterreicher's stand seems more realistic.

46. *On the Eternal in Man*, p. 269; *cf.* Brunner, *op. cit.*, p. 8.

47. *Ibidem*, pp. 85 ff.

48. *Ibidem*, pp. 107, 109 ff.

49. *Ibidem*, p. 12. Scheler is discussing here the notion of true repentance. The entire essay is quite remarkable. Repentance touches not merely a guilty action, but transforms our whole being. Our "being" must repent.

50. *Ibidem*, pp. 345 ff. Christianity is not a sacrifice of the intellect, but a discovery, really a rediscovery. *Cf. Ibidem*, pp. 113–15 and *Ressentiment*, pp. 130 ff.

51. *Ibidem*, pp. 107–108.

52. *Ibidem*, pp. 220, 287 ff. Also, p. 286, wherein he criticizes Rudolph Otto for maintaining that the Christian doctrines are "free floating utterances and trial flights at expression of numinous feeling."

53. *Ibidem*, p. 123.

54. *Ibidem*, p. 122.

55. *Ibidem*, p. 127.

56. *Ibidem*, p. 119.

57. *Ibidem*, pp. 332–56.

58. *Ibidem*, pp. 161–332.

59. *Ibidem*, pp. 258–59, 273–81. *Cf.* Aubert, *op. cit.*, pp. 518–19.

60. *Ibidem*, pp. 281 ff., wherein Scheler has a fine discussion of how the proofs came to be used.

61. *Ibidem*, pp. 297–99: "If we are to apply the principle that metaphysics and natural theology (not to mention religion itself) are

essentially different right down to the ultimate roots of theology, if accordingly we must reject the doctrine that the supreme bases of metaphysics are at the same time fundamentals of theology, we must be all the more careful to recognize that religion and theology *without* metaphysics would lack all those points of contact and communication with secular knowledge and practice that they require for their own subsistence." *Cf.* Stark, *op. cit.,* p. xx.

62. *Ibidem,* pp. 146–60. *Cf.* McCool, "Primacy of Intuition," pp. 58–66.

63. *Ibidem,* pp. 85–86. *Cf.* Frings, *op. cit.,* p. 159.

64. *Ibidem,* pp. 142, 164. Scheler sees metaphysics dealing with an *idea,* even though it is an idea of reality. He sees the pursuit of the "holy" through value-intuition as a journey toward a person who "opens." *Cf.* also, p. 85, where he says: "A man has first to learn in a more or less blind way to will and act rightly and well, objectively speaking, before he is in a position to see good *intuitively* as good and *intuitively* to will and actualize what is good. . . . There are always certain practical ways of life which, having taken the wrong course at some time in the past, draw *down* our sense of values and relative worth, and thereby lead us into blindness to values or illusions of value-perception." *Cf.* Stark, *op. cit.,* pp. xviii–xix and Acworth, *op. cit.,* p. 367.

65. *Ibidem,* pp. 273–74: "But is it not perverse to *employ* science to belittle our a-rational insight into nature, to remove from consideration its components' symbolic reference to God, and *then* to go on maintaining that God's existence can be inferred from purely objective, logical, causal arguments?" *Cf.* Stark, *op. cit.,* p. xvii: "Because the control of nature is its [intellect] aim, it tends to conceive all phenomena . . . as functions of a universal mechanism—for only in so far as the world resembles a mechanism can we dominate and exploit it for our own purposes." *Cf.* also, McCool, "Primacy of Intuition," p. 62.

66. This will become clearer from our discussion of the "religious act." *Cf.* Frings, *op. cit.,* pp. 149 ff.

67. Frengs, *op. cit.,* pp. 58, 63.

68. *On the Eternal in Man,* pp. 246–70.

69. *Ibidem,* p. 164. "If the metaphysical idea of the *ens a se* coincides in this way with the primary religious definition of the divine, it none the less remains true that the religious and metaphysical paths to knowledge are altogether different." *Cf.* Frings, pp. 68–69.

70. Bochenski, *op. cit.,* p. 153. *Cf.* also, Schneider, *op. cit.,* pp. 174 ff.

71. Carlos Cirne-Lima, *Personal Faith,* trans. G. Richard Dimler, S.J. (New York: Herder and Herder, Inc., 1965), Foreword by James Collins, wherein he gives credit to Max Scheler, p. 8. Cirne-Lima makes an important distinction between *intellectus* and *ratio* in St. Thomas: "Intellectus is that simple undivided knowledge of a single veritas, in which, however, there is revealed a content full of individual objects of knowledge. . . . Ratio, on the other hand, extends itself to many things. . . . Intellectus is the point of departure for ratio. . . . If we were to translate these words of St. Thomas into our technical language, they would read: Intuition is the starting-point as well as the goal of discursive, conceptual thought.

Intuition is that undivided simple kernel, that oneness in which many things are made manifest. Out of this intuition then arise by analysis . . . concepts, judgments and syllogisms. Conceptual knowledge is therefore nothing more than the unfolding of intuition." (pp. 103–104) *Cf.* also, the remarkable commentary on Cirne-Lima by McCool, "Primacy of Intuition," pp. 57–73, wherein he shows that the use of the "Thomistic" theory of knowledge which Scheler knew was actually the product of Cajetan, not true Thomism. *Cf.* p. 58. Also, Brunner, *op. cit.*, p. 8.

72. James Collins, Foreword to Cirne-Lima, p. 8. Collins gives exceptional credit to Scheler and shows how Karl Jaspers and Gabriel Marcel "worked upon this clue." *Cf.* Aubert, *op. cit.*, pp. 522–64, showing development after Scheler.

73. *On the Eternal in Man*, p. 16. Collins, *op. cit.*, p. 8, calls it the fact that "these thinkers guided their analyses by the actual human relationships presented by living believers." The emphasis was on "one's personal existence and in the interpersonal community of men."

74. *Cf.* Schneider, *op. cit.*, pp. 201, 203.

75. *Cf.* Stark, *op. cit.*, p. xii for influence of Brentano. *Cf.* Lauer, *op. cit.*, p. 185, wherein the author insists that Scheler had to "break through traditional cognitive functions to be rational but not Kantian or Scholastic." *Cf.* Aubert's treatment and the insistence that the "disciples" of Scheler recognized the need to add the "Augustinian dimension" to contemporary Scholasticism, *e.g.*, Otto Grundler, pp. 549 ff.; M. J. Hessen, pp. 561 ff; J. Engert, pp. 551 ff., who makes clear that Thomas himself "did not reduce faith to a purely rational knowledge"; K. Eschweiler, pp. 556 ff. These men had their differences with Scheler, as Aubert points out, but they recognized the scholasticism that Scheler was fighting. Marius Schneider seems to overlook the historical problem that Scheler was facing. Erich Przywara was aware of the same problem. *Cf.* his *Polarity*, trans. A. C. Bouquet (London: Oxford University Press, 1935), especially pp. 94–116. Thus Scheler's remarks (*On the Eternal in Man*, p. 16) had valid meaning, when he saw the beginning of a break from traditional cognitive forms: "There are also attendant signs that both Thomism and Kantianism, whose supremacy over whole insulated groups had until lately blocked the path to union, are being radically called into question . . . the ever growing interest of learned Catholic circles in the Platonic-Augustinian tradition of thought." (Scheler's Preface to the second German edition) Scheler was aware that "even in Aquinas there are far more numerous traces of concessions to the older trend of theology . . . than are admitted by modern Thomists." (p. 284) On p. 20 he shows his indebtedness to Eschweiler for showing the corruption of pure Thomism at the German universities.

76. *On the Eternal in Man*, pp. 107 ff., 284 ff.

77. *Ibidem*, pp. 109–128, 284 ff., 359 ff.

78. *Ibidem*, pp. 164 ff.

79. *Ibidem*, pp. 119 ff. This is an important passage in the light of Bonhoeffer's views on a "stop-gap Christianity." *Cf. Letters and Papers from Prison*, trans. R. H. Fuller (New York: Macmillan Paperback, 1965), especially pp. 190–201 and 208–210. Bonhoeffer was inveighing against a theology, or a religion, which relied on its problem-solving value. He well

said that "man has learned to cope with all questions of importance without recourse to God." (p. 195) He resents the "Christian apologetic" that tries to "prove to a world thus come of age that it cannot live without the tutelage of God." (*Ibidem*) He calls it an attack "by Christian apologetics on the adulthood of the world" since it tries to "demonstrate to secure, contented, happy mankind that it is really unhappy and desperate." (p. 196) He concludes (if notes of a condemned man can be "concluded") that "God should not be relegated to some last secret place, but that we should frankly recognize that the world and men have come of age, that we should not speak ill of man in his worldliness, but confront him with God at his strongest point." (p. 214) Bonhoeffer's views, certainly colored by his prison experience, are not totally clear. When we confront man "at his strongest point," do we not ultimately say that he "needs" God? Bonhoeffer was against a Christianity that brought a man to God only in view of death, which presumably he saw in prison. He was against a Christianity that did not want man to involve himself in the challenge of the world's progress. (p. 201) He does not seem to be opposed to a Christianity that showed man— in his strength—that Christ could give the real meaning to his life. If this is what Bonhoeffer meant (opinions on his meaning are diverse), we are in agreement. He hardly does justice to the thought of Paul Tillich, *Dynamics of Faith* (New York: Harper & Row, Publishers, 1958) pp. 197 ff., nor is his exegesis of Christ's attitude toward the weak and needy in any way probatory. (pp. 209–210) Scheler's point was different. He saw the advantage of "need" if Christianity could provide a needy man with answers. Thus, *On the Eternal in Man*, p. 119: "It is possible for the world's cry of need to hold great meaning only when it generates motion and activity in man's positive springs of religion, only when it brings our reason to act in renewed concentration on the idea of God and opens our mental eye to the positive benefits of revelation and grace which are already *present* in the world. . . . Need, the empty heart, the heartfelt want, can and should have this effect." Our speculations—later in this dissertation—will discuss this problem in modern perspective.

80. *Philosophical Perspectives*, p. 11: "The modern metaphysics is no longer cosmology and metaphysics of concrete objects, but *metanthropology* and metaphysics of *action*. . . . The only access to God is, therefore, not theoretical contemplation which tends to represent God as a concrete being, but personal and active commitment of man to God and to progressive self-realization." Cf. *On the Eternal in Man*, pp. 89 ff. Also, Bochenski, *op. cit.*, p. 143 and Frings, *op. cit.*, p. 28.

81. Scheler shows this with repentance on p. 63 of *On the Eternal in Man:* "I find that the deepest understanding of the meaning and significance of repentance is to be found in Christianity, and within Christianity, in the Catholic Church." As we will see, this part of Scheler's argument is somewhat weak and does not seem to be an important insight in his apologetic. Cf. also, Koehle, *op. cit.*, p. 131, and Scheler's assertion that the true idea of community is only within Christianity. We will discuss this also a bit later.

82. *On the Eternal in Man*, pp. 269, 399. Stark treats this extremely well, *op. cit.*, pp. xxii–xxiii. Cf. Frings, *op. cit.*, pp. 73 ff., pp. 153 ff.

83. *Ibidem*, pp. 267–68. Also, p. 27 and pp. 399 ff. It is hard not to mention here the similarity in Tillich's thought, *e.g.*, Paul Tillich, *op. cit.*,

Chap. I, where he develops the idea of the "ultimate concern." Tillich speaks of such idols as "ultimate concern with 'success' and with social standing and economic power. It is the god of many people in the highly competitive Western culture. . . . It demands unconditional surrender to its laws." (p. 3) With Tillich, too, there is no middle ground. A man must have an ultimate concern if he is to have faith, since "Faith is the state of being ultimately concerned. The content matters infinitely for the life of the believer, but it does not matter for the formal definition of faith." (p. 4) Tillich sees the possibility of a man not having "faith," since "if unconscious forces determine the mental status without a centered act, faith does not occur, and compulsions take its place." (p. 5) In principle, Scheler would seem to hold the same view about "compulsions," or "vital urges," as he called them. (*Cf. supra*, Chap. I, note 16, especially reference to *Ressentiment.*) Tillich acknowledges no debt to Scheler. In a summer course at Union Theological Seminary in 1965, I asked the Tillichian scholar, Heywood Thomas, if he thought Scheler had exerted direct influence on Tillich. He answered that he did not know, and that he himself was unaware of the work of Scheler.

84. *On the Eternal in Man*, p. 180.

85. *Ibidem*, p. 180. *Cf.* also, the Introduction to *Ressentiment* by Louis Coser, p. 12. Concerning "guilt" as an idol, *cf.* Stark, p. xxii. Also, *On the Eternal in Man*, pp. 60 ff.: "His own unrepented guilt, or that of his forefathers, takes on for modern man the outward form of a spectre in which his soul no longer recognizes itself. . . . The spectre demands whole, complex scientific theories for its 'explanation'."

86. "No doctrinal position—unless it wishes to surrender entirely—will be able to content itself with a mere wish to maintain its status quo; every such position will have to exert itself in addition to demonstrate positively to the world its overriding worth—and to be the warrant of its own truth." *On the Eternal in Man*, p. 121.

87. *Ibidem*, pp. 332 ff.

88. *Ibidem*, pp. 339–40, 344–45; pp. 373 ff. and p. 401. On the types of community, *cf.* Bochenski, *op. cit.*, p. 148. Also, Koehle, *op. cit.*, p. 95. *Ressentiment*, pp. 120–34.

89. *Ressentiment*, pp. 88–89; *On the Eternal in Man*, p. 180. Frings, *op. cit.*, pp. 81 ff., has a thorough development of *Ressentiment* as disturbing the true *ordo amoris*.

90. *On the Eternal in Man*, p. 268: ". . . the permanent self-delusion of putting a finite good (*e.g.*, the State, art, a woman, money, knowledge) in place of God, or of *treating* it 'as if' it were God."

91. *Cf.* Meyerhof, *op. cit.*, p. xix; Bochenski, *op. cit.*, p. 149.

92. *On the Eternal in Man*, p. 268. When Scheler speaks of the "spontaneous quest of its proper object," he did not intend to confuse the insights of "faith" and "intuition." In the Preface to the second German edition, he cites the objections of the critics, and insists that "the author was and remains clearly conscious of having strictly distinguished on all occasions between what rests in his theses on essential *insight* and what is matter of positive faith." (p. 17) Some called his system a "common whore," since he pressed phenomenology "into the service of the apologetics of a positive

Church and its dogma." (p. 18) Scheler agrees that his method may well be a "common whore," but not because it confuses faith with reason, but rather because it is a method of "reducing given religious and metaphysical systems . . . to their *original empirical contents, i.e.,* of *reconstructing* and re-intuiting the basis of what appears in them as matured, developed, rationalized, ossified—thereby revitalizing its *original meaning* and restoring its perceptual validity for today—*this*, as the method used in the descriptive study W*eltanschauungen*, is in fact a 'common whore'." (p. 18) He rejects the labor of "ontologist" or "fideist" (p. 20), and says that the German neo-Thomists accuse him of belittling "spontaneous reason as a source of knowledge," while the Protestants object that he leans too heavily on "natural theology" and he has "allotted metaphysics much too important a place in the book." (p. 21) Scheler insists that his method is valid because it relies on experience and self-evidence, while it is "constituted by the fact that an intentional object, whether entity or value, is clear to the mind in its essential *thus*ness . . . when there is an utter *congruence* among the contents of all noetic acts which are possible in reference to that object." (pp. 22–23) This seems close to the Aristotelian principle of evidence as the *fulgor veritatis*.

93. *On the Eternal in Man*, p. 273. McCool, "Primacy of Intuition," p. 62: "The dominance of the mathematical and natural sciences, however, has produced in the modern mind an ideal of objective and impersonal knowledge which looks upon faith as an uncertain and provisional form of knowledge which is destined to make way for the apodictic certitude of science. . . . Yet science, it must be admitted, owes its perfection to the ontological poverty of its object. The realms of being above the purely material, the undetermined richness of human liberty and the unrepeatable unicity of the historical event cannot be expressed in the categories of necessity and universality which have been drawn from the world of inorganic matter. . . . If the human being is aware of the presence in his consciousness of other, higher realms of being, it must mean that in some inobjective, not directly conceptualizable way, they have been grasped together with the objective aspects of an experience."

94. *On the Eternal in Man*, pp. 107 ff. *Ressentiment*, pp. 153, 165. Man becomes a prisoner when society replaces community.

95. *Ibidem*, pp. 340–41, 368–73.

96. *Ibidem*, pp. 368–72.

97. *Ibidem*, pp. 107 ff.

98. *Ibidem*, p. 331.

99. *Ibidem*, pp. 373 ff. *Ressentiment*, pp. 108, 115–16, 174: "If we consider the transvaluation of the relation between tool and organ in its totality, we must conclude that the spirit of modern civilization does not constitute 'progress' . . . but a decline in the *evolution* of mankind."

100. *Ressentiment*, p. 152.

101. *Ibidem*, p. 153.

102. *Ibidem*, p. 159. Similarity with the thought of Max Weber, *The Protestant Ethic and the Spirit of Capitalism* (New York: Charles Scribner's Sons, 1948), is apparent.

103. *Ibidem*, pp. 56, 159. Actually, Scheler wanted to retain the "estates."

104. *On the Eternal in Man, cf.* footnote, p. 270.

105. *Ibidem*, p. 95. *Cf.* Lauer, *op. cit.*, p. 187.

106. *Nature of Sympathy*, p. 168; Stark, *op. cit.*, p. xix; Lauer, *op. cit.*, p. 187; McCool, *op. cit.*, pp. 63–64: "The highest dimension of earthly being, unique, free, personal reality, can only be touched in such a comprehension of another person. Such knowledge is intuitive; it is not the general law of a world of objects . . . it is the presence of a single, subjective whole, the free person in his uniqueness." Bochenski, *op. cit.*, p. 150: "When we analyze our love for a person it becomes apparent that the sum of values attached to the beloved person can never come near to accounting for that love . . . there always remains an unaccountable . . . the concrete person of the beloved." *Cf.* Frings, *op. cit.*, pp. 50 ff., 67–70.

107. *On the Eternal in Man*, p. 335.

108. *Ibidem*, pp. 164, 308 (note 2), 334, and the need for personal witnesses within the community, pp. 340–48.

109. *Cf.* Bochenski, *op. cit.*, pp. 150–51; *On the Eternal in Man*, p. 266.

110. *Cf. Ressentiment*, p. 99, wherein the person refuses to allow his acts to be mere reactions. *Ibidem*, p. 141. *Cf. On the Eternal in Man*, pp. 58, 377: "We should feel ourselves truly co-responsible in all guilt." *Cf.* Koehle, *op. cit.*, pp. 112, 132; Schutz, *op. cit.*, p. 501.

111. *On the Eternal in Man*, pp. 368–71; *Ressentiment*, pp. 115–16.

112. *Ibidem*, pp. 85, 286.

113. Lauer, *op. cit.*, p. 187.

114. *Ressentiment*, pp. 172–73.

115. *On the Eternal in Man*, p. 95.

116. *Cf.* Chap. I, note 16. Also, *On the Eternal in Man*, p. 95; Schneider, *op. cit.*, pp. 9 ff. *Ressentiment*, pp. 103 ff., wherein he discusses the true and false asceticism. Meyerhof, *op. cit.*, p. xxi.

117. *On the Eternal in Man*, p. 107. *Cf.* similarity with Tillich, *op. cit.*, pp. 5 ff. and "faith as a personal and centered act." *Cf.* Koehle, *op. cit.*, p. 72.

118. *Ibidem*, pp. 246–47, 275–76. *Cf.* Aubert and the discussions following the impact of Scheler, *op. cit.*, pp. 561 ff. Even Przywara did not accuse Scheler of sentimentality.

119. This was what he criticized in Schleiermacher and even in Otto.

120. *On the Eternal in Man*, pp. 268–69. *Cf.* also, Stark, *op. cit.*, p. xxi. Scheler did not deny the reality and importance of lesser values, but insisted that man could not be satisfied ontologically without seeking out the "holy."

121. *Ibidem*, p. 168. Scheler would not deny that there is an evolution of values historically, and that man is conditioned by his society. His quarrel is with those who stop short of the holy, or make some lesser value their holy. See Frings, *op. cit.*, p. 45, where Scheler is seen to have viewed man far more optimistically than his contemporaries. Scheler's attack on idols and his

refusal to allow man to rest at false absolutes was the result of his appreciation of the human depths, not a mere negative criticism of man's weakness. *Cf. Ibidem*, pp. 57 ff., for a discussion of Scheler's awareness that the pursuit of the holy takes place within the "background of a historically changing content of the sphere of the absolute."

122. Bochenski, *op. cit.*, p. 149. *Cf.* Stark, *op. cit.*, p. xxxi: "He realized that in the 13th century the cosmological proof was by no means so unconvincing as it is today. Today the creatureliness of the creature, which is the foundation of the whole argument, is not admitted."

123. *On the Eternal in Man*, pp. 16, 260; Brunner, *op. cit.*, p. 13; Acworth, *op. cit.*, p. 367.

124. *Ibidem*, p. 147 (p. 143 in German edition): "*Alles religiöse Wissen um Gott ist ein Wissen auch durch Gott im Sinne der Art der Empfängnis des Wissen selber.*" *Cf.* Bochenski, *op. cit.*, p. 149.

125. *On the Eternal in Man*, p. 268.

126. *Ibidem*, p. 250. *Cf.* Frings, *op. cit.*, pp. 156 ff.

127. *Ibidem*; *cf.* John Courtney Murray, *The Problem of God* (New Haven: Yale University Press, 1963), pp. 95–97. *Cf.* also, Ignace Lepp, *Atheism in Our Times*, trans. Bernard Murchland (New York: The Macmillan Company, 1964), pp. 97–107.

128. *Ibidem*, p. 251.

129. *Ibidem*, pp. 252–53.

130. *Ibidem*, pp. 253–54, 335; Stark, *op. cit.*, p. xix; Bochenski, *op. cit.*, p. 149.

131. *Ibidem*, p. 254.

132. *Ibidem*, p. 254.

133. *Ibidem*, p. 253.

134. *Ibidem*, p. 263.

135. *Ibidem*, p. 17.

136. *Cf. supra*, note 93.

137. Karl Rahner, *Nature and Grace*, trans. Dinah Wharton (New York: Sheed & Ward, 1963), p. 114. *Cf.* also, *Theological Investigation*, I, trans. Cornelius Ernst, O.P. (Baltimore: Helicon Press, Inc., 1961), pp. 297 ff. Rahner gives a brief historical background and a good bibliography.

138. *Ibidem*, pp. 115–16.

139. *Ibidem*, p. 118.

140. *Ibidem*, p. 119.

141. *Ibidem*, p. 120.

142. *Ibidem*, p. 122.

143. *Ibidem*, p. 124.

144. *Ibidem*.

145. *Ibidem*, p. 127.

146. *Ibidem*.

147. *Ibidem*, p. 129.

148. *Ibidem*, p. 133.

149. *Ibidem*, p. 132.
150. *Ibidem*, p. 134.
151. *Ibidem*, p. 139.
152. *Ibidem*, p. 140.
153. We do not presume to treat the long controversy leading to Rahner's supernatural existential, but one of the key works in the growing awareness of the danger of viewing grace as something "extrinsic" to man in an effort to safeguard the gratuity of God's gift is De Lubac's *Sûrnaturelle: Études Historiques* (Paris: n.p., 1946). Rahner gives a list of articles discussing the work of De Lubac on pp. 147–49 in *Nature and Grace*. Most authors are aware that De Lubac's point is well taken, but many think that he has gone too far in avoiding the "extrinsicist" view, and has actually threatened the gratuity of grace. Among such criticism, *cf.* C. Vollert, review of De Lubac's *Sûrnaturelle, Theological Studies*, XIII (1947–49), 288–93, wherein he shows De Lubac's position to be that of a gradual theological evolution, whereby the natural order came to mean a closed order. De Lubac shows that this was not the case with the Fathers, who were not afraid to see an exigency for grace on man's part. Vollert asks De Lubac what this desire is. An act? An instinct? He goes on to say that De Lubac does not give adequate patristic evidence, nor does he do justice to the "obediential potency" in St. Thomas. (For more, on this point, *cf.* H. Rondet, "Nature et sûrnatural dans la théologie de St. Thomas D'Aquin," *RSR*, XXXVI [1947], 379–95.) P. J. Donnelly, "Current Theology . . . on the Supernatural," *Theological Studies*, VIII (1947), 483–91, criticizes De Lubac, insisting that no theologian ever held "pure nature" as anything more than a possible hypothesis. He says that Malvez refutes De Lubac's argument from the Fathers, since they were dealing with concrete man and weren't concerned with the order of essences. Donnelly says that most theologians hold that a state of pure nature with a natural destiny is entirely possible. (p. 489) In another article, "Discussion on the Supernatural Order," *Theological Studies*, IX (1948), 213–49, Donnelly lists other critics of De Lubac: a) de Blick, who points out that revelation does not tell us whether spirit *qua* spirit or spirit as grace produces the germ within man that responds to the call of God. In other words, De Lubac is asserting more than revelation can itself establish. Our own thought would be that this depends on our interpretation of spirit. To discuss this question would take us too far afield. b) Bouyer says that De Lubac is not rejecting "pure nature," but a nature not elevated. Bouyer sees "pure nature" as going back to the Fathers and is in St. Thomas. c) Donnelly's own criticism wonders if De Lubac ultimately preserves the real liberty of choice in God, or ends up with some kind of spontaneity only questionably free.

It will appear in our treatment of Blondel, whom De Lubac favored strongly, that later in his life Blondel was forced to admit that he had been mistaken in ignoring the theological concept of "pure nature." When Blondel spoke of nature, he was dealing with the observable man, and he was bypassing the question of the gratuity of grace. Rahner's viewpoint, offered here, provides a solution to the problem. Another point of view, attempting to resolve the same question, is offered by E. Schillebeeckx, "L'Instinct de la foi selon St. Thomas d'Aquin," *NRT* (1964), 377–407, in which he criticizes the view of M. Seckler's views on the *"instinctus fidei."* It is hard for me to see how Schillebeeckx differs fundamentally from Rahner. But our point here, in this long note, is to show that Max Scheler anticipated a problem that was by no means resolved in theological history. Today, Scheler can be heard more favorably after the theological debates. This will be true also of Blondel, who was criticized for his denial of the gratuity of grace. Blondel's point of view, defended as we shall see by Bouillard, is intelligible today in the light of modern developments. In his own day, as with Scheler, it was hard to take seriously his treatment of man's need of God, since it seemed to endanger the gratuity of grace. For a splendid article stressing the history of the vitalist approach in theology and the obstacles to its growth, *cf.* Weigel, "The Historical Background of the Encyclical *Humani Generis,*" *Theological Studies,* XII (1951), 208–32.

154. Collins, *op. cit.,* p. 8.

155. *On the Eternal in Man,* p. 61. As we shall see in Chap. IV, this is similar to Newman's argument for the existence of a personal God in the voice of conscience. Scheler was familiar with much of Newman's work.

156. *Ibidem,* pp. 284–90.

157. *Ibidem,* pp. 15–31, Preface to the second edition.

158. Collins, *op. cit.,* pp. 8–9.

159. *On the Eternal in Man,* p. 264.

160. *Ibidem,* p. 265.

161. *Ibidem.*

162. *Ibidem,* p. 266.

163. *Ibidem,* pp. 275, 281.

164. Schneider, *op. cit.,* pp. 196 ff.

165. *Ibidem,* p. 107.

166. *Ibidem,* p. 124.

167. *Ibidem,* pp. 168–69.

168. *Ibidem,* pp. 180, 162: "In view of the essentially *social* nature of religion, another discipline which must be accepted into the essential phenomenology of religion is the study of the *essential forms of sociological structure* taken by communities to whom revelation is proclaimed as collective revelation." Koehle, *op. cit.,* pp. 129 ff. *Cf. Der Formalismus,* pp. 523–62.

169. *On the Eternal in Man,* p. 180.

170. *Ibidem,* p. 381.

171. *Ibidem,* pp. 382–84.

172. *Ibidem,* pp. 28, 383. *Cf.* also, Koehle, *op. cit.,* pp. 130–31.

173. *Ibidem,* p. 134.

174. Koehle, *op. cit.,* p. 121.

175. *Ibidem,* p. 122, a paraphrase of *Der Formalismus,* pp. 586–588.

176. *On the Eternal in Man,* p. 71.

177. *Ibidem,* p. 341.

178. *Ibidem,* p. 162.

179. *Cf. supra,* Chap. I, note 5.

180. *On the Eternal in Man,* pp. 135, 341.

181. *Cf.* Preface to *On the Eternal in Man*, second edition.

182. Koehle, *op. cit.*, pp. 121 ff., gives an excellent summary of this matter from *Der Formalismus*. *Cf. Der Formalismus*, pp. 584–96. *Cf.* also, *Schriften aus dem Nachlass*, I (Bern: Francke Verlag, 1957), 288 ff.

183. *On the Eternal in Man*, p. 273. *Cf.* Frings, *op. cit.*, p. 43, where he says that Scheler's tendency to stress the purification of the spirit sought to achieve a "devotion to the world."

184. *Ibidem*, pp. 326, 331.

185. *Ibidem*, pp. 325–26.

186. *Ibidem*, p. 125.

187. *Ressentiment*, pp. 121–22.

188. *On the Eternal in Man*, p. 245.

CHAPTER III

1. Aubert, *op. cit.*, p. 266.

2. Maurice Blondel, *L'Action, Essai d'une critique de la vie et d'une science de la pratique.* (Thèse presentée à la Faculté des lettres de Paris.) (Paris: Ancienne Librairie Germer Baillière et Cie, 1893), p. 396. There are two works by Blondel entitled *L'Action*, one a single volume written as his doctoral thesis in 1893. This is the volume that concerns us here. The other *L'Action*, a two-volume work, appeared in 1937. The latter is far more than a revision of the first *L'Action*. Henri Bouillard, *Blondel et le Christianisme* (Paris: Editions du Seuil), p. 173, calls the first *L'Action* a phenomenology and the second an ontology. The second *L'Action* attempted to resolve metaphysical problems aroused by the first, and was part of a trilogy which will be mentioned later.

3. Aubert, *op. cit.*, pp. 279, 289.

4. Dru, in Alexander Dru and Illtyd Trethowan, Introduction to Blondel's *Letter on Apologetics and History and Dogma* (New York: Holt, Rinehart and Winston, Inc., 1964), pp. 34–35. This hundred-page Introduction is the best single source we found in English in helping to uncover the mind of Blondel.

5. *Ibidem*, pp. 35–36.

6. Henri Bouillard, "The Thought of Maurice Blondel: A Synoptic Vision," *International Philosophical Quarterly*, III (1963), 392.

7. *Ibidem*.

8. Dru, in *Letter*. *Cf.* also, Jean-Paul Gélinas, "*La Restauration du Thomisme sous Léon XIII et les philosophies nouvelles*," (an unpublished doctoral dissertation, Catholic University of America, Washington, D.C., 1959), p. 51. *Cf.* also, Blondel's *Lettres Philosophiques* (Paris: Aubier, 1961), pp. 72–73.

9. Gélinas, p. 37.

10. Bouillard, "The Thought of . . . ," p. 399. Dru, *Letter*, pp. 38–39, erroneously states a professorship in 1894. Actually, not until 1897. *Cf.* Bouillard, *Blondel*, p. 30. *Cf.* also, the interesting comment of Valensin in *Maurice Blondel* (Paris: Librairie Lecoffre, 1934), p. 8, wherein he says that the study of "Leibnitz, Descartes, Spinoza, St. Augustine, and Ollé-

Laprune" were *"ne lui ont sans doute jamais été qu'un prétexte . . . de mettre en valeur ses propres idées."*

11. Maurice Blondel, *Les Premiers Écrits* (Paris: Presse Universitaire, 1956), p. 114: *"L'Action et L'idée de l'action sont hétérogènes et irréductibles."* Dru, *Letter*, pp. 40–43.

12. Dru, *Letter*, pp. 40–41, where he quotes from Blondel's *Une Soutenance de Thèse*, the first volume of *Études Blondéliennes* (Paris: Presse Universitaire, 1951). Cf. also, Frederick Scott, S.J., "William James and Maurice Blondel," *New Scholasticism*, XXXII (1958), 32–44.

13. Cf. *Une Soutenance de Thèse*, p. 88. Translation from Dru, p. 41, and improved by the author with recourse to the original.

14. Maurice Blondel, *Carnets Intimes, 1883–1894* (Paris: Editions du Cerf, 1961), Vol. I, p. 526. This is a kind of diary Blondel kept from 1883 to 1894.

15. Bouillard, "The Thought of . . .," p. 392. Cf. Bouillard, *Blondel et le Christianisme*, pp. 16–17.

16. *L'Action*, pp. xxi, xxii.

17. *Maurice Blondel et Auguste Valensin: Correspondence*, Vol. II (Paris: Aubier, 1957), 174. Blondel had directed Valensin to the religious life, and their growing friendship is both interesting and enviable to recall.

18. Aubert, *op. cit.*, pp. 277–82. Blondel, *Carnets Intimes*, Vol. II, p. 86. Cf. also, Dru, *Letter* and Blondel, *Les Prémiers Ecrits*, the section entitled "L'Illusion idéalist," pp. 97–122.

19. Blondel, *Carnets Intimes*, Vol. II, p. 526. Translation from Dru, p. 45.

20. *Lettres Philosophiques*, p. 10. Translation ours.

21. *Ibidem*, pp. 12–13.

22. Cf. *Carnets Intimes*, Vol. I, pp. 23–24, 496. The translation used here is that of Dru on p. 37 of *Letter*.

23. Bouillard, *Blondel*, p. 277. Cf. Dru, *Letter*, p. 45, recording Blondel's comment regarding his future wife: "I never dreamed that someone could love me. A wonderful discovery. . . ."

24. *L'Action*, p. ix. Cf. also, *Letter*, pp. 37 ff.

25. *Ibidem*, pp. 6 ff. Cf. "Une Dialectique de la conversion: L'Action de Maurice Blondel," *Revue Philosophique de Louvain*, LVII (1959), 550.

26. *Ibidem*, p. x.

27. *Ibidem*, p. xii.

28. *Ibidem*, pp. ix, xvi.

29. *Lettres Philosophiques*, pp. 16–17.

30. *L'Action*, pp. viii, ix. Page xxi, where Blondel demands that we enter into every way of life with these bold words: *"Il faut, au contraire, accueillir toutes les négations qui s'entre-détruisent, comme s'ils étaient légitimés; dans toutes les erreurs, comme si elles étaient sincères; dans toutes les passions, comme si elles avaient la générosité dont elles se vantent; dans tous les systèms philosophiques, comme si chacun étreignait l'infinie verité qu'il pense accaparer."* This was a long way, as we shall see, from the plans of the early neo-Scholastics, and the extreme anti-Modernists.

31. Maurice Blondel, *La Semaine Sociale de Bordeaux et le Monophorisme* (Paris: Bloud and Gay, 1910), originally published in a series of articles in *Annales de Philosophie Chrétienne*, 1909–1910, p. 103. The translation is that offered by Dru, "From the Action Française to the Second Vatican Council," *Downside Review*, LXXXI (1963), 245. The Semaines Sociales was the name of a "sort of perambulating, yearly university for the study of social questions." *Cf. Letter*, p. 39. One of the founders, Adéodat Boissard, was a relative of Blondel's wife, and Henri Lorin, a former president and active supporter of the group, admired Blondel's thought enthusiastically. For these reasons, Blondel's criticisms of veterism in the Church, which were written at the request of Henri Lorin, took the name of *La Semaine Sociale de Bordeaux*. Blondel was very much concerned with the need for the type of social action which the Semaine Sociale undertook. The specific form of Blondel's attack on veterism in the Church will become clearer in our development.

32. *Ibidem*, pp. 162 ff. As we shall see later in our development, this was an extremely sensitive area with Blondel. He was more patient with the Church's authoritarianism than was Laberthonnière (*cf.* Dru, *Letter*, pp. 67–79), and was willing to recognize progress with the condemnation of Action Française (*cf.* below) and a more liberal attitude after the death of Pius X. Yet, he continually fought the Church's policy of ultramontanism, integrism, or monophorism (words used indiscriminately and called by Blondel, "rigid thought without entrails, without openness, without movement, without suspicion of anything within itself, conceited, intolerant, and despotic." [A. Cartier, "Le Philosophie de L'Action," in *Archives de Philosophie*, XXIV (1961), 20.] This quotation is from Blondel's *L'illusion idéaliste*.) and saw the root of the problem in the shackle that bound revelation to an intellectualist Scholasticism. As long as the Christian thinker was governed by closed categories of thought, the social policy of the Church would be tied to whatever institutions, however compromising, that gave it security. This is ultimately why Blondel, though inclined to social works, fought at the level of the intellect. *Cf. Carnets Intimes*, Vol. I, pp. 23–24. He saw truth as a dynamic growth, and not as a static category. He was pained by the Church's denial of human liberty and the exaggerated view of human malice. He touches upon this idea in many places, but perhaps most thoroughly in *La Semaine Sociale*. His essay on *History and Dogma* shows the same danger in an exclusively historical approach to religion, whereby revelation can be intellectually conceived as independent of its contemporary recipients, and its dynamic growth (follows the *Letter on Apologetics* in the 1964 English translation), pp. 211–87.

33. *Lettres Philosophiques*, pp. 30–31. Letter to Gabriel Seailles.

34. *Ibidem*, p. 20. Letter to A. Maurice Lena, Professor of Rhetoric.

35. *Ibidem*, p. 21.

36. *Ibidem*, p. 28.

37. *Ibidem*, p. 32.

38. *Ibidem*, p. 34. *Cf.* also, Blondel's Introduction to *L'Action*.

39. *Ibidem*, p. 35.

40. *Ibidem*, p. 34.

41. *Ibidem*, p. 36. *Cf.* also, pp. 38–39.

42. *Ibidem*, p. 37.

43. *Ibidem*. Letter to Albert Bazaillas, pp. 40–42.

44. *Ibidem*. Letter to Adolph Lasson, a professor at the University of Berlin, pp. 72–73. *Cf.* influences in his younger days, Bouillard, *Blondel*, p. 17. *Cf.* also, the influence of Leibnitz on his thought, *Ibidem*. *Cf. Lettres Philosophiques*, pp. 9, 11, 12.

45. *Cf. Correspondence Philosophique*, p. 80; *Lettres Philosophiques*, p. 33; Dru, *Letter*, pp. 47–48, 60. Blondel, of course, mentions the worthy efforts of Chateaubriand and others in the spirit of Pascal. We shall see more of the French scene in our historical discussion of the age of Blondel.

46. Bouillard, "The Thought of . . . ," p. 399. Blondel's abstention from controversy for "fourteen years" was on the advice of others. *Cf.* Trethowan, *Letter*, pp. 123–24.

47. *Cf.* Émile Poulat, *Histoire, dogme et critique dans la crise moderniste* (Paris: Easterman, 1962), pp. 513–73, for a discussion of Blondel's correspondence with Loisy and Hugel, and his answer to the position of the Gayraudists (the disciples of l'Abbé Gayraud). Poulat also presents a fine discussion of Blondel's *Histoire et dogme* in the context of the Modernist crisis.

48. Valensin, *op. cit.*, pp. 6–7. Dru, *Letter*, p. 48. Bouillard, *Blondel*, p. 33.

49. This was the united view he shared with Laberthonnière; *cf.* Dru, *Letter*, pp. 58–66. *Cf.* Poulat, *op. cit.*, p. 15, wherein he defines Modernism in this way. Poulat also shows Blondel's sympathy for the position of Loisy, especially in the matter of miracles and in the willingness of the veterists to disregard the valid methods of historical criticism (pp. 515 ff.). It is difficult to define veterism, but in general it included any adherence to decaying forms of thought. In the view of the veterists, political systems, philosophic systems, or theological expressions seemed always to be unchanging absolutes (*cf.* Poulat, *op. cit.*, pp. 567 ff.).

50. The *Annales de Philosophie Chrétienne* was a well-known periodical, which Blondel ultimately bought in 1905, and installed Laberthonnière as editor. In the decade following Blondel's ownership, it "played an important part in the controversies of the period and provided a platform for writers sympathetic to Blondel's ideas." It represented an attempt to break away from the narrow line of Roman Catholicism in its most conservative form, and to incorporate some of the romantic and Germanic insights. "It contained reviews of George Goyau's *Johann Adam Möhler*, of Bremond's first study of Newman. . . . Bremond was one of the most regular contributors." It later (1913) was put on the Index, retroactively to 1905, although the works of Blondel were excepted. It was actually the most important periodical of its kind in the early 1900's. *Cf. Letter*, Introduction, pp. 58–61.

51. The *Letter*, which was originally published in *Annales de Philosophie Chrétienne*, was not even available in book form until 1956. *Cf.* Preface to *Letter*, p. 121.

52. This information is contained in Bouillard, *Blondel*, pp. 279 ff. Bouillard offers a fivefold division of the works of Blondel. Most of the works were articles written in various periodicals. The division offered by Bouillard

is: a) Philosophy of action—eleven items, mainly periodical writings, with the exception of the first *L'Action*. b) Apologetic writings—nine items, five of which are listed above. c) Transition writings—numerous philosophical items. d) A trilogy on the metaphysics of *L'Action* and a discussion of *La Philosophie et l'esprit Chrétien* in two volumes. This is the heaviest concentration of metaphysical writings. The full value of the trilogy has not been finally assessed. This is discussed briefly in note 56 below. e) Posthumous works. This collection contains most of the correspondence of Blondel, his diary-like notes, and other unedited works.

The best commentary on the work of Blondel, far and away, is the book of Henri Bouillard, *Blondel et le Christianisme*. In English, the Introduction to the *Letter on Apologetics* by Trethowan and Dru is very good. Other than that, we have only occasional periodical literature in English. This will rapidly change.

53. Bouillard, *Blondel*, p. 277.

54. Dru, *Letter*, pp. 68–69.

55. Bouillard, *Blondel*, pp. 48 ff. On Blondel's exemption, *cf. L'Itinéraire Philosophique*, pp. 99–102.

56. *Cf.* Bouillard, *Blondel*, pp. 49 ff. A comparison of the first *L'Action* with the *L'Action* of the trilogy is contained in the Introduction to the *Letter*, pp. 67–79. Herein is explained how Blondel was obliged to temper his thought by Laberthonnière. Aubert, *op. cit.*, p. 293, seems to see the first *L'Action* as a necessary exaggeration: "The exaggerations of Maurice Blondel regarding the sufficiency of traditional apologetics, and which he himself recognized later, have been fortunate in producing a reaction." The first *L'Action* was such a strong reaction against sterile intellectualism that it seemed to jeopardize even sound rational thought. That this was not the intention of Blondel becomes clear in his controversies with Laberthonnière. *Cf.* Maurice Blondel, *L'Itinéraire Philosophique de Maurice Blondel* (Paris: Spes, 1928). Blondel remained open, and the correspondence between the two reveals Blondel's growing awareness of the value of St. Thomas. *Cf. Correspondence Philosophique*, pp. 298–99. Blondel had recognized the obscuring of Thomas by the neo-Thomists. For a more extended discussion of the evolution of Blondel's thought, *cf.* Tresmontant, *La Metaphysique de Maurice Blondel* (Paris: Editions du Seuil, 1963) and Étienne Borne, *Passion de la Verité* (Paris: Librairie Arthème Fayard, 1962). It is interesting to note that J. Marechal, S.J., found no objection to the metaphysics of the first *L'Action* in 1912. *Cf.* Dru, "From the Action Française . . . ," p. 245.

57. Dru, *Letter*, p. 25; "From the Action Française . . . ," p. 228. Poulat, *op. cit.*, pp. 514 ff.

58. Trethowan, *Letter*, p. 124. For the opening of the Blondel archives, *cf. Nouvelle Revue Théologique*, book reviews, LXXXV (1963), 424–25.

59. Poulat, *op. cit.*, pp. 17 ff. shows that Modernism had a different coloring in each country in which it grew. It was in France, he says, that Modernism found its "*terrain d'élection.*" (p. 19)

60. Henri Bremond, *A Literary History of Religious Thought in France*, Vol. I: *Devout Humanism*, trans. K. L. Montgomery (New York:

The Macmillan Company, 1928), pp. 305–395. Bremond is considered by some to be overly sympathetic to the Modernists.

61. *Ibidem*, p. 310, a quotation from de Caussade.

62. Dru, *Letter*, p. 20.

63. Bremond, *op. cit.*, p. 305.

64. *Ibidem*, pp. 395–96.

65. Dru, *Letter*, p. 21.

66. *Ibidem*, p. 22.

67. *Ibidem*, pp. 23–24 and *History and Dogma*, pp. 226 ff. For a discussion of Blondel's struggle with *l'extrinsécisme*, *cf.* Poulat, *op. cit.*, pp. 567 ff.

68. Aubert, *op. cit.*, pp. 114–22. *Cf.* J. M. Faux, S.J., a book review of *Un Essai de philosophie chrétienne au xixe siècle: L'Abbé Louis Bautain*, *Nouvelle Revue Théologique*, LXXXI (1963), 423–24. *Cf.* Denziger-Bannwart (New York: Benziger Bros., 1954), 1622–27.

69. Aubert, *op. cit.*, p. 265.

70. *Ibidem*, p. 266.

71. *Ibidem*, p. 267–68.

72. Aubert, *op. cit.*, pp. 270–75. He discusses the efforts of Janet, Payot, Box, Bazillas, the work of England's Balfour, which was immediately translated into French, Bruntière, and others.

73. *Ibidem*, p. 277. *Cf. La Semaine Sociale*, p. 93; Bouillard, *Blondel*, p. 15.

74. Aubert, *op. cit.*, p. 276. *Cf.* Scott's interesting article on the correspondence of James and Blondel, note 12.

75. *Ibidem*, p. 275. Sabatier was received with great excitement by the Catholic intellectuals in 1897 upon the publication of his *Esquisse d'une philosophie de la religion d'après la psychologie et l'histoire. Cf.*Vidler, *The Church in an Age of Revolution*, p. 183.

76. Aubert, *op. cit.*, p. 269. Quotation from Ollé-Laprune's *La Certitude Morale* (pp. 413–14).

77. Aubert, *op. cit.*, p. 277. *Cf.* also, Dru, "From the Action Française . . . ," pp. 226 ff.

78. This, as we have seen, and will see more clearly, was the burden of *L'Action*.

79. Dru, *Letter*, p. 24. This is the thesis of Henri Bremond. *Cf.* his Introduction to de Caussade's book, *Bossuet, maître d'oraison*.

80. Dru, "From the Action Française . . . ," pp. 226–32 and *Letter*, pp. 19–33. *Cf.* also, Bouillard's discussion "noetic" and "pneumatic" in Blondelian thought, *Blondel*, pp. 55 ff.

81. Actually, *La Semaine Sociale de Bordeaux et le Monophorism*. "Monophorism" (one-way thinking) permitted that the "Catholic apostolate would be made sterile, religious meaning destroyed." (p. 93)

82. Denis Gwynn, *The Action Française Condemnation* (London: Burns & Oates, Ltd., 1928), pp. 21–22.

83. *Ibidem*, p. 18.

84. Dru, *Letter*, pp. 24–25.

85. Vidler, *The Church in an Age of Revolution*, pp. 180 ff.

86. Dru, *Letter*, p. 27.

87. Gwynn, *op. cit.*, p. 17.

88. Edward R. Tannenbaum, *The Action Française: Die-hard Reactionaries in Twentieth Century France* (New York: John Wiley & Sons, 1962), p. vii.

89. Eugene Weber, *Action Française: Royalism and Reaction in Twentieth Century France* (Stanford: Stanford University Press, 1962), pp. 10–13.

90. *Ibidem*, p. 13.

91. *Ibidem*, pp. 10–13.

92. *Ibidem*, p. 16.

93. *Ibidem*, p. 219.

94. *Ibidem*, p. 220.

95. *Ibidem*, p. 219.

96. Tannenbaum, *op. cit.*, pp. 163–64.

97. Dru, *Letter*, pp. 31, 39–40.

98. A fuller treatment would involve a careful study of *La Semaine Sociale*. Dru, "From the Action Française . . .," gives a fine historical treatment, and suggests that the work of Blondel "may well have turned the scales."

99. Eugene Weber, *op. cit.*, p. 219.

100. *Correspondence Philosophique*, e.g., pp. 250–75.

101. Dru, *Letter*, p. 31.

102. See the complaints of William James, Scott, *op. cit.*, pp. 42–43; Dru, *Letter*, pp. 13, 15–16.

103. Bouillard, *Blondel*, pp. 33 ff., lists the criticism of Schwalm and H. Gayraud. *Cf.* Dru, *Letter*, p. 36. Especially *cf.* Jean-Hervé Nicolas, O.P., "Le Centenaire de Maurice Blondel," *Revue Thomiste*, V, No. 62 (1962), 444.

104. Dru, *Letter*, p. 36; Aubert, *op. cit.*, p. 266.

105. *Ibidem*, p. 64.

106. *Ibidem*. For Blondel's admission of his excesses in criticism of the Scholastics, *cf. Le Problème de la Philosophie Catholique* (Paris: Bloud and Gay, 1932), pp. 22 ff. Trethowan, *Letter*, p. 122, upholds Blondel's denunciation. For a discussion of Laberthonnière's bitterness toward Thomism, *cf.* Étienne Gilson, *Le Philosophe et le théologie* (Paris: Librairie Arthème Fayard, 1960), pp. 60 ff.

107. H. Duméry, *La Philosophie de L'Action* (Paris: Aubier, 1948), p. 16. Duméry calls the changes in the work of Blondel an *"approfondissement interne,"* and not *"adjonctions externes."* *Cf.* the openness to criticism and the effect it had on him in the *Lettres Philosophiques*, e.g., to Adolph Lasson, p. 71. *Cf. Le Problème*, pp. 28 ff., wherein Blondel discusses his revision of the *Letter on Apologetics*, and why the criticism of Scholasticism was less valid in 1932 than in 1896.

108. *Lettres Philosophiques*, p. 87.

109. *Ibidem*, pp. 121 ff.

110. *Ibidem*, p. 122.

111. *Ibidem*, pp. 102 ff., 122–23.

112. *Ibidem*, p. 123, 139; *cf.* Bouillard, *Blondel*, p. 72.

113. *Ibidem*, pp. 123–24.

114. *Ibidem*, pp. 128 ff.

115. *Ibidem*, p. 96. Blondel responded to this article by Père Schwalm in 1896. M. B. Schwalm (1860–1908) wrote several articles in the *Revue Thomiste*, this particular one in Vol. IV (1890), 412–41. *Cf.* Gardeil, "Le Synthèse Apologétique du P. Schwalm," *Revue Thomiste*, XXI (1913), 413–36.

For an interesting criticism of Blondel's theological ignorance and his boldness for entering an area where he was not at home, *cf.* Gilson, *op. cit.*, pp. 71–72. Our disagreement with Gilson is represented by our approval of Blondel's apologetic insights.

116. *Ibidem*, p. 105.

117. *Ibidem*.

118. *Ibidem*, p. 102.

119. Aubert, *op. cit.*, p. 280. For fuller treatment, *cf. L'Action*, pp. 395–97: "*L'idée de lois fixés dans la nature n'est qu'une idole; chaque phénomène est un cas singulier et une solution unique*," p. 396.

120. Dru, *Letter*, p. 26.

121. *Ibidem*, p. 29.

122. *Lettres Philosophiques*, p. 104; *L'Action*, pp. 395–96.

123. Dru, *Letter*, pp. 33–34.

124. *L'Action*, p. xxxiii.

125. Henri de Lubac, "Maurice Blondel et le Père Teilhard de Chardin," (Dec. 1919), *Archives de Philosophie*, XXIV (1961), 123–56. The quotation appears on p. 129.

126. *Ibidem*, p. 130. Valensin, who studied with Chardin, had asked Blondel to look over some of his ideas, and the correspondence of 1919 is the result of this most interesting communication of two kindred souls. We will discuss differences later on in this work.

127. *Ibidem*.

128. Trethowan, *Letter*, p. 86. For "non-anticipation," *cf.* Bouillard, *Blondel*, pp. 217–18.

129. Aubert, *op. cit.*, pp. 282–83. *Cf.* Valensin, "Immanence," in *Dictionnaire Apologétique*, II (1st ed.), 579–612. Also, *Lettres Philosophiques*, pp. 36–39. This discussion will come up later.

130. Aubert, *op. cit.*, p. 282.

131. Trethowan, *Letter*, p. 120. H. Duméry is quoted here as an interpreter of Blondel's theory of *L'Action*, not in his own right. Many of Duméry's own views do not seem to be orthodox from a Christian standpoint.

132. *Ibidem*.

133. *Ibidem*, p. 124.

134. *Ibidem*, p. 120.

135. *Letter*, p. 128.

136. *Ibidem*, pp. 129–30.

137. *Ibidem*, p. 130.

138. *Ibidem*.

139. *Lettres Philosophiques*, p. 150.

140. Bouillard, *Blondel*, p. 74. *Cf. Lettres Philosophiques*, pp. 115–16, 139.

141. *Ibidem*, p. 75.

142. *Letter*, p. 131.

143. *Ibidem*, p. 133.

144. *Cf. supra*, p. 157.

145. *Letter*, p. 133.

146. *Ibidem*, p. 134; Aubert, *op. cit.*, p. 279.

147. *Ibidem*, p. 135. *Cf. Lettres Philosophiques*, pp. 104–105. *Cf.* Blondel (under pseudonym of Bernard de Sailly) in *Annales de Philosophie Chrétienne*, CLIV (July, 1907), 337–62: "*La notion et le rôle du miracle.*" Aubert, *op. cit.*, p. 293; Bouillard, *Blondel*, pp. 42–43.

148. *Letter*, p. 135.

149. *Ibidem*, p. 134. *Cf. Lettres Philosophiques*: "I say merely that miracles are a speech written in a language of which philosophy is no judge." (p. 104) *Cf. History and Dogma*, p. 226.

150. *Lettres Philosophiques*, pp. 99 ff.

151. *Ibidem*, p. 103.

152. Bouillard, *Blondel*, p. 42.

153. *Letter*, pp. 145–47.

154. *Ibidem*, pp. 136–37. *Cf.* the interesting attempt of this type of apologetics by J. Coppens, "Un Éssai de synthèse apologétique," *Ephemerides Theologicae Lovanienses*, XIV (1937), 447–66: "The figure of Jesus is so transcendent and unique in its religious beauty, for Jews and pagans as well, that the souls in the quest of truth will not hesitate . . . to make an act of faith in Him as the best guide that history presents." (p. 453) Coppens would begin his apologetics almost at the point that Blondel would complete his. Coppens makes an interesting and a serious attempt, but we think that he takes a lot for granted in his appraisal of modern man. *Cf.* similar attempts by Eugene Joly, *What Is Faith?*, trans. Illtyd Trethowan (New York: Deus Books, 1963), pp. 19–26. *Cf.* also, Karl Adam, *The Christ of Faith*, trans. Joyce Crick (New York: Mentor-Omega, 1962), pp. 115–19. Adam's effort balances well with Blondel's requirements. He is well aware of the preparation of the subject.

155. *Letter*, p. 137.

156. *Ibidem*.

157. *Ibidem*, p. 140.

158. *Ibidem*, pp. 196–97. This passage is an outstanding one. *Cf.* also,

Gerard Fourez, S.J. and Jean Jacob, S.J., "Une Dialectique de la conversion," *Revue Philosophique de Louvain*, LVII (1959), 551.

159. *Letter*, p. 142.

160. *Ibidem*, p. 144.

161. *Lettres Philosophiques*, p. 102.

162. His criticism of "science" above was a general one, directed principally at positivists who saw truth only where it could agree with conditions they arbitrarily established. Here is a more specific application.

163. *Letter*, p. 145.

164. *Ibidem*, pp. 145–46.

165. *Ibidem*, p. 147.

166. *Ibidem*, pp. 196–97.

167. *Ibidem*, p. 142.

168. *Ibidem*, p. 148.

169. *Ibidem*, p. 155.

170. *Ibidem*.

171. *Ibidem*, p. 156.

172. The *Letter* can be understood only in terms of *L'Action*. *Cf.* Bouillard, *Blondel*, pp. 103 ff., the section, "Reflets de *L'Action* dans la *Lettre*."

173. *Letter*, p. 157.

174. *Ibidem*.

175. *Ibidem*, p. 183; *L'Action*, p. 235; Scott, *op. cit.*, pp. 33 ff.; Trethowan, *Letter*, pp. 87 ff.; Bouillard, "The Thought of . . . ," p. 393.

176. Macquarrie, *op. cit.*, p. 174.

177. Bouillard, "The Thought of . . . ," p. 394.

178. Bouillard, *Blondel*, p. 78; *cf.* also, pp. 16–22.

179. *L'Action II* (1937), p. 354.

180. Bouillard, *Blondel*, p. 78.

181. Aubert, *op. cit.*, pp. 279–80. "Profound will," of course, is the *volonté voulante*.

182. *Lettres Philosophiques*, pp. 14 ff. *L'Action*: "The true will of man is the divine will." (p. 387) *L'Action*, pp. 422–23.

183. *L'Action*, Introduction, especially pp. xxv ff.; pp. 23–42, pp. 354–55; Fourez and Jacob, *op. cit.*, p. 550; Bouillard, "The Thought of . . . ," p. 393 ff.; Bouillard, *Blondel*, p. 83.

184. *L'Action*, pp. 372–73.

185. *Ibidem*.

186. Bouillard, "The Thought of . . . ," p. 78.

187. Cartier, *op. cit.*, p. 10.

188. *L'Action*, p. 467. This is from the last chapter, which was not in the dissertation, but added. It is interesting to note how the Blondelian thought has crept into modern philosophy without any acknowledgement of the role of its author. In John MacMurray, for example (*The Self as Agent*

in the Gifford Lectures for 1953 [London: Faber and Faber, Ltd., 1955], p. 84) we read: "What is here proposed is that we should substitute the 'I do' for the 'I think' as our starting point and center of reference; and do our thinking from the standpoint of action. . . . Any reasoned objection to its possibility would presuppose the primacy of the theoretical and would therefore be invalid." It is hard not to see in this statement some careful acquaintance with the work of Blondel, but it indicates how thoroughly the philosophy of *L'Action* has become a part of contemporary thought. *Cf.* also, Chap. IV, "The Agent as Subject" and Chap. VIII, "Reflective Activity." Both Aubert and Bouillard bring out the influence of Blondel on all of modern theology, but it is rare that we see direct credit given to him. De Lubac is a notable exception.

189. *Les Premiers Écrits*, p. 115.

190. Unedited notes, in Cartier, *op. cit.*, p. 9.

191. *Ibidem.*

192. *L'Action*, pp. 39, 85, 390: ". . . *une incurable disproportion entre l'élan de la volonté et le terme humain de l'action.*" Bouillard, *Blondel*, pp. 91 ff.

193. Bouillard, "The Thought of . . .," p. 397, seems to indicate the influence of Husserl's *Epoche.*

194. *L'Action*, p. 493.

195. *Ibidem*, pp. 45–305.

196. *Études Blondéliennes*, I, 78.

197. *Letter*, p. 158.

198. *Ibidem*, p. 160.

199. *Ibidem*, p. 161. *Cf.* also, p. 160. There is a good discussion of his meaning in *Lettres Philosophiques*, pp. 91 ff. He insists that he wishes to remain a philosopher, and writes only of observable phenomena. He can only write about a subjective faith, or a kind of "baptism of desire." This will become clearer when we discuss his use of "nature."

200. *Letter*, p. 161.

201. *Ibidem*, p. 162.

202. *L'Action*, p. 372; Fourez and Jacob, *op. cit.*, p. 551.

203. *Letter*, pp. 162–63; *L'Action*, pp. 354–55; Bouillard, "The Thought of . . .," p. 395 and *Blondel*, pp. 67 ff.

204. *Lettres Philosophiques*, pp. 91 ff.; Bouillard, *Blondel*, pp. 34 ff.

205. Nicolas, *op. cit.*, pp. 433–44, especially pp. 443–45. On p. 439, he insists that Blondel introduces theological conclusions into philosophy, and Bouillard does not resolve this objection. On p. 441, he insists that the critics find in Blondel what they want, which is probably the attitude most take concerning Nicolas' objections. *Cf.* Trethowan, *Letter*, pp. 98–105.

206. Bouillard, *Blondel*, p. 75. Bouillard maintains here that Blondel never spoke of the man of "pure nature."

207. *Lettres Philosophiques*, p. 91.

208. Aubert, *op. cit.*, p. 282. For Blondel as a phenomenologist, *cf.* Bouillard, *Blondel*, p. 169. *Cf. Lettres Philosophiques*, p. 105.

209. *Ibidem*, pp. 282–83.

210. *Ibidem*, pp. 283–84.

211. *Ibidem*, p. 282.

212. *Lettres Philosophiques*, pp. 138–39.

213. De Lubac, *Sûrnaturelle*, p. 129.

214. Karl Rahner, *Nature and Grace*, p. 298. *Cf.* Trethowan, *Letter*, p. 104, in which he gives the quotation which Malevez used: "It is unquestionably an error to argue as though the natural *state* of the unbeliever, the agnostic or the apostate were the state of "pure nature," a state which no doubt could have existed, which never has existed, whose real conditions we cannot even precisely define." (*La Semaine Sociale*, p. 268) For a more complete treatment of the supernatural existential, *cf. supra*, Chapter II, on Max Scheler.

215. Cartier, *op. cit.*, p. 20. Bouillard, *Blondel*, pp. 198–269.

216. *Lettres Philosophiques*, p. 91.

217. Unedited note, Cartier, *op. cit.*, p. 9.

218. Bouillard, "The Thought of . . .," p. 398; Bouillard, *Blondel*, pp. 173 ff.

219. *L'Action*, p. 379.

220. Macquarrie, *op. cit.*, p. 174.

221. *L'Action*, p. 352.

222. *Letter*, p. 180; *Les Premiers Écrits*, pp. 113–17.

223. *L'Action*, p. 454.

224. Fourez and Jacob, *op. cit.*, p. 555.

225. *L'Action*, pp. 476–77.

226. *Ibidem*, pp. 491–92.

227. Bouillard, "The Thought of . . .," p. 396 and Bouillard, *Blondel*, pp. 221 ff.; *cf.* a complete discussion of the process of *reflection* and *progression* in Blondelian thought in Cartier, *op. cit.*, pp. 13–17; Scott, *op. cit.*, pp. 33–34.

228. *L'Action*, pp. 400–403; Aubert, *op. cit.*, p. 280.

229. *L'Action*, p. 454.

230. Aubert, *op. cit.*, p. 293.

231. R. Marle, S.J., *Au Coeur de la crise moderniste* (Paris: Aubier, 1960), gives an excellent account of the Blondel-Loisy struggle.

232. Gélinas, *op. cit.*, pp. 326–28, insists that Laberthonnière did not hold that man's needs produced the dogmatic truths, but he is less clear in this matter than Blondel. *Cf.* Dru, *Letter*, where it seems (pp. 58 ff.) that their differences were highlighted by temperamental responses.

233. De Lubac, *Archives de Philosophie*, Vol. XIV (1961), correspondence with Chardin, pp. 145 ff.

234. *L'Action*, p. 391.

235. Cartier, *op. cit.*, p. 5.

236. *Letter*, p. 186. The whole latter part of the *Letter* seeks to establish this. *Cf.* also, Bouillard, *Blondel*, pp. 244–71.

237. *Ibidem*, p. 206.

238. *L'Action*, p. 372; Bouillard, "The Thought of . . .," pp. 394, 396, 398; *Lettres Philosophiques*, p. 150; Fourez and Jacob, p. 553.

239. Bouillard, *Blondel*, p. 79: "*susciter*."

240. *Lettres Philosophiques*, p. 150: "*Vous estimez qu'il est impossible défaire la science de la preparation subjective de la foi; comme si le subjectif, le volontaire et le libre, etant synonyme de capricieux, d'arbitraire et indeterminé, ne comportaient aucune méthode générale ni aucune précision philosophique.*"

241. *L'Action*, p. ix; also, p. 372.

242. Quoted in Aubert, *op. cit.*, p. 285 (footnote).

243. *Letter*, pp. 163–64.

244. *Ibidem*, p. 196; Fourez and Jacob, 551.

245. *Lettres Philosophiques*, p. 126.

246. Valensin, *op. cit.*, pp. 11–12; De Lubac, *Archives de Philosophie*, Vol. XIV (1961), p. 130; Bouillard in *Blondel* establishes this in his work: *cf.* pp. 133, 197, 221; also p. 69: "*La philosophie blondélienne s'arrête au seuil de la dogmatique, elle n'absorbe (et un partie seulement) que la théologie fondamentale en la posant comme fondamentale. La première (la philosophie hegélienne) est une théologie rationalisée, la second (Blondel), une apologétique rationelle.*" Cf. the following paragraph: "*Elle a un caractère apologétique.*"

247. *Letter*, p. 170.

248. *Ibidem*, p. 200.

249. De Lubac, *Archives de Philosophie*, Blondel-Chardin correspondence. Cf. Christopher Mooney, "Blondel and Teilhard de Chardin, *Thought*, XXXVII (1962), 543–62.

250. *Ibidem*, p. 127. Also, for the Sacrament of the Eucharist as a picture of *L'Action*, cf. *Lettres Philosophiques*, pp. 18–19.

251. *Ibidem*, p. 129.

252. *Ibidem*, pp. 130–31.

253. *Ibidem*, p. 132.

254. *Ibidem*, p. 145. For the apologetics of Chardin, *cf.* Henri De Lubac, *La Prière du P. Teilhard de Chardin* (Paris: Librairie Arthème Fayard, 1964), pp. 145–222.

255. *Letter*, p. 197.

256. Aubert, *op. cit.*, p. 289.

257. De Lubac, "Maurice Blondel et . . . Chardin," pp. 145–50.

258. *Ibidem*, p. 140.

259. Mooney, *op. cit.*, p. 555.

260. Gélinas, *op. cit.*, p. 59.

261. *L'Action*, p. 148.

CHAPTER IV

1. Borghild Gundersen, *Cardinal Newman and Apologetics* (Oslo: I Kommisjon Hos Jacob Dybwad, 1952), pp. 125 ff.

2. Aubert, *op. cit.*, pp. 348 ff. According to Aubert, Newman was known in France largely through his *Oxford University Sermons*. Ollé-Laprune, however, who was extremely indebted to Newman in his *La Certitude morale*, was familiar with the *Grammar of Assent*, and made liberal use of Newman's contrast of real and notional assent. *Cf.* Edmond D. Benard, *The Problem of Belief in the Writings of Newman, James, and Aquinas* (unpublished doctoral dissertation, Catholic University of America, Washington, D.C., 1948), pp. 23 ff.

3. Aubert, *op. cit.*, pp. 564 ff. Erich Przywara, S.J., Germany's great Newman scholar, divided Newman's apologetic into the threefold "*Glaubensbegrundung*," "*Glaubenspflicht*," and "*Hingabe des Verstandes*." From Aubert's evaluation of Przywara's thought it appears to us that Przywara exaggerated the third part of Newman's apologetic to prevent revelation from appearing as a fulfillment of man's inner need, a revelation supported by mere intrinsic criteria. It will appear from our development that Newman did, indeed, stress the extrinsic evidence to support revelation, but at the same time it fulfilled the need of personal conscience. We shall point out later that Newman's *Grammar of Assent* separated him from any dangerous immanentism, but faith was not a simple matter of man submitting from the force of extrinsic evidence. Newman saw the relationship between faith and simple nature and looked for the need in man to which God would respond. It was a different thing to say that man's need created revelation than to say that nature would look for revelation. This is the distinction that Blondel, Scheler, and Newman all made, and it was interpreted as a kind of Modernism. Guitton brings this out clearly when he says that Newman's apologetic starts with a kind of dilemma and finds that the mind contains the solution within itself if it is true to its nature. *Cf.* Jean Guitton, *La Philosophie de Newman* (Paris: Boivin et Cie, 1933), pp. xxvi–xxix. Following out Przywara's interpretation of "*Hingabe des Verstandes*," we end up close to an obediential concept of faith, as in Billot, and not with Newman's existential and personalist view.

4. Martin C. D'Arcy, S.J., *The Nature of Belief* (London: Sheed & Ward, 1931), pp. 147 ff.

5. Contemporarily, the *Newman-Studien* series (Nuremberg: Glock und Lutz, 1955–   ) is perhaps the best in the Newman field.

6. *Cf.* the excellent bibliography in the fourth volume of the *Newman-Studien* series.

7. Newman is primarily an apologete. This characteristic is expressed in all that he writes, but the *Grammar of Assent* is recognized as his most complete and mature effort in this area. It contains essentially his complete apologetic. *Cf.* Heinrich Fries, *Newman und Grundprobleme der Heutigen Apologetik*, Vol. III, *Newman-Studien* (Nuremberg: Glock und Lutz, 1957), 225–48. *Cf.* especially pp. 231 ff. *Cf.* also, Gundersen, *op. cit.*, p. 38.

8. *Cf.* Newman's letter to the Reverend R. Greaves, Feb. 27, 1828 (Oriel Library): Meriol Trevor, *Newman: The Pillar of the Cloud*, Vol. I (New York: Doubleday & Company, Inc., 1962), 17, 34. Miss Trevor lists the important books that Newman borrowed from Mayers: Beveridge's *Private Thoughts*, which contained his first exposure to the rationalistic apologetics; Milner's *Church History*, which opened to him the world of the

Fathers; Newton's *On the Prophecies*, which painted the Pope as anti-Christ, a prejudice from which Newman had difficulty freeing himself; and Thomas Scott's *Force of Truth*, which might have been the seed of Newman's later development of the growth of doctrine and the growth of the individual faith. *Cf.* also, A. Dwight Culler, *The Imperial Intellect* (London: Yale University Press, 1955), pp. 4–6. Mayers warns Newman of the dangers to faith in an Oxford University education. It is a kind of foreshadowing of the warning that Pius IX would give with regard to secular education in the midst of the Dublin University question. Culler, *op. cit.*, p. 127. *Cf.* Gundersen, *op. cit.*, p. 31, wherein he rejects the idea that Newman's Calvinistic bent came from his family, as F. X. Connolly asserts in his *Newman Reader* (New York: Image Books, 1964), p. 14.

9. Culler, *op. cit.*, pp. 38 ff. J. H. Newman, *Apologia Pro Vita Sua* (New York: Image Books, 1956), pp. 130 ff.

10. On Newman's nervous breakdowns, *cf.* Culler, *op. cit.*, pp. 20, 31, 59 *et passim*; also, Trevor, *op. cit.*, Vol. I, 30, 43, 44, 69–70, 130, 139, 338–39, 436. On Newman's personal thoughts about his deep-rooted pride, *cf.* his *Autobiographical Writings* (New York: Sheed & Ward, 1955), pp. 159–60, 179, 210.

11. Owen Chadwick, *From Bossuet to Newman* (Cambridge: Cambridge University Press, 1957), p. 10. Regarding Newman's optimism, *cf.* Culler, *op. cit.*, p. 62. Concerning Newman's early preoccupation with sin, *cf.* J. H. Walgrave, *Newman the Theologian*, trans. A. V. Littledale (New York: Sheed & Ward, 1960), p. 20.

12. H. Francis Davis, Introduction to Erich Przywara, *The Heart of Newman* (Springfield, Ill.: Templegate Publishers, 1963), pp. xiii ff.

13. Newman, *Apologia*, pp. 125 ff; Culler, *op. cit.*, pp. 1–22; Trevor, *op. cit.*, pp. 15–31.

14. *Grammar*, pp. 354–59.

15. Chadwick, *op. cit.*, p. 176.

16. *Grammar*, p. 243.

17. *Apologia*, pp. 140 ff., wherein Newman discusses his changing view of the miracle. For his mature view of the miracle, *cf. Grammar*, p. 243 and especially p. 333, where Newman explains that a coincidence seen through the eyes of Providence has the effect today of the miracles of another time. *Cf.* also, Culler, *op. cit.*, pp. 249–50.

18. *Apologia*, pp. 135 ff.; Culler, *op. cit.*, pp. 36–45; Trevor, *op. cit.*, pp. 44 ff.

19. Vidler, *The Church in an Age of Revolution*, pp. 45 ff.

20. Gunter Rumbold, *Das Wesen der Person Nach John Henry Newman*, Vol. IV, *Newman-Studien* (Nuremberg: Glock und Lutz, 1964), pp. 9–138. *Cf.* especially pp. 11–17.

21. Rumbold, *op. cit.*, p. 25. For evidence of Newman's awareness of Pascal, *cf. Grammar*, pp. 244–46. *Cf.* also, Gundersen, *op. cit.*, pp. 49–51. F. Copleston, S.J., *A History of Philosophy*, Vol. IV (New York: Image Books, 1963), p. 180, sees Pascal as a stimulus to philosophers rather than as a systematic thinker whom one might adopt.

22. Rumbold, *op. cit.*, p. 25; Copleston, A *History of Philosophy*, Vol. IV, 147–60.

23. Cragg, *op. cit.*, pp. 75–79.

24. *Ibidem*, pp. 37 ff.; Rumbold, *op. cit.*, pp. 27–37; Copleston, A *History of Philosophy*, Vol. IV, p. 159.

25. *Ibidem*, pp. 75 ff.; Rumbold, *op. cit.*, pp. 42–47.

26. Rumbold, *op. cit.*, pp. 42–47; Gundersen, *op. cit.*, pp. 26–30; Copleston, A *History of Philosophy*, Vol. V, Part 1 (New York: Atheneum Publishers, 1964), 151–52. For a treatment of empiricism in Locke, *cf.* Copleston, V, Part 1, 76–88.

27. Cragg, *op. cit.*, pp. 157 ff.; Copleston, V, Part 1, 118–32.

28. *Ibidem*. C. J. H. Hayes, A *Political and Cultural History of Modern Europe*, Vol. I (New York: The Macmillan Company, 1944), 496–576. On Newton, *cf.* Copleston, Vol. V, Part 1, 153–67 and on Samuel Clarke, pp. 168 ff.

29. Cragg, *op. cit.*, pp. 170 ff.; Vidler, *The Church in an Age of Revolution*, pp. 39 ff.; Copleston, Vol. V, Part 1, 206 ff.; Johannes Artz, *Der Ansatz der Newmanschen Glaubensbegrundung*, Vol. IV; *Newman-Studien*, 249–68, especially pp. 254–55; Rumbold, *op. cit.*, pp. 61 ff.; Vincent Blehl, *The Essential Newman* (New York: Mentor-Omega, 1963), p. 284.

30. Cragg, *op. cit.*, pp. 163 ff.; Artz, *op. cit.*, pp. 254 ff.

31. Copleston, Vol. V, Part 1, 176–81, 195–202; Gundersen, *op. cit.*, pp. 41–48, offers an excellent treatment of Butler and attempts to show that Butler skirts the eighteenth century and returns to the spirit of Pascal; for Newman's personal approval of Butler, *cf. Apologia*, p. 132; Chadwick, *op. cit.*, p. 78; Cragg, *op. cit.*, pp. 165 ff.; Walgrave, *op. cit.*, pp. 221 ff.; Rumbold, *op. cit.*, pp. 50 ff.

32. Cragg, *op. cit.*, p. 167; Copleston, Vol. V, Part 1, 198 ff.

33. Cragg, *op. cit.*, p. 168; Copleston, Vol. V, Part 2, 63–196, especially pp. 92–96, 109–121; Rumbold, *op. cit.*, pp. 57–61; Chadwick, *op. cit.*, pp. 176–77; Blehl, *op. cit.*, p. 284.

34. Culler, *op. cit.*, p. 36.

35. *Apologia*, pp. 125–97; *Autobiographical Writings*, pp. 86 ff.; Culler, *op. cit.*, pp. 23–78; Blehl, *op. cit.*, pp. 31 ff., especially p. 43.

36. *Autobiographical Writings*, on student drinking, p. 158, and on forced attendance at Communion services, pp. 89 ff.; Culler, *op. cit.*, pp. 116 ff., speaks of the "*Credo in Newmannuum*" espoused by many young men; *cf.* also, Culler, Chap. 3, pp. 46–79 ("Tutorship at Oriel") and Chap. 5, pp. 96–120 ("Tractarian Education"); *cf.* Trevor, *op. cit.*, pp. 62 ff.

37. *Autobiographical Writings*, pp. 92 ff.; *Apologia*, pp. 137 ff.; Culler, *op cit.*, pp. 46–79; Walgrave, *op. cit.*, p. 15, explains the importance of human contact for Newman, as does Trevor, *op. cit.*, pp. 78 ff.; Connolly, *op. cit.*, p. 12. For a good, short summary of the principles of the Oxford movement, *cf.* Blehl, *op. cit.*, pp. 45 ff.

38. Culler, *op. cit.*, pp. 96–120; *Autobiographical Writings*, on the Irish University question, pp. 280–333.

39. *Ibidem*, pp. 123–70.

40. *Ibidem*, pp. 89–92; Przywara, *The Heart of Newman*, pp. 232–35.

41. J. H. Newman, *The Idea of a University* (New York: Image Books, 1959), pp. 413–32; Culler, *op. cit.*, pp. 113, 255 ff.

42. Cragg, *op. cit.*, pp. 141 ff.

43. *Ibidem*, pp. 154 ff.; Vidler, *The Church in an Age of Revolution*, pp. 36 ff.

44. Stephen Dessain, "'Cardinal Newman on the Theory and Practise of Knowledge: The Purpose of the *Grammar of Assent*," *Downside Review*, LXXV (1957), 1–25, especially p. 3.

45. Rumbold, *op. cit.*, p. 71.

46. *Ibidem*; *cf*. also, Gundersen, *op. cit.*, p. 47, where he shows Newman's possible dependence on Butler for the often-used argument from the common testimony of men: *Securus judicat orbis terrarum.*

47. *Ibidem*, pp. 70–72.

48. Culler, *op. cit.*, p. 229. It should be noted that part of the merit of Copleston's *History of Philosophy* is the extremely positive view he takes of the British philosophers of the eighteenth century.

49. *Grammar*, p. 187.

50. Chadwick, *op. cit.*, p. 111.

51. Trevor, *op. cit.*, pp. 65 ff.; Culler, *op. cit.*, pp. 60–61.

52. *Apologia*, p. 133; Culler, *op. cit.*, pp. 150–52.

53. *Apologia*, pp. 144 ff.; Walgrave, *op. cit.*, pp. 17 ff.; Blehl, *op. cit.*, pp. 81 ff.; Chadwick, *op. cit.*, p. 118.

54. On the influence of S. T. Coleridge, who is Newman's connection with the world of German thought, *cf*. Culler, *op. cit.*, pp. 180, 218; *cf*. also, Chadwick, *op. cit.*, p. 125; also, Vidler, *The Church in an Age of Revolution*, pp. 79 ff. Chadwick, pp. 102 ff., has a lengthy discussion of the question of Newman's awareness of Möhler's work. Acton believed that Newman had read Möhler, but his evidence is unconvincing at best. Newman had been encouraged to read Möhler by Wiseman, but it is difficult to disagree with Chadwick that Newman knew of Möhler by articles and hearsay, and was not dependent on him for his thought. Chadwick says: "He was not reading Möhler, nor Wiseman, nor Perrone, nor even Petau. He was reading Justin Martyr, Athanasius, Tertullian, Ambrose, Lactantius, Cyprian." (p. 119) Newman quotes Möhler in *On Consulting the Faithful*, referring to the French translation, *Symbolique*, of Möhler's work. He also refers to him, linking him with De Maistre, in the *Essay on Development* (New York: Image Books, 1957), p. 53.

55. Vidler, *The Church in an Age of Revolution*, p. 81.

56. Chadwick, *op. cit.*, pp. 130–38.

57. *Ibidem*, p. 195; *Essay on Development*, pp. 57–76, 115–74.

58. Concerning Newman's awareness of the parallel between personal and ecclesiastical development and growth, *cf*. Fries, *op. cit.*, pp. 242, 246; *cf*. also, Walgrave, *op. cit.*, pp. 221 ff. Regarding Newman's extension of Butler's idea, *cf*. Walgrave, *op. cit.*, p. 223. Gundersen, *op. cit.*, pp. 46–47, 81–82, does not seem to be aware of Newman's departure from Butler on the matter of miracles. For a contrast, *cf*. Culler, *op. cit.*, p. 250.

59. Culler, *op. cit.*, pp. 72–77, 116. Newman wanted to teach subjects and not just a given book, as was the Oxford custom. *Cf.* also, David, *op. cit.*, p. xiii.

60. Trevor, *op. cit.*, pp. 328–43, 395–404. *Cf. Autobiographical Writings*, pp. 254–61, wherein Newman says that as a Protestant his religion was dreary, whereas as a Catholic his life was. In the Church he felt "nothing but failure," and insisted strongly both that the Church must prepare for the entrance of the convert and that Catholics need to be educated to be aware of their own narrowness and bigotry.

61. *Grammar*, p. 207.

62. Culler, *op. cit.*, p. 70, refers to a letter Newman wrote to his mother, March 13, 1829.

63. Fries, *op. cit.*, p. 231.

64. Dessain, *op. cit.*, p. 2. *Cf.* also, Francis Bacchus, "How to Read the *Grammar of Assent*," *The Month*, CXLIII (1924), 106–15.

65. *Cf.* Boyd C. Shafer, "The Study of History in the United States," *Bulletin of the American Association of University Professors*, L, No. 3 (1964), 232–40. The author blames historians themselves for making of history an irrelevant study for the students. (p. 233)

66. Fries, *op. cit.*, p. 232. Fries considers the *"demonstratio catholica"* of Newman as presently valid. We do not. However, we are concerned in our study with the modern unbeliever, and to develop a *"demonstratio catholica"* would be foreign to our present purpose.

67. Newman, too, has this optimistic approach; *cf.* Fries, *op. cit.*, pp. 241–42 and Culler, *op. cit.*, pp. 245 ff.

68. *Apologia*, p. 319.

69. Fries, *op. cit.*, pp. 234 ff. Fries quotes approvingly the philosophers, such as Jaspers, who have taken up the stimuli of Max Scheler, and sees such efforts as being in accord with that which Newman proposed to do in the religious demonstration. Jaspers says: *"Keine Existenz ohne Transzendenz, kein wahres Bild des Menschen ohne Gott. Existenz die wir sein können, ist nur in eins mit der Transzendenz, durch die wir sind. . . . Atheismus ist nicht Erkenntnismangel, sondern Existenzverlust."*

70. *Grammar*, pp. 329–32, has a criticism of William Paley.

71. *Ibidem*, p. 319; Artz, *op. cit.*, p. 255. Newman's awareness of the futility of mere rationalistic argument and logic in religious matters was evident as early as 1821 in the *Christian Observer* and in sermons from 1826 to 1843; *cf.* Franz Willam, *Die Vorgeschichte des Begriffes "Konvergiende Probabilitaten,"* Vol. IV; *Newman-Studien* (Nuremberg: Glock und Lutz, 1964), 138–43. *Cf.* also, "The Nature of Faith in Relation to Reason," from the *Oxford University Sermons* in Connolly, *op. cit.*, pp. 315 ff.

72. We have borrowed this term from Alfonso Nebreda, S.J., *Kerygma in Crisis* (Chicago: Loyola University Press, 1965), p. viii. Nebreda seems to have taken the term from The East Asian Study Week on Mission Catechetics in Bangkok, 1962.

73. Fries, *op. cit.*, pp. 235–36; *Grammar*, pp. 95–109.

74. *Grammar*, pp. 98 ff.; Walgrave, *op. cit.*, p. 25.

75. Dessain, *op. cit.*, p. 3.

76. *Grammar*, pp. 49–92.

77. *Ibidem*, p. 52.

78. *Ibidem*, p. 85.

79. *Ibidem*, p. 90.

80. *Ibidem*, p. 93.

81. Walgrave, *op. cit.*, p. 234.

82. *Grammar*, p. 250.

83. *Ibidem*, pp. 136–39.

84. *Ibidem*, p. 227.

85. *Ibidem*, p. 275.

86. *Ibidem*, pp. 161, 165 ff. as compared with p. 172.

87. *Ibidem*, p. 207.

88. *Ibidem*, p. 194.

89. *Ibidem*, p. 270.

90. *Ibidem*, p. 139.

91. *Cf.* Walgrave, *op. cit.*, pp. 225 ff., who sees Providence as the more general principle in Newman and sees analogy and nature as developments of the Providence-theme. *Cf.* Gundersen, *op. cit.*, pp. 41 ff., who has done a fine job of summarizing Butler's influence on Newman. Chadwick, *op. cit.*, pp. 86 ff., questions Butler's influence in Newman's *Essay on Development*, but does not question Butler's general influence on Newman.

92. *Grammar*, p. 96.

93. *Ibidem*, pp. 256–60.

94. *Ibidem*, pp. 246 ff., 321.

95. Chadwick, *op. cit.*, pp. 151 ff. Walgrave, *op. cit.*, pp. 221 ff.

96. *Grammar*, pp. 242, 251.

97. *Ibidem*, pp. 303 ff. Newman's famous *Securus judicat orbis terrarum* was used by Butler.

98. J. H. Newman, *On Consulting the Faithful in Matters of Doctrine* (New York: Sheed & Ward, 1961), pp. 53–107, where he cites example after example from the early history of the Church.

99. For Newman's description of his own conversion and his personal illative sense, *cf. Apologia*, pp. 216 ff.; *Grammar*, pp. 217, 223, 232.

100. *Grammar*, pp. 109, 323. F. J. Kaiser, *The Concept of Conscience According to John Henry Newman* (unpublished doctoral dissertation, Catholic University of America, Washington, D.C., 1958), exaggerates this sense of community that Newman felt with all men. Newman knew he could not draw all, but only the many like himself. *Cf.* Kaiser, p. 1.

101. Walgrave, *op. cit.*, p. 14, note 3.

102. *Grammar*, p. 143.

103. *Ibidem*, p. 229.

104. *Ibidem*, p. 230; Walgrave, *op. cit.*, p. 234, speaks of Newman's existentialism.

105. *Ibidem*, pp. 240 ff.; *cf. Essay on Development*, pp. 115–34.

106. *Ibidem*, p. 269.

107. *Ibidem*, pp. 265 ff.

108. *Ibidem*, pp. 268 ff.

109. *Ibidem*, p. 275.

110. *Ibidem*, pp. 216 ff.

111. *Ibidem*, pp. 281–99.

112. *Ibidem*, p. 263.

113. *Ibidem*, pp. 162–63.

114. *Ibidem*, p. 174.

115. *Ibidem*, p. 301.

116. *Ibidem*, p. 109.

117. *Ibidem*, p. 293.

118. *Ibidem*, pp. 181 ff.

119. On Newman's reopening of the question of universals, *cf.* an excellent discussion by Dessain, *op. cit.*, pp. 17 ff. He includes Van Steenberghen's comments that the abstract must rely on the concrete. He also approves Newman's statements about the inadequacy of words. *Cf. Grammar*, pp. 281 ff., 379, where Newman mentions "arguments too deep for words."

120. Fries, *op. cit.*, p. 234.

121. *Grammar*, pp. 242–50.

122. *Ibidem*, p. 333.

123. Gundersen, *op. cit.*, pp. 75–80; Kaiser, *op. cit.*, pp. 271 ff., takes the same approach in attempting to crowd Newman's concept of conscience into the traditional view of Catholic moral theology. To be seen properly, Newman should not be crowded into any system.

124. *Cf.* Benard, *op. cit.*, pp. 159 ff., for a more realistic approach to Newman. Benard brings out that Thomas was not nearly as personal and concrete in his treatment of faith as was Newman, and Thomas barely mentions action as a demonstration of faith. Furthermore, Thomas clearly distinguishes between faith and knowledge, whereas Newman, more modernly, does not see the importance of this distinction in any clear-cut way.

125. *Grammar*, p. 90.

126. *Ibidem*, pp. 66 ff., 284 ff. Newman uses many terms, such as "presumption," "tacit understanding," and "preconception." The value of antecedent probabilities is brought out better in the *Oxford University Sermons* and in the Essay on Development. *Cf.* Walgrave, *op. cit.*, p. 227 and *Essay*, pp. 125 ff.

127. *Grammar*, p. 97. Walgrave's treatment of conscience, *op. cit.*, pp. 203–240 and appendices D and E, is excellent. Our treatment of conscience in Newman owes him a great deal.

128. *Ibidem*, pp. 301–303 shows Newman to be safely free of the modernist error of immanent revelation. Chadwick's effort to show that Newman's *Development of Doctrine* includes a new revelation (p. 195 *et passim*) is inconclusive. In answer to Chadwick's question, "These new

doctrines of which the Church had a feeling or inkling but of which she was not conscious—in what meaningful sense may it be asserted that these new doctrines are not 'new revelation'?", I think the solution lies in the distinction between word and reality. If revelation is identified with words, then it will appear that there is a new revelation. If revelation is the reality, it can be there in fullness long before the words can express it. I find Rahner's thought more in accord with Newman, in *Theological Investigations*, Vol. I, trans. Cornelius Ernest (Baltimore: Helicon Press, Inc., 1961), pp. 39–78.

129. *Ibidem*, pp. 98 ff., 304 ff.

130. *Ibidem*, p. 318.

131. *Ibidem*, p. 308.

132. *Cf.* Kaiser, *op. cit.*, pp. 138 ff., 240 ff., for a thorough treatment of Newman's consideration of the forms of escaping conscience.

133. *Grammar*, p. 107. Kaiser, *op. cit.*, pp. 183–225, says that in Newman the "supremacy of conscience is the essence of natural religion and the supremacy of Apostle, Pope, or Church, or Bishop is the essence of the revealed." This exaggerated treatment of the objective norm of conscience in Newman does not do justice to Newman's more personal and individual view. Newman saw the place of the individual conscience within the Church and even the need of an apparent believer to search for true faith within the institutional Church.

134. *Ibidem*, p. 100.

135. *Ibidem*, p. 97.

136. *Ibidem*, pp. 103 ff., 303 ff.

137. *Ibidem*, pp. 98 ff. *Cf.* Walgrave, *op. cit.*, pp. 347 ff., where he discusses Lappel's tripartite view of conscience. Lappel makes instinct a separate part of the conscience, and Walgrave shows that instinct rather operates within and around the moral sense and the sense of duty. It is the "sense" part of moral knowledge and moral action.

138. *Ibidem*, pp. 318 ff.

139. *Ibidem*, pp. 305 ff.

140. *Ibidem*, p. 308.

141. *Ibidem*, p. 311.

142. *Ibidem*, p. 314.

143. *Ibidem*, p. 313.

144. *Ibidem*, p. 321.

145. *Ibidem*, pp. 138 ff., 179 ff. Here Newman touches on the need for a will to believe.

146. *Ibidem*, pp. 375–80. *Cf.* also, the *Apologia*, pp. 317–53, Newman's general answer to Mr. Kingsley, in which he points out that Catholicism was not an untroubled mental experience.

147. *Ibidem*, pp. 330–59. Here Newman points out that a man reaches the point that he needs: Christianity. This does not mean that there is not a definite body of doctrine or a definite revelation. It only means that the man of natural religion reaches a point where he looks for revelation to resolve his need for forgiveness and meaning. Newman gives conscience value as "extrinsic" evidence in this search. *Cf. Grammar*, p. 302.

148. *Ibidem*, p. 330.

149. *Ibidem*, p. 224.

150. *Ibidem*, p. 160.

151. *Ibidem*, p. 159.

152. *Ibidem*, pp. 268, 301.

153. *Ibidem*, pp. 178 ff.

154. *Ibidem*, p. 180.

155. *Cf.* Walgrave, *op. cit.*, p. 225.

156. *Cf.* Culler, *op. cit.*, pp. 123–70.

157. *The Idea of a University*, p. 429.

158. *Grammar*, pp. 200 ff.

159. *Essay on Development*, pp. 189 ff.

160. *Grammar*, p. 159.

161. *Ibidem*, p. 165.

162. *Ibidem*, p. 376.

163. *Cf. Essay on Development*, pp. 51, 54, where he criticizes the dictum of Vincent of Lerins.

164. Chadwick, *op. cit.*, pp. 180–84, 195.

165. Walgrave, *op. cit.*, pp. 218–19.

166. As was indicated above, Ollé-Laprune had read Newman and much of Newman is reflected in *La Certitude morale*. It will be remembered that Ollé-Laprune played a formative part in Blondel's education. *Cf.* Aubert, *op. cit.*, p. 346. *Cf.* also, Walgrave, *op. cit.*, pp. 237 ff., wherein he denies any connection between Newman and Blondel.

167. Walgrave, *op. cit.*, pp. 239 ff.

168. In the *Grammar*, as in the *Apologia* (especially pp. 315–355), Newman wanted to establish his own sincerity and honesty.

CHAPTER V

1. *Supra*, pp. 17–21, 41–44, 84–85.

2. *Letter on Apologetics*, pp. 145–47, 215.

3. Coppens; *supra*, pp. 7–9.

4. *Supra*, pp. 18 ff., 56 ff., 90 ff.

5. *Letter on Apologetics*, pp. 129–30.

6. *Supra*, p. 108.

7. *Lettres Philosophiques*, p. 32.

8. *Supra*, p. 17.

9. Yves Congar, *Lay People in the Church*, trans. Donald Attwater (Westminster, Md.: The Newman Press, 1957), p. 395.

10. Gerard Philips, "The Church in the Modern World," *The Church and the World*, trans. Aimée Berneuf. (Concilium Series; New York: Paulist Press, 1965), pp. 12–13.

11. Charles David, *Theology for Today* (New York: Sheed & Ward, 1962), p. 42.

12. Hannah Arendt, *The Human Condition* (New York: Anchor Books, 1959), especially pp. 225–95; *cf.* also, Kenneth Keniston, *The Uncommitted—Alienated Youth in American Society* (New York: Harcourt, Brace & World, Inc., 1965).

13. *Constitution on the Church in the Modern World*, art. 7.

14. *Ibidem*, arts. 4, 5.

15. *Ibidem*, art. 5.

16. *Supra*, pp. 31, 56.

17. *Constitution*, art. 19.

18. *Supra*, pp. 59–60.

19. *Supra*, p. 69.

20. *Supra*, pp. 59–60.

21. *Constitution*, art. 76.

22. *Ibidem*, art. 21. The serious questions raised by the unbelievers is the subject of a growing literature. Some material that we have found helpful is: *Council Speeches of Vatican II*, eds. Hans Kung, Yves Congar, and Daniel O'Hanlon (Glen Rock, N.J.: Deus Books, 1964), especially pp. 231–88; John Courtney Murray, *The Problem of God* (New Haven: Yale University Press, 1963), especially pp. 77–121; Jean Danielou, *God and the Ways of Knowing*, trans. from the French (New York: Meridian Books, 1964), especially pp. 52–94; Ignace Lepp, *Atheism in Our Times*, trans. Bernard Murchland (New York: The Macmillan Company, 1964); John Macquarrie, *An Existential Theology* (New York: Torchbooks, 1965), especially pp. 29–134; Gabriel Marcel, *Creative Fidelity*, trans. Robert Rosthal (New York: The Noonday Press, 1964), especially pp. 82 ff.; Gustave Weigel, *The Modern God* (New York: The Macmillan Company, 1963); Joseph Walsh, "The Confrontation between Belief and Unbelief," *Cross Currents*, L (1965), 43–56; Michael Novak, *Belief and Unbelief* (New York: The Macmillan Company, 1966).

23. *Ibidem*.

24. Philip Rahv, "For External Use Only," review of *The Triumph of the Therapeutic*, by Phillip Rieff, "Book Week," *Washington Post*, Feb. 6, 1966, p. 4.

25. *Constitution*, art. 19.

26. *Ibidem*, art. 4.

27. There is a good treatment of the modern problems of ecclesiology contained in Jerome Hamer, *The Church Is a Communion*, trans. Ronald Matthews (New York: Sheed & Ward, 1964); *cf.* also, *The Church, Readings in Theology*, comp. at the Canisianum, Innsbruck (New York: P. J. Kenedy & Sons, 1964), especially pp. 64 ff.; *cf. Council Speeches of Vatican II*, especially pp. 145 ff.

28. *Constitution*, art. 17.

29. *Ibidem*, arts. 13, 17.

30. *Ibidem*, art. 13.

31. *Ibidem*, art. 16.

32. *Ibidem*. *Cf.* also, Karl Rahner, "Christianity and Non-Christian Religions," *The Church, Readings in Theology*, pp. 112–35.

33. *Declaration on the Relation of the Church to Non-Christian Religions*, art. 1.

34. *Ibidem.*

35. *Ibidem*, art. 3.

36. *Constitution*, art. 62.

37. *Ibidem.*

38. *Ibidem*, art. 60.

39. *Supra*, p. 16.

40. *Supra*, p. 39.

41. Hamer, *op. cit.*, pp. 90–91, note 1.

42. *Constitution*, art. 22.

43. *Supra*, p. 26.

44. *Letter on Apologetics*, p. 92.

45. *Constitution*, art. 42.

46. The names of Paul Tillich, Reinhold Niebuhr, and Martin Buber deserve a special place because of their effort to make theology relevant to the unbeliever world. An outstanding periodical with a similar concern is *Christianity and Crisis*, published biweekly through the efforts of Union Theological Seminary, New York.

47. *Decree on Ecumenism*, art. 12.

48. *Declaration*, art. 4.

49. *Decree on Ecumenism*, art. 4.

50. *Cf. supra*, note 46, this page.

51. *Cf.* Dietrich Bonhoeffer, *Letters and Papers from Prison*, trans. Reginald H. Fuller (New York: Macmillan Paperback, 1962); John A. T. Robinson, *Honest to God* (London: SCM Paperback, 1965); Harvey Cox, *The Secular City* (New York: Macmillan Paperback, 1965); a representative work of Paul Tillich is *Theology of Culture* (New York: Oxford University Press, 1964); an interesting series of the "God-is-dead" controversy was contained in three lengthy articles by Ved Metha, "The New Theologian," *The New Yorker* (Nov. 13, 20, and 27, 1965). This series offers an interesting picture of the more liberal of modern Protestant theologians.

52. Karl Rahner, *Nature and Grace*, p. 113. We find Rahner's use of the word "enemy" offensive, but agree with the basic idea he describes.

53. During the summer of 1964 we attended a theological seminar in Europe and did some parish work there. Our general impression was that the problem of unbelief was much like our own American problem.

54. *Cf. supra*, Introduction, note 7.

55. *Supra*, pp. 9–10, 18 ff., 56 ff., 92 ff.

56. *Supra*, p. 21.

57. *Supra*, pp. 61 ff.

58. *Supra*, pp. 102 ff.

59. *Constitution*, art. 12.

60. *Ibidem*, art. 10.

61. *Supra*, p. 57.

62. *L'Action*, p. ix.

63. *Supra*, pp. 21–22.

64. *Supra*, pp. 60, 70.

65. *Supra*, pp. 104 ff.

66. Tillich, *Theology of Culture*, p. 207.

67. Philips, *The Church in the Modern World*, p. 14.

68. Alfred Dondeyne, "The Existence of God and Contemporary Materialism," *God, Man, and the Universe: A Christian Answer to Modern Materialism*, trans. from the French (New York: P. J. Kenedy & Sons, 1953), p. 11.

69. *Constitution*, arts. 10, 11.

70. *Ibidem*, art. 43.

71. *Ibidem*, art. 34.

72. *Ibidem*, art. 11.

73. *Supra*, p. 32.

74. *Supra*, p. 69.

75. *Constitution*, art. 18.

76. *L'Action*, p. ix.

77. *Supra*, pp. 39–41.

78. *Supra*, p. 54.

79. *Supra*, p. 16.

80. *Supra*, p. 110.

81. *Declaration*, art. 2.

82. *Constitution*, art. 27.

83. *Ibidem*, art. 31.

84. *Ibidem*, art. 16.

85. Ely Chinoy, *Society* (New York: Random House, Inc., 1961), pp. 19 ff., 48 ff.

86. *Grammar*, pp. 290 ff.

87. *Cf. supra*, pp. 30–32.

88. *Cf. supra*, p. 69.

89. *Supra*, pp. 30, 68.

90. *Supra*, pp. 102–103.

91. *Constitution*, art. 12.

92. *Ibidem*, art. 21.

93. *Supra*, pp. 23–24, 67 ff.

94. *Supra*, pp. 104, 105 ff.

95. *Supra*, pp. 15, 26, 43, 66, 103.

96. Lepp, *op. cit.*, pp. 31, 34.

97. Cox, *op. cit.*, p. 71.

98. Bonhoeffer, *op. cit.*, pp. 209 ff.

99. *Supra*, p. 15.

100. Bonhoeffer, *op. cit.*, p. 214.

101. *Constitution,* art. 3.

102. *Ibidem,* art. 4.

103. *Ibidem,* arts. 21, 22.

104. *Ibidem,* art. 41.

105. *Supra,* pp. 00 ff.

106. *Lettres Philosophiques,* p. 34.

107. *Supra,* p. 109.

108. *Supra,* p. 110.

109. *Supra,* p. 13.

110. Monica Lawler, "The Catholic Undergraduate," *Theology and the University* (Baltimore: Helicon Press, Inc., 1964), pp. 26, 30 ff.

111. Gerhard Lenski, *The Religious Factor* (New York: Anchor Books, 1963), p. 298.

112. *Declaration on Religious Freedom,* arts. 1, 3.

113. *Ibidem,* art. 9.

114. Robert McAfee Brown, *Observer in Rome* (New York: Doubleday & Company, Inc., 1962), p. 162.

115. *Constitution,* arts. 16, 17.

116. *Ibidem,* art. 28.

117. *On the Eternal in Man,* pp. 267–68.

118. *Supra,* pp. 21 ff.

119. *Supra,* pp. 47 ff.

120. *Constitution,* art. 58.

121. *Ibidem,* art. 57.

122. *Declaration,* art. 5.

123. *Supra,* pp. 20 ff., 61 ff.

124. *Supra,* pp. 61 ff.

125. *Supra,* pp. 17–18.

126. *Supra,* pp. 109 ff.

EPILOGUE

1. *Cf.* Gerard Sloyan, "The Parish as Educator," *Commonweal* LXXIV (1966), 20 ff.

2. *Constitution,* Church in the Modern World, Preface. Par. I.

BIBLIOGRAPHY

Adam, Karl. *The Christ of Faith.* Translated by Joyce Crick. New York: Mentor-Omega, 1962.

Alexander, Anthony. *College Apologetics.* Chicago: Henry Regnery Company, 1954.

Arendt, Hannah. *The Human Condition.* New York: Anchor Books, 1959.

Artz, Johannes. *Der Ansatz der Newmanschen Glaubensbegrundung.* (*Newman-Studien series,* Vol. IV.) Nuremberg: Glock und Lutz, 1964.

Aubert, Roger. *Le Problème de l'act de la foi, donnes traditionelles et resultats des controverses recents.* Louvain: E. Warny, 1950.

Blehl, Vincent. *The Essential Newman.* New York: Mentor-Omega, 1963.

Blondel, Maurice. *L'Action, Essai d'une critique de la vie et d'une science de la pratique.* (Thèse presentée à la Faculté des lettres de Paris.) Paris: Ancienne Librairie Germer Baillière et Cie, 1893.

———. *Carnets Intimes, 1883–1894.* Paris: Editions du Cerf, 1961.

———. *Études Blondéliennes.* Paris: Presse Universitaire, 1951.

———. *L'Itinéraire Philosophique de Maurice Blondel.* Paris: Spes, 1928.

———. *Letter on Apologetics and History and Dogma.* Introduction by Alexander Dru and Illtyd Trethowan. Translated by Dru and Trethowan. New York: Holt, Rinehart and Winston, Inc., 1964.

———. *Lettres Philosophiques.* Paris: Aubier, 1961.

———. *Le Problème de la Philosophie Catholique.* Paris: Bloud and Gay, 1932.

———. *Les Premiers Écrits.* Paris: Presse Universitaire, 1956.

———. *La Semaine Sociale de Bordeaux et le monophorisme.* Paris: Bloud and Gay, 1910.

Bochenski, I. M. *Contemporary European Philosophy.* Translated by Donald Nicholl and Karl Aschenbrenner. Berkeley: University of California Press, 1965.

Bonhoeffer, Dietrich. *The Cost of Discipleship.* Translated by Reginald H. Fuller. New York: Macmillan Paperback, 1963.

————. *Letters and Papers from Prison*. Translated by Reginald H. Fuller. New York: Macmillan Paperback, 1962.

Borne, Étienne. *Passion de la Verité*. Paris: Librairie Arthème Fayard, 1962.

Bouillard, Henri. *Blondel et le Christianisme*. Paris: Editions du Seuil.

Bremond, Henri. *Devout Humanism*. Vol. I of A *Literary History of Religious Thought in France*. Translated by K. L. Montgomery. New York: The Macmillan Company, 1928.

Brown, Robert McAfee. *Observer in Rome*. New York: Doubleday & Company, Inc., 1962.

Brunhes, Gabriel. *La Foi et sa justification rationelle*. Paris: Bloud and Gay, 1928.

Brunner, Emil. *Man in Revolt, A Christian Anthropology*. Translated by Olive Wyon. Philadelphia: The Westminster Press, 1957.

Chadwick, Owen. *From Bossuet to Newman*. Cambridge: Cambridge University Press, 1957.

Chinoy, Ely. *Society*. New York: Random House, Inc., 1961.

The Church, Readings in Theology. Compiled at the Canisianum, Innsbruck. New York: P. J. Kenedy & Sons, 1964.

Cirne-Lima, Carlos. *Personal Faith*. Translated by G. Richard Dimler, S.J. New York: Herder and Herder, Inc., 1965.

Congar, Yves. *Lay People in the Church*. Translated by Donald Attwater. Westminster, Md.: The Newman Press, 1957.

Connolly, F. X. *Newman Reader*. New York: Image Books, 1964.

Copleston, F., S.J. A *History of Philosophy*. Vol. IV. New York: Image Books, 1963.

————. A *History of Philosophy*. Vol. V, Parts 1 and 2. New York: Atheneum Publishers, 1964.

Coser, Louis A. Introduction to Max Scheler's *Ressentiment*. Translated by William Holdheim. New York: Crowell-Collier Press, 1961.

Cox, Harvey. *The Secular City*. New York: Macmillan Paperback, 1965.

Cragg, G. R. *The Church and the Age of Reason*. ("The Pelican History of the Church," Vol. 4.) Baltimore: Penguin Books, Inc., 1961.

Culler, A. Dwight. *The Imperial Intellect*. London: Yale University Press, 1955.

Danielou, Jean. *God and the Ways of Knowing*. Translated from the French. New York: Meridian Books, 1964.

D'Arcy, Martin, S.J. *Mirage and Truth*. New York: The Macmillan Company, 1933.

————. *The Nature of Belief*. London: Sheed & Ward, 1931.

David, Charles. *Theology for Today*. New York: Sheed & Ward, 1962.

De Lubac, Henri. *La Prière du P. Teilhard de Chardin.* Paris: Librairie Arthème Fayard, 1964.

————. *Sûrnaturelle: Études Historiques.* Paris: n.p., 1946.

De Montcheuil, Yves. *Mélanges Théologiques.* Paris: Aubier, 1946.

De Sailly, B. [Maurice Blondel] *Comment réaliser l'apologétique intégral?* Paris: n.p., 1913.

Devivier, Walter. *Christian Apologetics.* Translated from the French. New York: Wagner Bros., 1924.

Dondeyne, Alfred. "The Existence of God and Contemporary Materialism," *God, Man and the Universe: A Christian Answer to Modern Materialism.* Translated from the French. New York: P. J. Kenedy & Sons, 1953.

Dulles, Avery. *Apologetics and the Biblical Christ.* Westminster, Md.: The Newman Press, 1964.

Duméry, H. *La Philosophie de L'Action.* Paris: Aubier, 1948.

Eliade, Mircea. *The Sacred and the Profane.* New York: Harper & Row, Publishers, 1961.

Fichter, Joseph. *Textbook in Apologetics.* Milwaukee: The Bruce Publishing Company, 1947.

Fries, Heinrich. *Newman und Grundprobleme der Heutigen Apologetik.* (*Newman-Studien* series, Vol. III.) Nuremberg: Glock und Lutz, 1957.

Frings, Manfred. *Max Scheler: A Concise Introduction into the World of a Great Thinker.* Pittsburgh: Duquesne University Press, 1965.

Gilson, Étienne. *Le Philosophe et le théologie.* Paris: Librairie Arthème Fayard, 1960.

Guitton, Jean. *La philosophie de Newman.* Paris: Boivin et Cie, 1933.

Gundersen, Borghild. *Cardinal Newman and Apologetics.* Oslo: I Kommisjon Hos Jacob Dybwad, 1952.

Gwynn, Denis. *The Action Française Condemnation.* London: Burns & Oates, Ltd., 1928.

Hamer, Jerome. *The Church Is a Communion.* Translated by Ronald Matthews. New York: Sheed & Ward, 1964.

Hayes, C. J. H. *A Political and Cultural History of Modern Europe.* Vol. I. New York: The Macmillan Company, 1944.

Heenan, John. *The Faith Makes Sense.* New York: Sheed & Ward, 1948.

Joly, Eugene. *What Is Faith?* Translated by Illtyd Trethowan. Glen Rock, N.J.: Deus Books, 1963.

Keniston, Kenneth. *The Uncommitted—Alienated Youth in American Society.* New York: Harcourt, Brace & World, Inc., 1965.

Kung, Hans, Congar, Yves and O'Hanlon, Daniel (eds.). *Council Speeches of Vatican II.* Glen Rock, N.J.: Deus Books, 1964.

Lammenais, F. *Essai sur l'indifférence en matière de religion.* Vols. I–IV. Paris: Garnier, 1895.

Latourelle, René, S.J. *Théologie de la révélation.* Paris: Desclée, 1963.

Lawler, Monica. "The Catholic Undergraduate," *Theology and the University.* Baltimore: Helicon Press, Inc., 1964.

Lenski, Gerhard. *The Religious Factor.* New York: Anchor Books, 1963.

Lepp, Ignace. *Atheism in Our Times.* Translated by Bernard Murchland. New York: The Macmillan Company, 1964.

Levie, Jean. *The Bible, Word of God in Words of Men.* Translated by Geoffrey Chapman. New York: P. J. Kenedy & Sons, 1961.

Macquarrie, John. *An Existential Theology.* New York: Torchbooks, 1965.

———. *Twentieth Century Religious Thought.* New York: Harper & Row, Publishers, 1963.

MacMurray, John. *The Self as Agent.* ("The Gifford Lectures for 1953") London: Faber and Faber, Ltd., 1955.

Madgett, Arthur Patrick. *Christian Origins.* Cincinnati: Xavier University Press, 1943.

Marcel, Gabriel. *Creative Fidelity.* Translated by Robert Rosthal. New York: The Noonday Press, 1964.

Marle, R., S.J. *Au Coeur de la crise moderniste.* Paris: Aubier, 1960.

Masure, E. *Le Signe.* Paris: Bloud and Gay, 1953.

Maurice Blondel et Auguste Valensin: Correspondence. Vol. II. Paris: Aubier, 1957.

Murray, John Courtney. *The Problem of God.* New Haven: Yale University Press, 1963.

Nebreda, Alfonso, S.J. *Kerygma in Crisis.* Chicago: Loyola University Press, 1965.

Newman, John Henry. *Apologia Pro Vita Sua.* New York: Image Books, 1956.

———. *Autobiographical Writings.* New York: Sheed & Ward, 1955.

———. *Essay on Development.* New York: Image Books, 1957.

———. *The Grammar of Assent.* New York: Image Books, 1955.

———. *The Idea of a University.* New York: Image Books, 1959.

———. *On Consulting the Faithful in Matters of Doctrine.* New York: Sheed & Ward, 1961.

Novak, Michael. *Belief and Unbelief.* New York: The Macmillan Company, 1965.

Ortegat, Paul, S.J. *Intuition et religion: le problème existentiale.* Louvain: Editions de L'Institute Supérieur, 1947.

Philips, Gerard. "The Church in the Modern World," *The Church and the World.* Translated by Aimée Berneuf. ("Concilium Series.") Glen Rock, N.J.: Paulist Press, 1965.

Poulat, Émile. *Histoire, dogme et critique dans la crise moderniste*. Paris: Easterman, 1962.

Przywara, Erich. *The Heart of Newman*. Springfield, Ill.: Templegate Publishers, 1963.

————. *Polarity*. Translated by A. C. Bouquet. London: Oxford University Press, 1935.

Rahner, Karl. *Nature and Grace*. Translated by Dinah Wharton. New York: Sheed & Ward, 1963.

————. *Theological Investigations*. Vol. I. Translated by Cornelius Ernest. Baltimore: Helicon Press, Inc., 1961.

Robinson, John A. T. *Honest to God*. London: SCM Paperback, 1965.

Rumbold, Gunter. *Das Wesen der Person Nach John Henry Newman*. (*Newman-Studien* series, Vol. IV.) Nuremberg: Glock und Lutz, 1964.

Scheler, Max. *Der Formalismus in der Ethik und die materiale Wertethik*. Bern: Francke Verlag, 1954.

————. *The Nature of Man*. Translated by H. Meyerhof. Boston: Beacon Press, 1961.

————. *On the Eternal in Man*. Translated by Bernard Noble. London: SCM Press, 1960.

————. *Theological Investigations*. Vol. I. Translated by Cornelius Ernst, O.P. Baltimore: Helicon Press, Inc., 1961.

————. *Vom Ewigen im Menschen*. Bern: Francke Verlag, 1954.

Sheed, F. J. *A Map of Life*. New York: Sheed & Ward, 1933.

Smith, Canon George. *The Teaching of the Catholic Church*. Vol. I. New York: The Macmillan Company, 1953.

Stark. Introduction to Scheler's *The Nature of Sympathy*. Translated by Peter Heath. New Haven: Yale University Press, 1954.

Steffes, Johann Peter. *Glaubensbegrundung: Christlicher Gottesglaube in Grundlegung und Abwehr*. I Band: *Methodische und Geschichtliche Einführung Anthropologische Grundlegung Religionsphilosophie*. Mainz: Matthias Grunewald Verlag, 1958.

————. *Religionsphilosophie*. Munich: Kösel and Pustet, 1925.

Tannenbaum, Edward R. *The Action Française: Die-Hard Reactionaries in Twentieth Century France*. New York: John Wiley & Sons, 1962.

Tanquerey, Adolph. *Synopsis theologiae dogmaticae fundamentalis ad mentem S. Thomae Aquinatis, hodiernis moribus accommodata*. Vols. I and II. 24th ed. New York: Benziger Bros., 1943.

Tillich, Paul. *Dynamics of Faith*. New York: Harper & Row, Publishers, 1958.

————. *Theology of Culture*. New York: Oxford University Press, 1964.

Tresmontant. *La Metaphysique de Maurice Blondel*. Paris: Editions du Seuil, 1963.

Trevor, Meriol. *Newman: The Pillar of the Cloud.* Vol. I. New York: Doubleday & Company, Inc., 1962.

Valensin, Auguste. *Maurice Blondel.* Paris: Librairie Lecoffre, 1934.

Vancourt, Raymond. *Le Phénoménologie de la foi.* Paris: n.p., 1953.

Vidler, Alec. *The Church in an Age of Revolution.* ("The Pelican History of the Church," Vol. 5.) Baltimore: Penguin Books, Inc., 1965.

————. *Prophecy and Papacy: A Study of Lammenais, the Church and Revolution.* New York: Charles Scribner's Sons, 1954.

Walgrave, J. H. *Newman the Theologian.* Translated by A. V. Littledale. New York: Sheed & Ward, 1960.

Weber, Eugene. *Action Française: Royalism and Reaction in Twentieth Century France.* Stanford: Stanford University Press, 1962.

Weber, Max. *The Protestant Ethic and the Spirit of Capitalism.* New York: Charles Scribner's Sons, 1948.

Weigel, Gustave. *The Modern God.* New York: The Macmillan Company, 1963.

Willam, Franz. *Die Vorgeschichte des Begriffes "Konvergiende Probabilitaten."* (*Newman-Studien* series, Vol. IV.) Nuremberg: Glock und Lutz, 1964.

Wilmers, Wilhelm. *Handbook of the Christian Religion.* Translated from the German. New York: Benziger Bros., 1905.

ARTICLES AND PERIODICALS

Acworth, Richard. Book review of *On the Eternal in Man,* by Max Scheler, *Heythrop Journal,* II (1961), 367–69.

Bacchus, Francis. "How to Read the *Grammar of Assent,*" *The Month,* CXLIII (1924), 106–115.

Bouillard, Henri. "The Thought of Maurice Blondel: A Synoptic Vision," *International Philosophical Quarterly,* III (1963), 392.

Cartier, A. "Le Philosophie de L'Action," *Archives de Philosophie,* XXIV (1961), 20.

Congar, Yves. "Théologie," *DTC,* XIV (1946), 440–46.

Coppens, J. "Un Essai de synthèse apologétique," *Ephemerides Theologicae Louvanienses,* XIV (1937), 447–66.

De Lubac, Henri. "Maurice Blondel et le Père Teilhard de Chardin," *Archives de Philosophie,* XXIV (1961), 123–56.

D'Epeymon, F. Taymans. "Le Miracle, signe du sûrnaturel," *Revue Théologique,* LXXVII (1955), 225–45.

De Sailly, Bernard [Maurice Blondel]. "La notion et le rôle du miracle," *Annales de Philosophie Chrétienne,* CLIV (July 1907), 337–62.

Dessain, Stephen. "Cardinal Newman on the Theory and Practise of Knowledge: The Purpose of the *Grammar of Assent*," *Downside Review*, LXXV (1957), 1–25.

Donnelly, P. J. "Current Theology . . . on the Supernatural," *Theological Studies*, VIII (1947), 483–91.

Dru, Alexander. "From the Action Française to the Second Vatican Council," *Downside Review*, LXXXI (1963), 245.

Faux, J. M., S.J. Book review of *Un Essai de Philosophie chrétienne au xix⁰ siècle: "L'Abbé Louis Bautain,"* *Nouvelle Revue Théologique*, LXXXI (1963), 423–24.

Fenton, Joseph C. "The Case for Traditional Apologetics," *American Ecclesiastical Review*, CXLI (December, 1959), 406–416.

Fourez, Gerard, S.J. and Jacob, Jean, S.J. "Une Dialectique de la conversion," *Revue Philosophique du Louvain*, LVII (1959), 551.

Gardeil, A. "Crédibilité," *DTC*, Vol. III. Paris: Librairie Letouzey et Ané (1931), 2300–2308.

———. "Le Synthèse Apologétique du P. Schwalm," *Revue Thomiste*, XXI (1913), 413–36.

Lauer, Quentin, S.J. "Four Phenomenologists," *Thought*, XXXIII (1958–1959), 184.

McCool, Gerard. "Primacy of Intuition," *Thought*, XXVII (1962), 68.

———. Book review of *On the Eternal in Man*, by Max Scheler, *The New Scholasticism*, XXXVII (1963), 91.

McNamara, Kevin. "Nature and Recognition of Miracles," *Irish Theological Quarterly*, V (1960), 295.

Maisonneuve, L. "Apologétique," *DTC*. Vol. I. Paris: Librairie Letouzey et Ané (1931), 1511–80.

"Max Scheler," *Lexikon fur Theologie und Kirche*, IX. Freiburg: Herder, 1964, pp. 383 ff.

Metha, Ved. "The New Theologian," *The New Yorker* (November 13, 20, and 27, 1965).

Murphy, John L. "Seventy-Five Years of Fundamental Theology in America," *American Ecclesiastical Review*, X (1964), 392–93.

Nicolas, Jean-Hervé, O.P. "Le Centenaire de Maurice Blondel," *Revue Thomiste*, V, No. 62 (1962), 433–44, especially pp. 433–45.

Oesterreicher, John M. "Max Scheler and the Faith," *Thomist*, XIII (1950), 175–76.

Pater, Thomas. Book review of *Apologetics and the Biblical Christ*, *American Ecclesiastical Review*, CL (1964), 453.

Philips, G. "Deux tendances dans la théologie contemporaine," *Nouvelle Revue Théologique*, LXXXI (1963), 227–29.

Rahv, Philip. "For External Use Only," book review of *The Triumph of the Therapeutic*, by Phillip Rieff, "Book Week," *Washington Post*, Feb. 6, 1966, p. 4.

Rondet, H. "Nature et sûrnatural dans la théologie de St. Thomas D'Aquin," *RSR*, XXXVI (1947), 379–95.

Schillebeeckx, E. "L'Instinct de la foi selon St. Thomas d'Aquin," *NRT* (1964), pp. 347–407.

Schutz, Alfred. "Max Scheler's Epistemology and Ethics," *The Review of Metaphysics*, IX (1957–1958), 306 ff.

Scott, Frederick, S.J. "William James and Maurice Blondel," *New Scholasticism*, XXXII (1958), 32–44.

Shafer, Boyd C. "The Study of History in the United States," *Bulletin of the American Association of University Professors*, L, No. 3 (1964), 232–40.

Sloyan, Gerard, "The Parish as Educator," *Commonweal*, LXXIV (1966), 20 ff.

"Une Dialectique de la conversion: L'Action de Maurice Blondel," *Revue Philosophique de Louvain*, XVII (1959), 550.

Valensin, Auguste. "Immanence," *Dictionnaire Apologétique*, II. 1st ed. 579–612.

Vollert, C. Book review of *Sûrnaturelle: Études Historiques*, by Henri De Lubac, *Theological Studies*, XIII (1947–1949), 288–93.

Von Hildebrand, Dietrich. "Max Scheler als Personalichkeit," *Zietliches im Lichte des Ewigin*. Regensburg: Habbel, 1932.

Walsh, Joseph. "The Confrontation between Belief and Unbelief," *Cross Currents*, L (1965), 43–56.

Weigel, Gustave. "The Historical Background of the Encyclical *Humani Generis*," *Theological Studies*, XII (1951), 208–230.

UNPUBLISHED MATERIAL

Benard, Edmond D. *The Problem of Belief in the Writings of Newman, James, and Aquinas*. Unpublished doctoral dissertation, Catholic University of America, Washington, D.C., 1948.

Gélinas, Jean Paul. *La Restauration du Thomisme sous Léon XIII et les philosophies nouvelles*. Unpublished doctoral dissertation, Catholic University of America, Washington, D.C., 1959.

Kaiser, F. J. *The Concept of Conscience According to John Henry Newman*. Unpublished doctoral dissertation, Catholic University of America, Washington, D.C., 1958.

Koehle, Eckhard Joseph. *Personality: A Study According to the Philosophy of Value and Spirit of Max Scheler and Nicolai Hartmann*. Unpublished doctoral dissertation, Columbia University, New York; Arlington, Va.: Catholic Protectorate Press, 1941.

Schneider, Marius. *Max Scheler's Phenomenological Philosophy of Values.* Unpublished doctoral dissertation, Catholic University of America, Washington, D.C., 1951.